On the Street

On the Street

Jack Kelly

with
Richard
Mathison

Henry Regnery Company · Chicago

Library of Congress Cataloging in Publication Data

Kelly, Jack, 1921-
  On the street.

    1. Narcotics, Control of—Atlantic City—Personal
narratives. I. Mathison, Richard R., joint author.
II. Title.
HV5833.A8K44   363.4'5'0924 [B]   74-6897
ISBN 0-8092-8357-3

Published by Henry Regnery Company
114 West Illinois Street, Chicago, Illinois 60610

Manufactured in the United States of America
Library of Congress Catalog Card Number: 74-6897
International Standard Book Number: 0-8092-8357-3

Contents

1

Kelly the Cop

They called him Kelly the Cop. He was five feet, nine inches tall and weighed 155 pounds. Both cheekbones were broken. His nose was smashed and a ragged scar ran down what had once been the bridge of it. The knuckles of both hands were warped and gnarled from the years of fighting. Everyone in Atlantic City knew him: some loved him; some hated him; all respected him. He was my dad—the toughest man I ever knew.

He worked the same beat for years. People turned to him for advice with family problems. They entrusted their kids to him to walk them across busy streets or boot them in the ass when he thought they needed it. Juvenile delinquency stopped right there with Dad.

Merchants slept well at night knowing he was checking their doors. When he found a would-be burglar or a hooligan he didn't lock them up. He slugged them and told them to stay the hell off his beat.

Dad survived the heyday of gangsters and the Prohibition era in Atlantic City with his own curious glory. Nucky Johnson was the town's political boss although he was later to be convicted of income tax evasion. When he was in control, bigtime hoods like Al Capone

1

and Dutch Schultz considered Atlantic City their private spa and resort. They ran their trucks of booze down Atlantic Avenue and nothing was said. You paid off everybody and everybody had a price. Dad was the exception.

Nucky Johnson may have been a gangster to the outside world, but in Atlantic City he was the hero. I remember as a kid going to a church social, when Nucky suddenly appeared. His pockets were filled with change and he threw handfuls of coins in the air. We scrambled on the sidewalk fighting over the nickels and dimes and—because it was the Depression—many of the adults did the same. Nucky roared with laughter at the sight of hungry men fighting for money. He was all class!

Rich and powerful as he was, he never awed my dad. Take the fateful day Nucky summoned Dad to his headquarters at the Ritz-Carlton.

"Kelly, I got your name down here because I hear you're one of the best cops on the force. I want to talk to you about being a sergeant."

My dad said nothing. He knew the game.

"For five hundred dollars you get promoted," Nucky went on.

Dad shook his head. "No, I'm not putting up anything. But I should be a sergeant."

Nucky turned red. "I know you should be a sergeant too, you Irish son of a bitch! But you've got to pay for it like everybody else."

"I don't pay anybody," Dad said. "I deserve it. I worked for it. You should make me a sergeant."

Nucky chuckled. "Yeah, I should. But I ain't going to ruin morale by giving it to you free."

"Go to hell!" Dad replied. He was never to become a sergeant. A companion of Dad's, Sam Barab, bought the job. A few years later he put up $1000 and went on to become a lieutenant.

I asked Dad about it one day. "What's the difference between a patrolman's pay and a sergeant's pay?"

"Five hundred dollars a year," Dad replied.

"In other words, you could have been collecting $500 a year

more for all these years? That's thousands of dollars. And all because you were too thickheaded to pay Johnson the $500. . ."

My dad just shook his head. "That wasn't the point. It wasn't the money. It's the idea of that bastard making me pay for a job when I deserved it." That was my dad.

So in this bare-fisted, corrupt, rough-and-tumble town where I grew up, Dad continued to walk his beat and keep the peace as he saw it, slugging burglars, rousting whores, passing out traffic tickets to elected officials, buying ice cream cones for lost kids, crying when friends on his beat died and, now and then, shooting it out in a fracas. He ran the cleanest beat in the toughest part of town this way, the only way he knew how—he was an anachronism in both the Police Department and all of official Atlantic City.

I asked him once—when I had returned from the Marine Corps and World War II—why he'd never gone along with it all. He simply looked puzzled. "Suppose all the cops gave in," he finally said. "You wouldn't have any law and order." It was as good an explanation as he could give to what seemed to him a stupid question.

Not that Dad didn't get angry and frustrated in his job. I recall the time he was working the midnight-until-eight shift in the Italian section of town. Someone had told him of a large bootlegging operation on Georgia Avenue. He set out to find it one night. He kept doubling back in the area again and again until he saw a car with four men turn into an alley.

"I knew it was no car on my beat," he told me later.

Dad ran along a fence on the side of the alley until he reached the point where the auto had stopped. Then he jumped the fence and pushed his gun into the ear of the driver. "Get out," he ordered the four men. They were all armed. He marched them, hands locked behind their heads, to a call box and ordered a paddy wagon from City Hall. The four men were put in a cell.

The driver, it turned out, was Dutch Schultz. Within half an hour Nucky Johnson had ordered their release. It came out later they'd come from New York City for a conference with some Philadelphia hoods and Dad had fouled up their plans.

Dad hadn't even completed his report when Dutch Schultz strolled up to him at the counter in City Hall. "You know, I'll tell you something, you got a lot of guts," he grinned.

Dad stood in red-faced rage holding the useless arrest forms. "Yeah, Dutch, and you got a lot of luck!" Dad shouted. "I made a mistake. Next time I won't bother to bring you here. I'll just take you to a hospital when I'm finished."

Mayhem was part of Dad's life. He came home constantly with black eyes, bruises, and injured hands. He took them all as just part of his job and was always nonchalant. His tangles also sometimes humiliated him. Once he ran into his match. A thug pummeled him with his own nightstick. The next morning when he showed up for inspection the lieutenant stopped as he walked down the line.

"Kelly, what you got those damned gloves on for?" he demanded.

My father stood silent. It turned out Dad had a broken arm. He'd rubbed it with Ben-Gay, then put gloves on to cover up his bruised hands. "Embarrassing," he told me later.

If street hooligans were Dad's special prey, crooked cops and their allies were his special hate. One parking lot owner near the Boardwalk had a fix in with motorcycle cops: he paid them off to use the red zone for autos near his lot when it was crowded. This infuriated Dad. Although the area was technically out of his jurisdiction, he'd spend hours giving out tickets for autos parked there on busy days. The parking lot owner had to pay the fine and howled foul. He once hinted to Dad that maybe something should be worked out. Dad hinted back that trying to bribe an officer was mighty serious. He just kept on giving out tickets.

This was an exception, as Dad actually preferred a roust to a formal arrest. Tickets caused trouble and confusion for him downtown, particularly if the man he arrested had the fix in—which in Atlantic City was nearly everyone. In addition, with those broken hands, his scribbling was often so confusing for a judge that he'd be called in to explain it.

As Dad's endless tangles with various kinds of trouble formed a pattern, I became accustomed to them. But there were times when real crisis came. When I was eleven years old I was awakened one night by Dad in the bathroom where he was running water for a long time. Mother had left me alone to visit my grandmother. Then I heard a knock at the front door and Dad in conversation with some men.

"Well, be as quiet as you can. My kid is asleep in the other room and I don't want to wake him," I heard him say. Then the front door closed. I got up and looked out the window. I saw Dad getting into a police car. I went to the bathroom. It was covered with blood. I was terrified and didn't know what to do. We had no telephone so I dressed and went to my grandmother's house on Bellevue Avenue to tell my mother. She called the Police Department. "Kelly is under arrest for murder," she was told by a friend in the department.

Some years before, Dad had arrested a man for burglary who had been given five years in prison. He was a huge blacksmith named Paul Mall. The day he got out of prison he set out to find my father. He found him in a bar. He leapt on Dad and began to beat him, breaking both his cheekbones. Everyone ran, including another policeman who was with Dad. After he'd been beaten mercilessly Dad apparently decided there was only one escape. He pulled out his gun and shot Paul Mall.

He was to spend two years in jail awaiting trial, charged with first-degree murder. The prosecutor of Atlantic County prepared carefully. Dad was defended by Thomas D. Taggert, Jr., who was later to become Mayor of Altantic City. Every day of the trial I sat in the front row filled with terror that he'd be found guilty. Finally the verdict came in. Dad was guilty of justifiable homicide. In New Jersey this was the usual finding for policemen who killed someone in performance of their duty. The episode was to leave a terrible scar on me. For years after I would awaken from nightmares of the trial.

I don't know why it didn't leave him embittered. I know it did me. I knew that I'd never be a policeman and risk such abuse. But Dad only said, "Look, if the courts weren't just, if law and order wasn't there, I would have been found guilty. But the fact that I was found innocent proves that I am doing the right thing."

I viewed his duties in a different light. I recall seeing him come home one night with his ears black and frozen from frostbite. I wondered, "What would bring a man to spend the night in the freezing cold and snow just to protect other people who were asleep?"

No, I would never be a cop.

Yet our memories have a way of discarding the unpleasant, probably for our own self-protection. I came back from the Pacific and was discharged from the U.S. Marine Corps on December 15, 1944. Two weeks later I was sworn in as a patrolman in the Atlantic City Police Department. I'm a little dim now why I ever made this hasty move. My father had tried to convince me that it would be a good idea on a temporary basis until I decided what I wanted to do with my future. Too, there was a shortage of personnel and it would help the department as a stop-gap measure, he explained. I'd been working for Proctor and Gamble before I joined the service, and the company offered me a better position. But Dad was a convincing opponent verbally as well as physically, and I reluctantly decided I'd spend a few months as a cop just to please him and, I think, to prove to him once and for all that it wasn't for me. It's now 30 years later. I'm still in law enforcement.

The Marine Corps had taught me the value of training, of being ready to meet any situation in the jungle. This belief in training was to stay with me when I got a look at our own urban jungles. That's why I can't forget the first day I reported as a patrolman. I'd bought some of my uniform and was self-conscious and nervous when a desk sergeant handed me a pistol, six cartridges, a badge to put on my cap, and a coat. He motioned me toward the drill room. "Go in there and wait for roll call," he grunted.

That was my "training" for the Atlantic City Police Department.

I know that because of Dad's reputation and name I was more concerned than the ordinary young officer reporting for duty. When we lined up the captain introduced me to the other officers on the shift and the sergeant walked down the line glancing at uniforms and handing out beat cards.

The concept was simplicity itself. You were assigned a specific territory and you walked from one end to the other, calling in at one post on the even hours and from the other end of the beat on the odd hours. You came to know every store, every face, every auto on your beat—and when something went astray, when the wrong light was on or a strange car was parked where it shouldn't be, you knew immediately something might be amiss. Too, you became a friend and intimate of all the people on the beat, knowing their habits and idiosyncrasies. Unfortunately, today the demands of efficiency and economy have replaced the cop on the beat; now we have that cold and impersonal form of enforcement which tends to make every kid, and even law-abiding citizens, fearful of The Man.

That first day my beat card had two numbers on it. I asked one of the officers as I went down the steps what they meant. He explained that that was my territory and suggested I come along on the streetcar with the others. I was the last one off at the end of the line. I'd been told I was to report in at 4:30 and I went directly to the call box. I opened it and found a handle and an earphone. But I didn't know what to do next. I started to pull the lever but decided against it, fearing it might signify some panic call like a four-alarm fire. There was no friendly sound from the earphone. Finally, I closed the box and went to a pay phone and called the station. The sergeant listened to my faltering questions and then explained with a tone of disgust in his voice how to pull the lever and contact the dispatcher. Such are the ways of police departments that I was already the butt of corny humor and kidding by the time I got back that night.

I learned that first week the quality of aloneness that comes with being a cop and walking a beat. The new uniform—contrary to the old saw about cops loving to strut around—doesn't make you feel important; it makes you feel naked. You feel everyone is watching you. You may act officious but end up wandering aimlessly. You don't know what to look for or how to check points or observe people along the way. You feel that you are doing nothing but killing time between the calls to the dispatcher. I found it all a bore on that first day and wondered how long I could stand it.

The following week I was assigned to the midnight-to-eight shift. What was more, I was given Dad's old beat—known for many years as the "ten and twelve"—that ran from South Carolina and the Boardwalk to Ohio and Atlantic. The game of Monopoly, as you have probably figured out, is based on the geography of Atlantic City, and this beat was to turn into one of the liveliest contests I ever played.

It was known as an extremely difficult beat and I wondered why they'd assign a rookie to it when, that first night, Dad appeared. A deal had been made, and with the indulgent sentimentality that is so often a part of the cop's inner world, I'd been given Dad's old beat with the idea that he would train me.

He did, waiting until late to arrive so as not to embarrass me. He showed me how to try doors, watch for certain people, investigate strange cars, go through back alleys, climb fences, and check narrow walkways. This was always Dad's favorite hunting ground and he spent more time in the backs of stores than on the sidewalk.

I'll never forget my first arrest. It was to hook me and I was for the first time to experience the thrill of being a cop, the same thrill I suppose a boxer feels when he wins his first fight.

It was about one A.M. on a humid, sticky night. I'd been working my way down a dark alley, climbing fences, crossing vacant lots, and checking back doors. I started down an alley when I noticed a light on in the rear of a dress shop. As I started toward it I heard a scraping sound. It was a sound that didn't fit, is all I can say. When we were fighting the Japanese on Guadalcanal we'd sometimes hear such an offbeat sound in the jungle night and immediately be on the alert.

I stopped and shined my flashlight at a rusty, discarded iron furnace in the alleyway. I knew by instinct—as well as I'd have

known there was something out in the jungle in the South Pacific—
that there was someone behind it!

I pulled my gun. "All right. I've got you covered. Come on
out," I ordered.

Yet, I was startled when a huge, rough-looking youth in a
leather jacket arose from behind the furnace with his hands up.
Immediately I wondered what to do next: do I let him walk in front
of me? Do I stand against the wall in this narrow alley and order him
to pass in front of me, then follow him? Do I back out and order him
to follow me, hands up?

I chose the latter action. I started backing out the length of the
long, narrow alley, only some four feet wide.

I suddenly tripped on some old boards, falling with a crash on
my back.

I saw his right arm raise and realized for the first time that he
was holding a piece of iron pipe.

Surprisingly, I didn't shoot. Rather, I felt curiously calm in
those few split seconds.

"I've still got my gun," I said softly. "Drop that pipe."

He did. I got out of the alley. I marched him to the call box,
ordering him to put his hands against a building as I'd seen police
do in the movies.

I called for assistance, then searched him for a weapon, finding
nothing. When the radio car arrived, we went back to the entrance
to the alley and found his car. It was filled with dresses.

The incident was to be a monumental moment of decision for
me. I knew now that I'd never go back to Proctor and Gamble. I was
a cop. I had it in my blood. Too, that arrest was to give me a sudden
new insight into my father, a new dimension.

Naturally, I followed the case of this young man, my first
arrest. His wife, I found, was in the hospital having a baby at the
time. He'd been desperate for money. He appealed to me and I tried
to talk to someone to help him. But the judge gave him five years in
prison. I felt terrible, guilty that I'd ruined this boy's life. I finally
decided to tell Dad about my dilemma.

I had hardly started explaining when he interrupted. "Wait a minute! Cut out thinking that way right now!" he snapped. "You didn't send him to jail. You did your job. You're a policeman. People break the law and you arrest them. A judge decides if they are guilty. It's his job to sentence them, not your job. Your job is to enforce the law. Now, when you lock a man up and the judge lets him go, that should be no personal concern of yours either. That's hard to take sometimes. But you've done your job, and if the judge feels there are extenuating circumstances he'll turn him loose. You'll find that happens many, many times. So don't ever feel responsible for him being in jail. He's responsible. He committed the crime. You enforced the law and protected the public good and the public right and that's what you're paid for. Never, never feel vindictive, and never feel bad. You should have no emotions about him at all. Always remember that."

It was a valuable sermon, that injunction by Dad as we sat at the kitchen table with a beer. Years later, when I was called upon to speak before young officers I always recited it as a creed for a law enforcement officer to live by if he doesn't want to lose perspective.

As I mentioned before, while I understand the pressures that led to the change, I believe the demise of the cop on the beat is one of the major tragedies of law enforcement. I learned that he was in many ways like a soldier taking the point on patrol. He never knew what crisis would occur. He had to know his area, the soft spots, where to look for a possible break-in, what to do with the neighborhood drunk. But, just as important, everyone knew him. Parents would tell their children if they got lost to find the local policeman. Buying an ice cream cone for a lost urchin was a standard part of the job. Today's generation of youngsters don't know the cop on the beat, only a black-and-white driving by that most of them fear.

Too, the man on the beat can recognize trouble better than the man in the black-and-white. He is aware when a strange car is in his area, he knows the unsavory people, he spots a strange face. The man who knew his beat well could smell trouble instantly when something was out of line.

My brief time as the cop on the beat convinced me of this. You can encounter a dozen problems on any night. You become conditioned to this. I recall a gunfight I had on the Boardwalk on the night of February 3, 1947. I was working the midnight-to-eight shift and it was bitterly cold with snow falling. I saw a hulking Negro standing in front of an open window at the Southern Sweet Shop.

"What are you doing?" I shouted.

He turned, pulled out a revolver, and started firing.

I fell to the Boardwalk and tried to get to my gun. But I was wearing a thick overcoat and had to unbutton it to reach my holster. (The episode was to result in a uniform change, with new coats that allowed us to reach through a coat pocket for our guns.) He fired several times before I could roll over and get my weapon out.

I fired a shot at him as a second man leapt out of the window and started firing too. Jimmy Peterson, who was working the beat next to me, had heard the shots and came running. He saw me stretched out and thought I was wounded. They took off. We chased them through alleys and finally stopped to call for a radio car. Several arrived but the two men were gone. We returned to find they'd been trying to blow a safe.

I went back and filled out my report, then went home to bed. A few hours later my wife awakened me crying and hysterical. A three-deck headline in the morning Atlantic City *Daily World* announced: "Rookie Cops Rout Two Burglars in Walk Gun Battle." I hadn't thought the incident important enough to disturb her.

Miracles, also, happen on the beat. I recall a woman who came to the curb pushing a baby carriage and casually pushed it down into the street. I shouted to her to get it back. She just stood, looking puzzled as I rushed toward her. A car hit the carriage as I ran toward it, crushing it like an accordion. The baby shot out of it and, like a star pass receiver, I caught the baby as it spun through the air. The woman was furious because the carriage was wrecked.

Now that I'd decided to stay on I set out to advance myself. If you visit any small-town police station in the country you're likely to see diplomas from the Institute of Applied Science. I signed up for the correspondence course, taking fingerprinting and photography. By then I was married with two children and making fifty dollars a week. I couldn't afford the course, but struggled through it as many young officers are doing today. It was difficult, learning how to classify prints by mail. But slowly I became proficient in taking prints, classifying them, and dusting the scene of a crime for prints. When an opening came in the Identification Bureau under Captain James Farley, I was qualified and got into plain clothes, the first step to becoming a detective.

For some months I was involved in fingerprinting defendants, sending copies to the FBI, going out on burglaries to dust blown safes, and fingerprinting cadavers. But it was also a wonderful chance to get to know the detectives. I'd go with them on jobs during my off hours and learn the refinements of their specialty.

Opportunity came when Sheriff Gerald Gormley decided to form a squad of his own to investigate county violations. The city's Police Department had its own vice squad but the sheriff wasn't pleased with the results. He wanted more coverage of the entire county. When I was asked if I wanted to join the squad I agreed immediately.

It was an unusual group. It consisted of John Berry, a white officer in charge, Robert Shepperson, a black officer, and myself. This was the nucleus, but we had a number of other officers who came and went as certain problems developed.

Our first target was gambling. It was common street talk that the city's vice squad was on the take from numbers men and bookies. A running gag was the way the vice squad dressed with expensive vicuna suits and diamond rings. As for gambling arrests, there just weren't any.

We were all crusaders. I was now a young idealist, convinced I could go out and slay the dragon. Within a month we'd made nearly a hundred gambling arrests. We also naturally became immediately the skunk at the lawn party. The vice squad denounced us, claiming we were usurping its authority. Higher-ups, captains and sergeants on the Police Department, suddenly wouldn't speak to us except to lecture us on our errant ways. We began to realize that this was no minor jurisdictional fight. There was an organized campaign against us. We'd make a bookie arrest and the man would be released immediately while we faced a dressing down from the brass for having made the arrest. Repeatedly, they let anyone we brought in go, hoping to break our spirit. If we complained, the sergeant or lieutenant would simply tell us to go to hell.

The day came when Sheriff Gormley called us in. "Look, I want to tell you boys how much I appreciate the job you've done, and I'm all for you. But I've been ordered to disband your squad and put you back in uniform. I don't want to do that. I've gone to the mat with the politicians and they've finally given me an ultimatum. You can't work any more gambling cases. In fact, they don't want you working in the daytime at all. They're afraid you'll run into things that they don't want you to run into. So that's about it. You work nights when the numbers and books are closed. How do you feel about that?"

By then we had a monkey on our backs. It wasn't so much that we cared about gambling in any moral way. It was the kick we got out of rousting the gamblers and outwitting them, knowing we were creating havoc with the big-shots. But it was clear that if we wanted to stay together there was nothing to do but accept the alternative. Otherwise we could go back in uniform or quit. We agreed to go to work at nine each night.

I was pissed off. Yet, as it was to develop, it was the best thing that ever happened to me. For we turned to narcotics, then a largely ignored and neglected field of enforcement. In the next few years I was to get my basic training on a hit-and-miss improvised basis as we worked the streets. Today, I tell young men at training schools that I come from the old school of narcotics law enforcement where the basic tool was a size twelve pair of shoes. It's true. In those days any illegal search became legal upon the finding of evidence. We never concerned ourselves with warrants. When we heard that someone had narcotics we simply went to the address and kicked in the door. Our intelligence gathering was just as primitive. We'd watch and listen until we got a rumble that someone was a user or peddler. Then we'd catch suspects and take them into an alley, tossing them against the wall, browbeating them and forcing them to tell who was scoring or peddling. When the battered suspect would talk and give us an address we'd let him go, knowing that he wouldn't admit he was a stoolie to whoever he'd named. Then we'd go to the address, watch until two or three people had entered, and kick in the door.

Improvising and devising ingenious schemes to corner a suspect were essential. Unlike federal agents, we had no money to make purchases of evidence or to pay informers. I remember when we came across a user who, after we'd banged him against the wall a few times, agreed to make a buy from the dealer for us. Three of us each chipped in enough to give him a five-dollar bill to buy a capsule of heroin. He led us to the apartment of Pencil Hersey, a black criminal we all knew. He went up and returned a few minutes later with the capsule. "They got it right in the living room," he told us. "There are about six of them sitting around. I saw Pencil go into the bedroom and take a paper bag from the third drawer in the bureau and bring it into the living room. He didn't know I could see him through the crack in the door. That bag's in the living room right now . . ."

Now was the time to hit them. We went to the fourth floor of the dingy building and could hear the murmur of voices in the apartment. Now Robert Shepperson, my partner, is the dearest friend I've ever had in life. He is an enormous man weighing about 260 pounds and standing six feet, four inches. Naturally he was nicknamed Teeny. He is known in the narcotics game as the finest door-buster in the United States and there's folklore about him. Certainly he's the finest I've seen in 29 years in law enforcement. He was particularly magnificent that day. When he hit the door he not only took it out, but the jamb around it and all the plaster. It hit with a crash. We rushed in so fast that no one was even able to get out of his chair.

But there was no paper bag in the living room. We felt confident, though. We had been assured that it was back in the third drawer in the bedroom.

We began to question everyone, playing cat-and-mouse. Pencil denied everything. Then we began to search, going through the kitchen and bath first to make it appear we didn't know where the heroin really was, to protect our informer in case anyone had seen him when he observed where Pencil had hidden it. Then we casually opened the drawer. It wasn't there! We began to search frantically. Nothing.

It was Pencil's turn now. "You bastards," he grumbled. "This is my aunt's place. When she comes home and finds that door she's going to get your jobs."

As I said, any illegal search became legal if you found evidence. If you didn't you could be in serious trouble. Pencil knew this, of course, and was making the most of it.

We tried to bully it through, threatening the six of them, but got nowhere. Then I had an idea. I went into the hall, unloaded my gun, put the cartridges in my pocket, and my gun back in my holster.

I went back in and whispered to Teeny, "Send Willie out to me." Willie Saunders was a burglar-addict we'd picked up many times before. I knew him well and what he was.

Willie came out, wide-eyed and puzzled. "Come on, Willie, let's go over to the stairs," I ordered.

He grinned. "Yeah, Mr. Kelly. Sure. It looks like you guys are in trouble, doesn't it."

I grinned back. "No, Willie, not really. We got a way out."

Willie shrugged, looking more puzzled. I pulled out my gun and stuck it in his ear.

"All right, Willie," I said softly. "You start running down those stairs."

"What you mean, Mr. Kelly?" he stuttered.

I tried to speak calmly. "Look, Willie! We don't have any reason for busting in that door. You know that. Now we've got to cover ourselves. I'm going to say you started a big hassle and tried to escape and I had to shoot you. With you wasted they aren't going to even think about the door."

"You wouldn't do that!"

I chuckled and pulled back the hammer.

Perspiration was pouring down Willie's face. "That's against the law," he moaned.

"Run!" I said.

Willie fell to his knees. "I'm not goin' to."

"Then I'm going to kick you down the stairs and shoot you when you hit the bottom," I said.

"What you want, Mr. Kelly?" he gasped.

"Where's the heroin, Willie?"

He looked fearfully at the apartment door, knowing what Pencil would do if he talked. But he was also now convinced of what I'd do if he didn't.

"When you hit that door Pencil just threw that bag out the window," he said. "It must be right down in the alley."

I pulled Willie to his feet and, gun still at his ear, went down to the alley and found the brown bag. I made him pick it up and we returned to the apartment.

Pencil began to curse, threatening Willie. But we took them all to jail.

Pencil was to appear in my life again and again. I'd already arrested him a year or so before. It was when I was assigned to traffic. I'd been directing cars on the corner of Tennessee and Pacific when I thought I heard a thud. I turned and a half block away saw an old woman falling on the street. I saw a truck turn down a narrow street which led into a maze of alleys. By the time I'd reached the street the truck couldn't be seen. I ran down and could see nothing. The rear entrance to the garage of the Senator Hotel seemed like the likeliest place to check. There was one truck in the garage and the attendant said one of the people who worked in the hotel, Pencil Hersey, had arrived in it just moments before. I checked the front for dents and found none. But I found Pencil and immediately arrested him for hit-and-run driving, gambling that he'd confess. He stuttered for a moment, then admitted he was the driver.

I was to encounter Pencil again in 1952 when I was a federal narcotics agent. I was ruffling through some wanted notices when I came across one from Philadelphia. An agent had bought some heroin from Pencil Hersey and he was a fugitive, thought to be in New York. I knew it had to be "my" Pencil. I called Teeny in Atlantic City to ask if he'd heard anything of our old friend. A few days later he called me back to say that he understood Pencil had a girlfriend who lived at 120th street and 8th Avenue in New York City. I asked him to check out any toll phone numbers from Pencil's old address inAtlantic City. He checked back and gave me one that had been called a number of times. It led to an apartment house. By now, nailing Pencil had become a hobby. The superintendent of the apartment house recognized Pencil from some pictures I showed him and promised to call me the next time Pencil arrived to visit his girl. He did—one Saturday night about seven when I was having dinner. He explained that he'd seen Pencil leaving and followed him to a poolhall on Fifth Avenue. I drove from Astoria on Long Island to the apartment house and the superintendent took me to the poolhall.

I was a lone white man in Harlem, but young and foolhardy. I went down a flight of stairs to the poolroom. There must have been a hundred black men there. When I walked in everything stopped. Players in the middle of a shot stopped, laughter and banter ended, and everyone turned to stare at me, an intruder into a private world. Everyone, that is, except Pencil, who was three tables down the narrow room with his back to me chalking his cue.

I walked quickly to the table.

"Pencil, look at me," I said.

He turned. "Oh, shee-at, Mr. Kelly. Not you again!"

"Listen, Pencil," I said softly. "I have a gun in my righthand coat pocket and it's pointed right at your heart. Let's walk out of here without trouble."

I knew that if there was a fracas I'd have everyone in the place swarming over me.

He grinned. "Hell, Mr. Kelly, I'd never give you no trouble." He turned and started for the stairway while the crowd stood staring. It was a long, long walk and the hairs stood up on the back of my neck. I was expecting a cuestick over my head each step. But we made it up the steps. Pencil seemed almost pleased to have me arresting him again and chatted merrily about old times, as I took him to the West Street House of Detention and locked him up. I never saw him again.

2

Little Bo Peep

If our little group of windmill-tilters had some moments of glory, we also made our ferocious blunders. Most were due to lack of training and a naive enthusiasm that leaves me bemused when I think of it nearly 30 years later.

I remember the spring night we were cruising—John Berry, Teeny, and myself—simply enjoying the warm weather and waiting for something to happen. Alan Gill, now a detective in Atlantic City, called our car and asked us to meet him at a northside bar. He was standing in front when we arrived and got into the car.

"Look at this," he said, handing us some ten-dollar bills. "Do they look okay to you?"

None of us knew anything about counterfeit money. But that didn't stop each of us from studiously fingering the bills for texture, holding them up to the light to study the markings, and finally concluding that they looked real enough to us.

Alan went on to explain that two couples had been drinking at the bar and paid their tab with one bill, then ordered more drinks and had given the bartender another ten rather than the change. Alan had wondered about that and followed them to another bar where they did the same thing. "It just seemed odd," he said.

As we had nothing better to do we decided to pursue it. We agreed that the others would tail the two men and women, who had a new blue Cadillac with New York plates, while I was sent to City Hall with the bills to get some expert advice.

I took them to the captain on duty, a double-chinned, bald curmudgeon noted for his authoritative ways.

"What do you make of these, Captain?" I asked, telling him the background and spreading the bills out on his oak desk. He gave me the sort of annoyed look kindergarten teachers reserve for their slower kiddies, then picked several up. After quickly glancing at them under the desk lamp he laconically let them flutter to the desk. "Perfectly authentic," he said with finality. I thanked him and went out, disappearing into the detective room. Here a couple of loungers put down their coffee cups and passed their judgment. "I've seen a barrel of funny money and this ain't it," said a lieutenant.

I doubted that. "I still think there's something going on," I replied. I turned to find the captain in the doorway glaring at me. "Listen, Kelly," he shouted, obviously angered that I had not taken his word as final. "These people are visitors. Don't harass them. Leave them alone. If they want to trot out big bills to show off in Atlantic City bars it's not your business. I know bad money when I see it."

I left and returned to my companions, who were in our car outside a dinette where the two couples were having dinner. "That captain says to drop it," I explained.

We sat wondering what to do and fingering the bills when something so simple a gas attendant would have recognized it occured to me. The serial numbers on all the bills were the same!

We were triumphant. We quickly got out of the car and went into the dinette where the foursome sat finishing the T-bone steaks and baked potatoes. We put the cuffs on them while they protested bitterly and drove them to City Hall..

At the station we found nineteen of the same bills on them. Then we started stripping down the Cadillac. In the arm rest between the seat we found $1950 in those bills. We called the Secret

Service and, by the time they'l finished their investigation, they had found over $10,000 in counterfeit money.

The total result was inevitable. Of course the captain was furious with me for embarrassing him before the detectives, and he read me off for not obeying orders.

We drifted more and more into narcotics work simply because we had been turned off from the gambling and corruption.

Nearly 30 years ago narcotics were still scorned by most racketeers as something that didn't pay beans for the risk involved and the unstable small market. Too, drugs were still oddities in crime. Even a stick of marijuana taken in a raid was cause for a news story. The result was that John, Teeny, and I were always being publicized in the local papers. As we kept lurching about in our amateurish way working more and more cases, one leading to the next, we sought the help and advice of two federal agents, Harry Sterling and Al Bendon, who worked out of Philadelphia. It was inevitable, I suppose, as I sat drinking martinis with them and listening to their tales of adventure, of million-dollar busts in exotic lands, of shootouts and intrigue in high places, that I decided there was only one job in the world—to be a federal agent. For the next year I spent my spare time daydreaming of getting into the Bureau of Narcotics.

Several things happened about then which were to destroy my fantasy. We had made a heroin case. Our user was a pathetic frycook who told us that he bought his stuff in New York City. "I'll tell you everything," he said. I called Joe Bransky, the District Supervisor in Philadelphia for the Bureau, aware that they'd have to pick up the case from here and make the arrest in New York.

I knew him casually and didn't like him. He was a curt and overbearing oldtimer who showed his contempt for local cops in every way he could.

He said he'd be in Atlantic City the next day. When he arrived I brought the prisoner from his cell to the detective bureau where Bransky sat waiting, smoking a cigar and glowering at me.

I sat in on the interrogation, as was the custom. Bransky began immediately to browbeat the prisoner, cursing him and calling him a lying junkie bastard.

"The man's telling the truth," I interrupted at one point, my Irish temper flaring.

Bransky turned to me. "What the hell do you know?" he said. "You're a punk who doesn't know what's going on. I've had years in the Bureau. Stay the fuck out of this!"

He turned back to the prisoner and started denouncing him again. I got up. I was furious, but had to concede that he must know a lot more. I went out to the hall to get a drink of water and cool down. I wasn't gone more than two minutes, then I went back into the detective bureau.

The wispy little prisoner was stretched out on the floor bleeding at the mouth. "All right, you lying son of a bitch!" Bransky was shouting. "Now start talking . . ."

"Get your ass out of here!" I yelled. Branksy turned with an amazed expression. He started to speak.

"Out! We don't need you," I shouted. "I'll throw you down the steps of City Hall myself!" I guess I'd gone slightly berserk from the reaming he'd given me and then this. "We don't beat up prisoners here."

I grabbed the prisoner from the floor and pushed him out while Bransky started swearing at me.

I took the stunned man to his cell, then went to the drill room downstairs. The phone was ringing as I entered. "The chief wants to see you," a voice said.

Chief Harry Saunders was sitting behind his battered desk and Bransky was in a leather chair with a fresh cigar.

"Mr. Bransky tells me you ordered him out of City Hall," the chief said.

"I did."

"Why?"

"He was beating up a prisoner of mine," I replied.

The chief turned to Bransky.

"The bastard was lying to me," Bransky snapped.

The chief stoof up abruptly. "Well, did you hear what Mr. Kelly told you?"

Bransky looked puzzled. "What do you mean?"

"He told you to get out. What he says goes. And don't ever come back as long as I'm Chief. . . ."

I'd won the battle but lost the war. As my application for the Bureau had to be processed through the Philadelphia office headed by Bransky I knew the incident had finished my hopes for a career with the Bureau before it ever started.

The reaction of the chief had been typical of him. He was a fine officer who backed up his men. But he could also be eccentric in many curious ways. I recall the winter night when John Berry and I chased a stolen car in a wild race that led all over town, then out to the highway bridge where we slipped and slid on the ice. Both cars spun around and ours struck the railing of the bridge and wedged there. The thief in the stolen car backed up and rammed us, trying to push us over the edge into the black waters below. Our police cars couldn't take much punishment. They were always in dreadful condition and disrepair. The front seat on the passenger side had fallen off in the one we were driving that night, which meant that I had to sit in the back while John drove. When the thief backed up to get ready for another ram at our car, I leaned out of the back window and fired my pistol at him. It made him pause and gave John enough time to start out, shift gears to reverse, and ram him. We ended up catching the man. But when I fired at him the fly window of the front was open and the bullet had gone through it.

I didn't give it a second thought, as we were both rather proud of the capture. A few days later the chief summoned me to his office. I expected some kind of congratulations for the way we had handled the chase. But then I thought it odd that John wasn't there.

Saunders sat back and eyed me coldly. "I understand you fired a shot the other night," he said.

I nodded smugly. "Yes, Chief. I was driving that guy away from us. He was trying to push us over the side and I put a shot through his windshield. That's how we were able to take him."

"But what about the fly window?"

"What fly window?"

"You put a bullet through it when you fired. You damaged city property. We have to keep our cars in good condition!"

"I don't understand what you mean, Chief," I said.

"I mean that window cost $2.10 and you're going to have to pay for it out of your salary!"

After the first shock of amazement I became furious. I took off my badge as I'd seen cops do in the movies and threw it on his desk. "If I have to pay for that Goddamned window I quit," I shouted.

He looked up at me a long moment, then shrugged. "Pick up your badge and get your ass out of here," he said.

For several weeks after the Bransky incident I mulled over other ways to get into the Bureau. I decided I'd simply have to try to bull it through with Bransky. If I had to qualify for the Bureau today, I wouldn't be able to make it. You need a college degree. In the 1950s, however, qualifying experience could be considered the equivalent of a college education. I applied to take the Civil Service test for the examination of a Treasury Agent, which the Bureau was under at the time. I scored high—91—and then got ten additional points as a disabled veteran of World War II. It was a very good score for the exam. But then I ran into the anticipated roadblock. I was called to Philadelphia for a personal interview with Bransky. It was his duty to talk to me.

The token interview was brief and to the point. He set out to make a fool of me and, knowing my weakness, succeeded in infuriating me. He blithely began to ramble on about the crooked police force of Atlantic City and explained how he knew that everyone—everyone on the force—was a thief.

"I resent that," I replied. "Not just for myself, but for all the honest members of the force, such as my father. I won't take that shit." The interview lasted perhaps three minutes. I left the Federal Building dejected and frustrated knowing that I had no chance as long as Bransky was District Supervisor in Philadelphia.

Sterling and Bendon tried to console me by explaining that

someday Bransky would be transferred. Bendon then suggested, "Why don't you go to New York and talk to the people there? Maybe there's some way to bypass Bransky."

I decided to try. I was sent to see one Irwin I. Greenfeld, who was later to become a dear friend. It was apparent that "Greenie" liked me. But there was little he could do. "You'll have to get transferred from the Philadelphia list to New York. I don't know if you can do that. Bransky would know what you're planning and refuse."

He also explained that even if I did get transferred it wouldn't help a great deal. My score of 101 was fine for Philadelphia, it seemed. But I would be quite far down the list with such a score in New York.

"There are a hell of a lot of college graduates coming back from the service who are taking the exam and scoring very high," he said.

I suppose I looked desperate, or maybe just pathetic. "I have one idea," Greenie said slowly, toying with a silver paperknife on his desk. "You're an ex-Marine. Mr. Harney, the Assistant Commissioner in Washington, D.C., is an ex-Marine and gung-ho as all hell. A Marine can do no wrong and all that crap. It might be worth a trip to talk with him."

I grabbed at the idea. A few weeks later I arranged an appointment. Mr. Harney was a gray-haired, dignified, and tough old man. His face lit up when he read my papers and saw I'd been in the Corps. "I like to think of the Bureau as a little Marine Corps," he told me.

He was most encouraging, telling me to go back to my job and wait. I returned to Atlantic City with new hope.

Meanwhile, the antics of the city's vice squad had reached a crisis. The entire squad was indicted for accepting bribes. We in the Sheriff's Squad joked about it. For years they'd been accepting bribes, stealing, not making cases—and now they were getting their comeuppance! When we saw any of them we'd needle them and generally be wise asses. Little did we know that it would all soon backfire. For the day came when we received a summons to come to the Police Department for a summit meeting.

Inspector Lou Arnheim wanted to talk with each of us, we were told. We sat in an outer office waiting our turn to be questioned one by one. None of us had any idea what to expect. When my turn came and I entered, the Inspector sat smoking and studying me coldly for a moment.

"I want to tell you something," he then announced. "You know the vice squad's in trouble. They need help and we're going to help them."

I shrugged. "We are?"

"Yes." He was stern.

"Okay, Inspector. What do you mean?"

He leaned back. "You and Berry and Shepperson have been out making all these narcotics cases. "I'm going to put those cases to use."

I was still puzzled. "What do you mean?" I repeated.

"Well, one of the things the grand jury is saying is that the vice squad isn't making any gambling cases. They're not locking up anyone. So we're going to give them credit for your narcotics cases to show the grand jury that they actually made those cases and you fellows were just in with them on the arrests."

I was outraged but tried to hold my temper. "How are you going to do that, Inspector? All the arrest records are in our names. I don't see how you can change that. . . ."

He rubbed his chin a moment. "It's simple. We're going to change all the reports."

I guess I showed the fury I felt at something as blatantly crooked as this.

"If you don't like it," he continued quickly, "just tell me and tomorrow you can go back in uniform."

"I don't give a damn about the cases, Inspector. I don't care who gets the credit. They're all in the past. We made them and we know it and I think the public knows it. I don't know who you expect to fool."

The Inspector was boring in now. "I'm going to carry it one step more, Kelly," he went on. "From now on when you or Shepperson or Berry get any information about narcotics I want you to call Sergeant Frank Sullivan at the vice squad and his squad will make the case. You fellows can go along with them but the sergeant is going to be in charge. That's all. . . ."

I walked out in a daze. Berry was waiting outside for me and Shep soon joined us. We adjourned to a bar and sat over beers puzzling over what to do. The alternatives were clear: go along, refuse and go back in uniform, or quit. We were all disgusted, angry and disappointed that law enforcement had come to this. We all said the same thing: the inspector could go screw himself. We weren't going to turn over our cases to the vice squad. What was more, we concluded on about the fifth beer, we were going on a rampage making some cases we'd held in reserve. Starting that very night.

We selected as our target for the night a place we'd had under surveillance. We parked in front of the old white house and sat there until dawn, then hit. It was pure luck. We found three suspects we were after as well as enough heroin to make a good case and a man from New York as well, their connection. It couldn't have been more fortuitous, and the following day, Sunday, there was a long newspaper story of our exploit. We chuckled among ourselves, knowing that something had to boil over.

It did. Monday we were called separately to Lou Arnheim's office. We knew why. It was so no two of us could testify or make any allegation against him. He was furious. A small man who weighed perhaps 120 pounds, he was in a white rage and waving his arms.

Our agreed-upon tactic was the dumb cop routine. "I just didn't understand your instructions," I explained innocently. "I thought you meant if there was time to call in the vice squad, we should. Well, there just wasn't enough time. It was nearly dawn when the case developed and you know all those vice squad boys go home at six at night. . . ."

Arnheim kept muttering "son of a bitch" under his breath, then finally got up and shook a bony finger under my nose.

"Look, Kelly," he shouted. "I'll be plainer with you. You leave this office and go down the street to the corner and a guy comes up to you and says, 'Hey, buddy, I got an ounce of heroin in my pocket to sell. Want to buy it?' Got that? Know what you are going to do? You turn and walk away. You're not to take any more narcotics arrests without Sergeant Frank Sullivan of the vice squad. Ever! Never! Got it? Is that clear?''

I nodded innocently. "Okay, Inspector. Now it's perfectly clear. You mean we are to supply the vice squad with narcotics cases at all cost.''

"Exactly! And if you can't turn the case over to them, forget it.''

Shep and Teeny and I were huddled over beers an hour later, more indignant than ever. The idea of a top police official ordering us not to make arrests! Immediately we set to plotting another arrest which would make the newspapers.

We went through our little black books. There was one iffy possibility: an apartment where three lesbians were supposed to have something going with heroin. We decided to take a chance. That night we hit the place and were in luck, finding a small supply of heroin. We called a reporter we knew immediately. The next morning, the day after Arnheim had read us off, there was another story and picture with our happy, smiling faces to greet Inspector Arnheim when he got up.

This time he didn't bother to call. By the time we arrived for duty he had drawn up reassignments for us. Johnny Berry was put on a motorcycle, Shep was assigned to walking a beat on the north side, and I was given the worst traffic corner in Atlantic City, Arkansas and Atlantic Avenue where all the trains came in. The next day's newspapers didn't carry a tale of our exploits, but the headline "City Dope Squad Abolished" with the explanation that the vice squad was taking over our duties.

Some officers enjoy working traffic. Dad did. But I despised it and my daily stint of trying to handle the milling summertime crowds who got off the trains and streamed down to the Boardwalk was eight hours of horror. If they wanted to persecute and punish me they certainly had picked the ideal job. Then, just to add to the torture, they began interspersing my traffic chore with eight hours at odd times walking a beat, shunting me from one beat to another from midnight to eight.

This went on for a month and I knew I had to quit. The future was apparent. Any career I might have hoped for in enforcement in Atlantic City was finished.

Then a miracle struck! Irwin Greenfeld, the acting District Supervisor in New York, called me. I was to report to him to become a Federal Narcotics Agent! Not only was my dream realized but I jumped from $2450 a year to $3400 a year.

I know I was snide when I notified William S. Cuthbert, the Director of Public Safety, that I was quitting the job to join the Bureau in five weeks. About two weeks before I was to depart I was directing traffic on the eight-to-four shift waving the tourists this way and that with carefree abandon, knowing that I'd be finished on July 30.

At about 11 A.M. I saw a black car pull up across the street. I recognized it as a police car and wondered what had happened. Then Inspector Arnheim emerged and walked out into the center of the street and held out his hand. "I just came down to congratulate you," he explained expansively. I guess I appeared dumbfounded. "I want you to know, John, that there was nothing personal in putting you back in uniform. It was just something that had to be done." "We both know why you put me back. I don't want to talk about it," I replied tersely, turning my attention back to the honking cabs.

He wouldn't give up. "Don't be bitter against me or the Department," he went on. "That's one reason I'm here. To tell you that when you get to be a Federal Narcotics Agent in New York I want you not to forget your old friends down here. You've seen a lot of things that are bad and probably know a lot of things that are bad in Atlantic City. I want you to forget them and remember us as old friends."

"What's that, some kind of threat?"

He shrugged, then chuckled. "In a way, I suppose. There are a lot of people in North Jersey who would like to make trouble for a lot of people down here. If you talked to them it would cause a lot of unhappiness."

I forgot all about traffic and turned on him. "Blow it out your ass," I said. "I'll do what I Goddamned please. I don't need you to tell me what I can and can't do."

His face hardened. "Okay. But just remember that your father is getting up in years and he's vulnerable. If you'd like him to keep his beat and make his pension you'd better listen to me."

I paused a moment. "Yeah," I said. "I'll tell you exactly what my dad would tell you. Go to hell. . . ."

Arnheim nodded. "We may just put him up in Venice Park or Chelsea Heights for awhile," he continued. They were the worst beats in Atlantic City.

"Get off my corner or I'll whip your ass," I ordered. It was the last time I ever spoke to him.

If my stint as a cop in Atlantic City taught me nothing else, I had become an expert in this kind of double-dealing chicanery and low-grade intrigue. I had learned from the ground up, starting with the most primitive form of stealing. Take my first encounter: I'd only been on the Boardwalk for a few weeks.

I'd found a window open at the back of Alfred's, an Italian restaurant. I climbed in, turned on the lights, and, as was standard procedure, called City Hall and gave them the owner's home phone number, which I found on a slip.

A few minutes later a radio car arrived. A burly veteran officer came in.

"What happened?"

"Nothing," I said. "Just a back window open."

"Did you check the cash register?" he asked.

I felt foolish. "I didn't look," I said weakly.

He grinned, went to the register. "Well, well—fifteen dollars," he announced, taking the three bills. "Alfred just had a robbery!"

He started to hand me a five. "Your cut, I'll give Billy out in the car one."

"Look," I said, confused. "Put it back. Alfred didn't have a robbery."

"So that's how you feel, is it?"

I nodded.

He stuck the bills in his pocket. "Okay, Little Bo Peep. If you don't want your cut, tough tittie."

He walked out.

What was there to do? If I reported him he had his partner in the car to back him up and call me a liar. I'd probably have been suspended or fired. Maybe it was the cowardly thing to do, but I simply forgot the incident.

It had its own ending. A few years later the officer was picked up for taking a bribe from a numbers man and went to prison.

Years later when I was a federal agent I ran into him on a visit to Atlantic City. He was on his uppers. "Do you remember that night at Alfred's?" he asked. I nodded.

"I wish you'd beat the hell out of me," he said.

If this was petty pilfering, some operations in the corruption of Atlantic City at that time were almost open warfare in the fight over loot. I recall Sergeant Milt Popowsky telling me about a crisis he had. Milt was honest and a fine officer. The Hall got word that one of the biggest bookies in town had died of a heart attack. Milt, who was the first one on the scene, called for an ambulance to take the body away and waited outside for its arrival. He didn't have the mind of a crooked cop. But others did, and within two minutes two officers were in the apartment shaking it down. They found thousands of dollars in small bills. Milt was dumbstruck when he saw them collecting the loot.

"I want everything left as it is," he ordered.

He started trying to gather up the bills. It ended in such a donnybrook that Popowsky had to pull his gun and hold his two fellow officers at bay until he could gather the money to turn it in.

I found out, too, how money can change the law. I recall Harold Scheper, a clever colored numbers man. This was during the period we'd been ordered to lay off gambling arrests. But one night we responded to a robbery call. We found Scheper in the front seat of his car, groggy and with his head split open. The gambler had tried to fight back, but the assailant, who had hid in the back seat, had slugged Scheper even though he'd been able to take one shot with the illegal gun he was carrying.

The only evidence was a hat in the back seat. We started questioning witnesses and one described a man getting into a cab. Teeny knew him immediately from the witness's details, a burglar and thief named Kirkland. We picked him up and took him in for questioning. The hat fit perfectly. As we questioned him I idly turned out the sweat band. There, printed in ink, was "KIRKLAND." I simply handed it to our suspect. He copped out immediately.

We were to encounter Scheper frequently. I developed a certain fondness for him even if he was a numbers man. Once, I recall, we had a hit-and-run case. We described the driver to Schep. He knew who it was immediately. Again, I remember during our counterfeit caper I'd later shown one of the bills to Schep who I knew was an expert in dealing with bills. He didn't even look, but simply felt the paper. "Nope, Jacko. That's counterfeit."

Scheper had his little flurries of trouble, which he had his own way of solving. Once he was arrested by the state police on a numbers charge after he had paid income tax on $175,000 for one year. He was convicted and sent to prison for five years. But within a few weeks he was back in Mays Landing at the Atlantic County jail. He did less than three months and then was released. The Attorney General gave some brief explanation about Schep's poor health and that he had to be near home as he had only a short time to live. A few weeks later we came across Schep smoking a cigar in a colorful purple suit and idling against a lamppost.

"It's great to see you out," I said. "Just for our own curiosity, nothing more, how did you do it?"

"Just personal, you promise?"

I nodded, "Scout's honor."

Schep flicked a bit of ash from his dollar cigar. "My attorney took me over to the Attorney General's office and I gave him $20,000 in cash, that's all."

It was such rough-and-tumble law and politics and enforcement that was to color my whole approach to being an officer, just as it had my dad's. I suppose it is a bit simplistic in these days of political subtleties. You were, quite simply, either crooked or honest. You enforced the law or you didn't. There were no grays in the spectrum of police work. My dad's solutions may have been primitive, but they worked. He illustrated his methods early in my days as a patrolman. I'd made an arrest on the Boardwalk about eight one evening. I was trying to keep my man in tow while phoning in on the call box. He was cursing me, yelling to the crowd that I was picking him up for no reason. Within minutes I had more than a hundred cop-haters around me, many of them angry and hostile. I tried my best to appear stern and businesslike as the mob swore and cursed me. But inside I was in panic. I knew if I tried to force my prisoner to quit raising hell it would only antagonize them more. I managed to get him to the other side of the Boardwalk and stood there helplessly until the wagon arrived listening to the jeers and taunts of the crowd.

That night I sat with Dad over a beer and told him of the incident. "They could've gotten out of hand and raised all kinds of trouble. I didn't know what to do," I explained.

Dad just listened, then replied. "It happens all the time. Someday I'll show you how to handle it."

Several months later I was on my way to work and passed Dad's corner at Tennessee and Pacific. He was struggling with a man who was shouting and swearing and a crowd had started to ·gather.

Dad saw me and called to me, meanwhile pulling the man toward a nearby call box. I started to help but he yelled above the crowd. "I don't want help. I just want to show you how to handle this." He put his key in the call box, opened the heavy iron door, and pulled his prisoner around with a fast jerk. He swung the door open, banging it against the prisoner's head. It happened so fast the crowd didn't know what was going on as Dad gently lowered the suspect to the street with a look of kindly compassion. "That's the way you handle it," he said quietly as he called for the wagon.

If my three years with the sheriff's squad lacked the refinements I was to learn later it was also excellent training for the years to come. Our boss, Jerry Gormley, believed in initiative and freedom. We worked every kind of case that came along although we were preoccupied with narcotics—of which we knew very little. But we also arrested parolees, prostitutes, hit-and-run drivers, burglars, and what-have-yous.

Typically, John Berry and I were cruising at 4 A.M. one night in December, 1949, in an unmarked patrol car. It was black, windy and cold.

We noticed a youth walking along Pacific Avenue and passed him. We drove aimlessly for some ten minutes and then started down Pacific again. Here was the young man again walking toward us in the opposite direction.

"What the hell's that kid doing strolling back and forth and freezing his ass off at this time of night?" Johnny asked.

We pulled up and stopped him.

His answers sounded awry. He was just out walking and thinking, he said. We shook him down. He had a pair of wirecutters in a back pocket. We took him to the station and began to question him again. He admitted that he was on probation for a minor infraction.

The wirecutters were more than just a tool to us at the moment. For weeks the city had been in an uproar about a "cat burglar," as he'd been dubbed by the newspapers, who cut his way through heavy wire screens. The name the press had selected was more pun than fact. The unknown criminal didn't scale walls to loot. He generally hit bars and had the curious habit of drinking the cream off the top of bottles of milk. Those were the happy days of the past when milk always had the little bulge at the top of the bottle for the day's cream ration. It was all fun for the newspapers.

and they'd report how many quarts of milk the cat burglar had taken the cream off of behind the bar before looting the cash register. But it wasn't fun for the Director of Public Safety, Chief of Police, or Chief of Detectives—who were all being made to look foolish in the press over the cream thief.

Our suspect had taken off his overcoat and thrown it carelessly on a chair in the interrogation room. John and I were getting nowhere. Then I noticed the label inside the coat: "HOFFMAN'S MEN'S STORE." It was one of the places that had been robbed and the style of the break-in—although it wasn't a bar—had been typical of the cat burglar. We had him take off his shirt. It was from HONEST ABE'S MEN'S STORE, which had been similarly robbed.

The rest was ritual. His fingerprints checked with those found in the stores. He broke down and admitted to 25 robberies.

It was the kind of gratification every officer finds the most satisfying, breaking a case through a sixth sense that something is amiss. Above all, the rough-and-tumble ways of Atlantic City prepared me for the daily horrors and agonies I was to see all around me in narcotics enforcement. I recall the night Teeny and I were working a radio car when we received an emergency call of trouble at a housing project.

Teeny was driving and I leapt out with my nightstick and rushed to the third floor where a crowd stood around a door. I slammed open the door. Despite my years in the South Pacific with the Marines the sight made me want to puke. Walls, ceiling, floor were covered with blood. A nude man and woman—at least what had been a nude man and woman—were sprawled on a bed, the man disemboweled, the woman sliced dozens of times across body, face, and limbs. A man stood next to them with a butcher knife, staring at me with a wild expression.

Instantaneously, I knew the story: he'd come home and found his wife in bed with another man. "You poor son of a bitch," I thought. This only took a flash. I shifted my club to my other hand. "Put down your knife," I ordered.

He let out a scream and lunged at me. I sidestepped and caught him with the club on the side of the head. He went out, but not before cutting me across the wrist and hand. I still bear the scars. Today, I would pull my gun, rather than sympathize over his marital problems.

Down through the years the image of Dad will never fade. It probably was all summed up on the Sunday morning I left for New York. We lived across the street from one another and had celebrated with a family dinner the night before. He had been cheerful and happy and gone home early, explaining that he was on duty directing traffic in front of St. Nicholas Church the next morning. The role of sort of unofficially being part of the Mass was one of his happier assignments as it gave him time to chat with dozens of friends and neighbors.

It was only nine in the morning when I came out with my bag and started down the street. I saw Dad waving cars this way and that way, in front of the church, his back to me.

As I came closer he turned. I gasped in amazement. He had two of the most beautiful shiners I've ever seen!

"And what the hell are you staring at?" he yelled.

I never did find out how he managed to get punched like that on the way to church. I was always afraid to ask.

3

The Bureau

I was appointed a narcotics agent in the Federal Bureau of Narcotics on July 30,1951. As a gag my wife tore a clipping from a newspaper astrology chart and had it framed. "You are now able to get out for the kind of social life which suits you to a T. Meet fascinating new personalities but don't neglect your civic duties."

Ah, prophecy! Those new personalities I was to meet over the next quarter century were indeed to be "fascinating."

My first glimpse of my new life was hardly one to send me into a jet-propelled tizzy of ecstasy. I was assigned to Enforcement Group Two in New York City after being sworn in by District Supervisor James C . Ryan. The Bureau was then under the U.S. Treasury Department and our offices were at 90 Church Street—the drab, cluttered, old Federal Building. It was a squat, block-square citadel that was a rabbit warren of confusion with various offices for the Post Office Department, the Internal Revenue Service, the Secret Service, and the Alcohol, Tobacco, and Firearms unit of the Treasury Department. To bring prisoners in we had to double-park and drag them handcuffed through the lobby as there were no facilities to jail them. The only cohesive element in the entire building was the uniformly dingy, gray walls. Several decades later

I made a pilgrimage back to the floor where our offices had been. I wasn't the least amazed to find the offices hadn't been painted in all those years.

As for the agents themselves, they come as a bit of a shock to a casual observer. Their "work clothes" are slovenly: unpressed pants, worn jackets, ragged sweaters, and often several days growth of beard. The reason is obvious—to look like an addict or street peddler. Today, a gathering of agents ready to go out on the street often looks like a hippie convention with love beads, beards, long hair, and all the other props of the street people. I have often wondered at the edict of the late J. Edgar Hoover, who ruled that all FBI agents look at all times like meticulous store dummies. Wasn't their neat Babbitty style often a giveaway to many an observant hood? I recall two of our agents who were working Skid Row in Los Angeles and—despite their beaten and tattered disguise—somehow couldn't make a buy of even a stick of pot. Then an informer tipped them off why they'd been tabbed as agents. Both were wearing good shoes. A night or so later they put on worn, beaten shoes with rundown heels and immediately started making some respectable busts.

Yet, the exception to the rule is always a rule of its own. Jack Cusack, my immediate boss in Group Two, was just that. And he also was the luckiest thing that ever happened to me. Jack—about 21 at the time—wore nothing but tailored Brooks Brothers business suits with button-down collars and expensive silk regimental stripe ties. He'd often wander through a back alley in Harlem in this outlandish high style to make a buy of heroin and come back with an arrest. I always held the theory that peddlers who dealt with him were so startled and amazed to find what appeared to be a Wall Street lawyer wanting to make a buy that they just *knew* he wasn't a narc. Too, Jack's blue eyes are forever twinkling. No peddler, I'm sure, could believe a man with such a merry glint could have nasty plans. I am convinced that Jack was born old. As a callow stripling he was bald with a dark fringe of hair. Today, he looks much the same—with a gray fringe of hair. Jack is still with the Drug Enforcement Administration of the Department of Justice—and still wears his Brooks Brothers suits. He was the most imaginative and brilliant agent I've ever known, even though he was only a youth at the time. Later, he was to start taking assignments in Europe and eventually became Regional Director for the Bureau in Europe. He was a Fordham graduate with several years' experience when I became more or less his apprentice. I was the 188th agent in those days but was to watch the Bureau burgeon with about a hundred additional men being sworn in during the next six months. Our group was a tight-knit unit. Ray Enright, who was to become my partner, had just turned 21. Howard Chappell, who today is the Los Angeles Commissioner of Parks and Public Property and Chairman of the Board of Commissioners of Los Angeles, was one of the top agents, and Stu Nadler, a pharmaceutical school graduate, and Ted Heisig, with whom I was to retire 22 years later, were some of the youngsters on the team. At 30 I was called "the old man" and had to take constant kidding.

Another of my mentors was Group Leader Sam Levine, one of the most beloved agents in the Bureau. Sam had what is now called charisma in the grand manner. He has a deep, soft voice that, at a crowded meeting, works like magic. When he begins to talk, everyone has to strain to hear him. Soon he is dominating the silent gathering. Too, he had the most articulate hands—and articulate is the only word—I have ever seen. I truly believe Sam could communicate most of his thoughts with his hands alone. A whimsical example of this was to come during the Kefauver Committee hearings on television. The Bureau requested that Sam not be photographed during the hearings for obvious reasons, but did agree to allow the television crews to show his hands on camera. The effect was startling and created a national stir as viewers listened to his soft, compelling voice and watched those expressive hands move with his monologue. The aftermath was that Frank Costello, when he was called to testify, insisted on equal rights with Sam and demanded that just his hands be shown on camera.

Jack Cusack's first assignment was to put me in a quiet room and start me rummaging through huge stacks of old reports, absorbing the techniques and methods previous agents had used. It was soon apparent that, despite what I thought of my derring-do days chasing peddlers in Atlantic City, I had much to learn.

The first was understanding the use of informers. In no branch of law enforcement is the informer so essential. Jack was a master at the psychology of developing and keeping informers. He taught me the subtle ways of treating them so that one combines friendliness with an aloofness that makes it always clear that you are the agent and he is the informer. Each, he taught me, must be treated as an individual and a unique human. Some you baby, some you treat in a harsh manner without being nasty, others you sympathize with and still others you flatter. But always you keep that proper balance between friendliness and sternness. Jack, while he respected my background as a police officer—which few of the other newcomers had—made constant suggestions of ways to correct my past habits, but he was never pompous or critical. Everyone knows, for example, of the good guy—bad guy technique of handling suspects. "Dragnet" made the scene a national institution with Jack Webb harassing and denouncing the suspect while his partner, Ben, acted as the sympathetic and understanding ally of the criminal.

Cusack was to take me far past this old gambit into the more devious refinements of interrogating a suspect. Once you have developed some rough appraisal of the personality you are dealing with, you plan your attack to get the information you need. Sometimes it's a series of jokes, again a nonchalant and rambling period of small talk that touches only vaguely on the issue of import. Others you simply threaten. Each is different.

Once you have established contact with the informer and he has become your tool it is time to adopt a new role. He must, above all, respect and fear you. This is vital as often an agent will have to live with an informer for weeks or even months at a time. The deadliest error an agent can make with an informer is to be judgmental. The informer knows that he, as a stoolie, is the lowest form of criminal life in the social strata of the underworld. To let him know that you agree he is scum will quickly destroy your effectiveness, as well as his.

Basically, there are three categories of informers. The most common and the most useful is the defendant-informer, the man you have made a case on and who is informing on his source of narcotics supply in order either to have his own charges dismissed or to receive a lighter sentence. His hope is the most primitive of all—simple survival. If he is assured he will be protected from retribution from the source he is about to destroy, he will usually cooperate completely.

Next, there is the informer who helps you for some financial gain or because he seeks revenge. Finally, there is the concerned good citizen who has come across some information about narcotics that he feels he must report. He is an unusual and uncommon figure and, in many ways, the most dangerous of all. He must be watched most closely, as he often, in his enthusiasm, can ruin a case. For example, he may make a purchase of evidence when an agent is not present or without the agent's authority. This can easily end up in a muddle of chaos with a case that cannot be prosecuted and with the peddler vanished.

Informers from the criminal world also present their own problems, which can lead easily to serious trouble. Let us assume you have arranged for your informer to make a buy of evidence from a peddler. You must search him before the operation begins, keep him in constant view during the purchase, and search him again after the buy. The reasons? He could have some narcotics on him and really not make a buy at all but simply return to the agent and sell him narcotics he has had hidden on his person, then blame the peddler you have seen him meet. Even while you think you've witnessed the actual purchase, you can be wrong. For perhaps the informer owes the suspect some money and simply uses the government money you have given him to pay off the peddler while the agent thinks the informer is actually making a buy. Again, you must search the informer after the buy to see if he might be holding out some of the narcotics he's bought or still has some of the government money you gave him. Of course, it's also always necessary to record the serial numbers of the purchase money.

Even here, with a clean buy and the proper legalities in order, the case is not over. Jack coached me carefully on the methods of testifying in court. I still believe the Bureau has failed to give enough instruction to agents on this vital step. I had testified many times before as a police officer. But I soon found that a Federal Court was another matter. It is highly restrictive and detailed, and an agent—to be effective—must do his homework, knowing all the facts of the case. Finally, appearance and attitude have destroyed many a good case, I'm sure. An uninformed agent in his sloppy work clothes and a shabby haircut is a joy and delight to a defense attorney. Too, a good lawyer can work on an agent's ego and destroy him. Too many agents are reluctant, when they don't know the answer to the most insignificant defense question, simply to say, "I do not know." They'll become belligerent or rattled and foul up the prosecution.

Perhaps it was simply that I was older than the other agents and had made narcotics arrests before in Atlantic City. Maybe it was that I was an eager beaver. Whatever the motivation, I was anxious to test my abilities to make a bust in the big city. I'd absorbed the reports and listened to the seasoned agents. I felt I was ready.

About two weeks after I joined the Bureau I saw my chance. Ray and Jack were out of the office on assignment. I was on my own and decided to take advantage of it.

I phoned Teeny, my old partner in Atlantic City.

"What's happened to Joe Sharkey?" I inquired. Sharkey was an informer and heroin addict we'd used before and I knew Teeny had arrested him just after I'd departed. I knew, too, that Sharkey had a source in New York where he bought regularly.

Teeny told me he had Sharkey wrapped up and could ship him to me anytime.

"Send him up on the next bus," I said. We arranged the timetable and a few hours later Sharkey, a lanky Negro about 32, got off the bus wearing his city clothes, an electric blue suit, yellow shoes, and an expression of resigned self-pity.

I took him to the office and put him in a conference room, then went to Sam Levine's office.

"Sam, I want to buy some evidence. What do I do to get some money?"

I was so self-assured Sam must have been smiling to himself.

"What are you going to do with it?" he asked. "Do you have a connection?"

I nodded smugly. "I've got an informer right here in the office. He's given me the name of his connection, a guy named Jose Sosa who's over in the Spanish section of Harlem."

I tried to sound casual, but I'm sure Sam suspected that I'd never seen Spanish Harlem—which was true.

He chuckled and told me how to draw the money. It was obvious he thought I was on an impetuous schoolboy lark, trying to make a fast bust in a city I didn't even know yet. "Good luck," he said in a kindly tone. I went to the squad room and put on some old clothes with a long-sleeved shirt, the mark of an addict.

I left the office with $100 I'd drawn from the Official Advance Funds with Sharkey reluctantly shuffling along beside me. I didn't even have an auto so we took a subway after I'd inquired directions from Sharkey.

We got off at the street Sharkey suggested and started toward the small park where he said Sosa usually dealt from a bench. I'd only seen Harlem a time or two before on orientation cruises during my first week but I had never been this close. It was a humid, sizzling day in August and all around us blacks sat on stoops or hung from rickety fire escapes. Flies swarmed over stinking garbage cans and kids ran about through the litter of trash.

My faded green flannel shirt with the long sleeves was an open invitation to sellers. Over the years I've thought time and again that I've solved the secret of how one addict knows another on the street. Such trademarks as long sleeves in hot weather to cover the needle marks are obvious. But there's something more subtle. A certain gait, expression, or desperate look in the eye. Whatever it is, I've repeatedly seen one user spot another by this sixth sense, but I've never really solved the mystery. That hot day, and probably it was Sharkey's aura, we were approached almost immediately with offers of heroin as we ambled down the crowded sidewalk. Sharkey knew such brazen offers were simply the old bunco game of selling a packet of milk sugar and paced on, just shaking his head as we pushed on through the crowd until we reached the small park. He greeted several loungers and asked for Sosa. An old man selling pretzels motioned toward a corner.

"Go wait there," he ordered.

A few minutes later Jose, a thin, sallow Puerto Rican of about 25, wearing the gaudy clothes of a pimp and a wide-brimmed white hat, approached us casually. Incongruously, my first bigtime Harlem peddler was happily gnawing on a red popsicle.

"Hello, Jose," Sharkey greeted him. Jose looked suspiciously at me, ignoring Sharkey.

"What you want?"

Sharkey turned to me. "Well, Jack, what do we want?"

"A quarter piece," I replied, the street terminology for a quarter ounce of heroin.

Jose turned to Sharkey and asked who I was. "A buddy from Atlantic City," Sharkey explained. "We just come up to score."

Jose nodded. "Where's the money?"

"How much?" I asked.

"Forty dollar, top stuff," Jose said.

I pulled my flash roll out and peeled off two twenties. Later, I was to learn this was an operational error. One of the tricks in making a buy is to use small bills because the serial numbers are recorded and you want the dealer to be holding as many recorded bills as possible for evidence when you arrest him later. With something like two twenties, the peddler is likely to return to his own connection and pay off, say, thirty dollars and get ten dollars in change. The recorded government money, which is your evidence in court if you arrest him, is gone. Yet, in the devious poker game of dealing, many peddlers know this and a payoff in large bills assures them that you aren't an agent.

Jose pointed to the park bench. "Go sit there", he ordered. We waited perhaps fifteen minutes and Jose returned, handing me a small brown bag secured by a rubber band.

"Listen, Jose," said Sharkey as we got up to leave. "If I can't make it next time Jack will come alone. . ."

Jose shrugged. "Just ask around for me."

It was about four in the afternoon when we arrived back at the office.

I told Sharkey to return to the conference room and knocked on Sam's door.

"Here's your quarter ounce," I announced proudly. "What do I do now?"

Sam laughed and called in Howard Chappell. "Show Jack how to process it," he said.

Howard was as amused as Sam at the idea of a neophyte bringing in a buy when he had to ask the addict how to get around town. He showed me how to remove the heroin from the glassine bag, weigh it on the scales, and place it in the evidence envelope, which is then locked and sealed. Sharkey was then called in to initial the glassine bag next to my initials and it was placed in a substitute container before being placed in the evidence envelope, which is then taken to the chemist, who initials it himself. It's then subsequently analyzed by him and he testifies in court as to the contents and chemical make-up. The agent and informer can then identify the package by their initials on the glassine bag and the date.

I returned to my desk and took a statement from Sharkey describing his participation in the purchase and then had to write him up as a "Special Employee," (at the time, the Bureau's euphemism for an informer) and draw more money to pay him for his services.

This system was, I believe, the cause of much of the dishonesty and stealing which were to lead to later scandals in the Bureau.

It invited chicanery. Agents were to pay informers out of their own pockets and often had the informer sign a blank receipt. Agents sometimes then filled in the figure for whatever amount they needed and applied it to an expense voucher each month to get their money back.

The flaw was that seldom did any of us have our own money. I, for example, was living at the YMCA in Jersey City and trying to maintain a home in Atlantic City for my family, hoping to save enough to move them later. As a Grade Seven agent I was making $3700 a year. It was always touch-and-go just for pocket money. Yet the system assumed we all had cash to advance. Again and again, the temptation was too much. An agent would draw money for the purchase of evidence. Some of it would be used to pay an informer. Later, the agent would need more money to pay an informer again and would draw still more money. The sum would escalate, and at the end of the month, the agent would owe the government anywhere from $50 to $100 which had been spent piecemeal during the nights of work on meals and expenses. The temptation to falsify one's receipts was constant. It was remarkably simple to pay an informer $50, have him sign a blank receipt, and then fill it in for $100.

This process was to come to a head in an investigation in 1970 by the Bureau of Narcotics and Dangerous Drugs. Informers were interrogated and their statements of sums paid were checked against agents' expense accounts. The inspectors relentlessly pried into the backgrounds of every agent for discrepancies. Many were arrested. Others were fired. Still others resigned. Before the furor was over, some fifty agents were through.

An even more frightening spectacle was the pilfering and use of drugs by the agents themselves.

A good undercover agent has to be an actor, an ardent liar, and he has to try to think like the peddler with whom he is dealing. It calls for cold nerve and logic. I've seen many agents crack under the pressures of undercover work. One, I recall, broke into tears because he couldn't lie in a convincing way to peddlers.

An endless hazard in working undercover is that the agent is asked again and again to smoke marijuana, sniff cocaine, or shoot heroin. If you are posing as a peddler the problem is less irksome. Dealers are wary of other dealers who use. But if your undercover role is that of an addict and the situation is tense, it could be easier sometimes to take a bit of drugs in playing out your role. Of course you don't, though.

I recall one agent who had been sent to Washington, D.C. on an undercover assignment from our New York office. He returned a month or so later and seemed introverted and strange. Gossip was that he hadn't done a very good job, that all he'd made were what is called "boot and shoe" cases, meaning arresting smalltime peddlers selling cut heroin at five or ten dollars a bag.

Soon after he resigned. "I can't take working undercover," he told me. "I'm just not built for it."

He got a job as a deputy sheriff. But within a few months he'd applied again for his old job in the Bureau. He'd had four years' experience and was reinstated. We seldom worked together and when he was made Agent-in-Charge in Newark, New Jersey, I lost all contact with him. He would arrive in New York now and again to get supplies. Then one afternoon I ran into him in the halls. We chatted and he explained he was in town to give a speech. Odd, I idly mused, that they had to import an agent from Newark to give a routine speech, with 50 agents in the office.

A few minutes later I was in my office when my group supervisor called me into his office.

"Listen, did you hear about that 30 ounces we got in that big seizure last night?"

"Yeah," I replied, "that was a dandy."

"How'd you like an ounce of it for some deserving informer? I was puzzled. "What do you mean?"

"I'll give you and your partner some. I know you've got some good informers and this is great stuff, 80 percent pure."

"We don't have anyone we want to give it to," I stalled.

"Talk to your partner and let me know," the supervisor insisted. "It's a great chance."

I told my partner, Ray Enright. "Like hell!" Ray exploded. "We aren't giving anyone any junk. That's what those old farts do, pull stuff like that. Not me!"

I didn't even bother to go back to refuse again but returned to cleaning up my paperwork. About 6:30 that evening the Newark agent came in.

He strolled around the office. "Just killing some time until the speech," he explained.

A half hour later I went over to the desk where he sat reading the **Daily News.** "I'm going across the street for a bowl of soup. Want to come along?"

He was flushed and nervous and jumped when I spoke to him. "No—I'll eat later."

"Are you okay?" I asked.

"Sure."

I returned to the office a bit later and he'd departed.

The next morning there was high excitement when I arrived. The Newark agent had been found dead in the bathroom of his parents' home where he'd been staying. A close friend, another agent, had gone to the house and found the Newark agent with the hypodermic needle still in his arm, dead from an overdose of nearly pure heroin. I knew immediately that it was the heroin that the group supervisor had offered me.

Investigation proved he'd become addicted in Washington, shooting up to please the peddlers. He'd quit as a deputy sheriff when he couldn't get heroin there and returned to the Bureau. We were to find that he'd cleaned out the vault in Newark of all the seized narcotics under his control. He had also somehow gained admittance to the vault in our New York office as well.

He was not alone. We all knew of another agent in New York who regularly came into the office late at night and went through everyone's desk looking for a stray bag of heroin. A brilliant agent, an attorney who had graduated first in his class at Harvard, he eventually took up with prostitutes and had them working for him to support his habit before the Bureau forced him to retire. Later, he was picked up repeatedly for possession.

If we lived in a climate of temptation in the Bureau in those days, we certainly had no one setting a good example in local law enforcement. I won't say that every New York City police officer was dishonest, but finding one who wasn't was an exception. Crooked cops were routine on the city's narcotics squad. And we had to work with them regularly because of the differences in federal and state laws. Typically, for example, under federal law perhaps you couldn't enter a place while under state law a city police officer could. Wiretapping was legal under state law, but not federal. To operate, we had to form alliances with city police.

A few years ago the five-man Knapp Commission formed by Mayor Lindsay and headed by Whitman Knapp, a former Wall Street attorney who is now a federal judge, started to investigate charges of police wrongdoing. The 283-page report issued after 31 months of investigation was about 25 years too late, as far as I'm concerned. It is the most exhaustive study of the New York Police Department ever made, and one of its findings was that more than 50 percent of the city's 29,600-man police force took part in corrupt practices in 1971. Corruption, the report also added, was most serious in narcotics law enforcement. Charges included keeping money for drugs confiscated in raids, selling drugs, storing needles and other drug gear in lockers, illegally tapping suspects' phones for blackmail purposes, and introducing potential users to pushers.

Two decades ago we heard daily stories even more dramatic than this: of top officers protecting narcotics dealers; of police murdering witnesses in drug cases. Those of us who had to deal with the city's narcotics squad took such stories as gospel.

The old hands in the Bureau in New York—Jack Cusack, Howard Chappell, Sam Levine, and Roy Morrison—advised us as new rookies in racketland that about the only thing we could do was hope. "Keep working with different partners," Sam explained to me, "and as you pair up with different teams, try to find someone honest or at least honest when they are working with you. They stay honest sometimes because they don't know what is going to happen on any given job."

Ray and I were fortunate. We found one man, Tony Peters on

the city's narcotics squad, we could trust. I couldn't say as much for his partner, Nick. While Nick wasn't greedy, he had a more curious trait. Again and again we'd make a bust at an apartment. During the routine shakedown, Nick would immediately grab any attractive woman and pull her into the bathroom, locking the door.

"What the hell is he doing that for?" I asked Ray several times. Ray would shake his head. "He thinks he can talk to women better than anyone else," he'd explain. "He's making a specialty of talking to broads."

Somehow the kickback and talk got too heavy even for the narcotics squad. Nick was arrested. He'd been forcing the women to go down on him for the promise of their freedom, then reneging later.

Within the department itself, it seemed apparent that the heisting of confiscated narcotics was organized and reached into high places. When one reads of missing narcotics in the department these days you can assume it is internal, just as when we read of the drugs missing in the 1960s at the time of the French Connection. We all knew they were obviously taken by men involved in the case. One agent in the Bureau was forced to resign after that particular case, as well as several policemen. The same agent was recently indicted for the sale of heroin.

I remember when Ray and I received a tip on the street of a stash pad which was thriving at the moment. "They're dealing big," our informant claimed. "Everyone's going there and scoring." Now a stash pad, meaning a dropoff spot for a supply of heroin, could turn into a big thing. Unfortunately, it was in Harlem. We knew the only way we could crack it was without a warrant. Our evidence was nothing more than the tipster's word, which wasn't enough to obtain a warrant. We would have to ask the city police to help out.

That created other problems. Tony Peters wasn't on duty and when we called his home we found he was out of town. We finally decided to risk calling Central Narcotics and asking for someone to work with us. Two young officers arrived a few hours later. It seemed hopeful, as neither had been on the squad long and we concluded they might still be straight.

We also needed a black as the easiest means of getting into the pad without a warrant. I called a friend, Coley Wallace, and told him what we had in mind. Coley, who later made the movie *The Joe Louis Story*, was a top-ranking heavyweight and was probably one of the top five fighters in the world at the time. He loved police work and I even once took him to meet Assistant Commissioner of Narcotics B.T. Mitchell when we were in Washington, D.C. When he was offered the chance by Mitchell to become an agent, he was enthusiastic but reluctantly had to turn it down as he had a fight coming up with Ezzard Charles which, if he won, could have led to a title fight. (Charles knocked him out and destroyed that dream.)

Coley was overjoyed when given a chance to participate in the bust.

We went to the address that evening and waited on the fourth floor for someone to arrive to make a buy. The scheme was that Coley would tag along with any visitor who appeared in the corridor, trading on his celebrity status as a fighter. Hopefully, he'd gain admission. Then the four of us would break in.

As it happened a fat black cat in a yellow turtleneck sweater came out of the apartment door before anyone arrived. We ran down the hall from the alcove where we'd been waiting and hit the door.

A half dozen junk dealers were sitting in the living room drinking beer. The supplier was lounging in an undershirt and his wife was in the kitchen frying hamburgers.

She was wearing a gingham apron which had bulging pockets. I simply reached into one of them and pulled out an ounce pack of heroin. I motioned her into the other room. "Dirty bastard!" she cried, waving the greasy spatula at me.

We made a respectable seizure. Nearly everyone was carrying at least an ounce, and secreted in a can in the closet was another 20 ounces.

In the bedroom I started emptying out the closet, throwing

dresses and shoes in a heap. Nothing. Then I took a battered man's hatbox from the shelf and opened it. It was stacked with tight rolls of ten- and twenty-dollar bills! Later, when we tried to estimate, we came up with the guess of five thousand dollars.

I took my find into the living room and showed it to the others.

As there's a law in New York City which calls for any money seized at the scene of a crime such as a narcotics raid to go automatically into the Police Pension Fund, we were delighted with the take, joking about how many old Irish cops would be saying their beads for us.

The two young officers departed with the evidence—the hatbox, the heroin, and the prisoners, all routine in such a bust involving city police.

Two days later Coley called me at the office.

"Do you know what happened up there in Harlem the other night?" he asked.

"What do you mean, Coley?"

"I mean with that case I helped you with. Remember that broad? The one you grabbed in the kitchen. . ."

"Sure," I replied.

"Well, she's out on the street."

I thought a moment. "Well, hell, she must have been bonded."

"Nope," said Coley. "She was never arrested. They released her along with a couple of others."

"Goddammit, Coley. I found an ounce in her apron pocket. How could they turn her loose?"

Coley grunted. "The word on the street is that the cops got the hatbox of money."

"I can't buy that," I said.

"Can you find out?"

I told him I'd try. I went to Ray's desk and told him. "Even those assholes wouldn't pull anything as crude as that," he gasped.

We called the Police Pension Fund. We named the two officers. "Did they turn in any money to the Fund?" I asked.

A moment later the clerk returned to the phone. "Yes, they did," she reported.

I looked at Ray and nodded and smiled. Almost as an after-thought I asked, "How much?"

"One hundred and three dollars," was the crisp answer.

We immediately called for the two young officers at city narcotics. One answered the phone. "What the hell happened?" I demanded.

"What do you mean?" he asked blithely.

"We hear the broad was released and is out on the street."

"Yeah," he said lazily. "She didn't have anything on her."

"Balls! I found an ounce on her and you know it!"

There was a pause. "Look at it this way, buddy," the punk cop went on, "her old man was the connection. She was probably just saving that stuff for him. He was the big gun and he's agreed to plead guilty if we let her go. Maybe it wasn't the right decision but we figured if he cops out we won't have to go to court and it will save the state a lot money."

To have him claiming he was worrying about the state spend-ing money made me want to climb the wall.

"Yeah, what about the money?" I asked angrily.

"What money?"

"That boxful of bills."

"Oh, we turned that into the Police Pension Fund."

I blew up. "Look, you bastard! We just called them. You turned in a hundred and three dollars. I know there was at least five grand there!"

"No, no, no," the voice replied soothingly. "There were a lot of ones there. Nearly all ones."

There was no use arguing. "I'm going to tell every agent in this office that you're a Goddamned thief," I threatened weakly.

There was a soft chuckle. "See you around, buddy," he said, hanging up.

Predators were everywhere in New York City: crooked cops, ruthless dealers, and the pathetic junkies who burglarized and robbed to support their gnawing agony. I was soon to realize that what I had to adjust to was the age-old dilemma of the smalltowner in the big city. Even in Atlantic City a certain criminal ethic existed—not out of any glowing morality but simply because criminals moved in a small social structure and had to preserve their local reputations to survive. Not in New York. Friendship, building a reputation for being a reliable dealer, or being known as an honest cop, meant nothing. There were always more suckers just a subway ride away. Typically, a rasping voice would call our office. "I know where you can pick up 20 ounces of heroin. If you knock him over will you give me two?" If we agreed—and sometimes we just said we would, the anonymous informer would continue: "Dominic Geosa will be at First and Grand in a blue Chevrolet at nine tonight and will have his stash under the front seat." We would make the bust and a shadowy figure would emerge from a dark doorway to demand his share. Later, we'd often find the informer was the prisoner's best friend. We would just threaten to tell the peddler who tipped us, and the informer would leave, cursing.

Too, I discovered that the peddlers and users were as star-struck and celebrity-conscious as teenage highschool girls. We heard constant rumors of actors, politicians, sports figures who were peddling or using. Such tales were generated on the street, gossip which gave a certain dignity to addicts who somehow felt that a famous actor snorting cocaine or shooting up brought some vague glamour to their own unhappy lives.

Once we picked up a street rumble that one Gus Levine was doing a thriving business as a peddler. All we had to go on was the name and that he was operating in Harlem. Assuming we were looking for a Jewish dealer, we tried in vain to get some information on him. We hit one blind alley after another.

Then one day one of our agents nailed a shaky, little addict who, with mucous streaming from his nose, said he had bought from Gus Levine. Gus, he explained, was a black bartender and ex-fighter. No wonder we'd struck out again and again.

Bill Jackson, the black agent who usually took over on such cases, was on another assignment. So our office arranged for another black agent, Bill Davis, to work with us on the Levine case.

The informer led Bill to Sugar Ray Robinson's bar on 8th Avenue in Harlem. Levine, who had fought Sugar Ray during his heyday, worked a day shift there. Bill made a few buys of heroin, then turned the case over to Ray Enright and myself for the cleanup as there was some suspicion that he'd been tabbed as a possible agent.

Sugar Ray owned an entire city block in Harlem. He had the bar, a beauty parlor, a barber shop, a dry cleaning and laundry business and other smaller enterprises all flourishing in his little feudal kingdom. He drove a custom-made fuchsia Cadillac around Harlem and was the neighborhood celebrity and hero. He was at the peak of his fame and the middleweight champion, having fought Randy Turpin and lost and then in a rematch won his title back. A constant mob of white admirers visited his saloon hoping to chat with him and he had also taken up tap dancing and was making still more money performing in nightclubs around New York.

Ray Enright and I became hangers-on at the bar, posing as worshipful fight fans. We developed a nodding acquaintance with him, as did many other habitues, and were dismissed simply as two more white sports lovers.

We were there, of course, to arrest Gus Levine, a sinewy, silent man who served drinks with a sullen air. Meanwhile, our office had picked up the usual celebrity rumors that Sugar Ray snorted cocaine. We more or less discounted this as the usual street gossip. But we weren't sure.

We watched them both for some weeks nursing our drinks at the end of the bar. Gus had a standard method of operation when dealing which we'd learned from Bill Davis. He would take orders at the bar for heroin during the day then when he'd finish work, meet his customers on the street to make the sale. It was obvious he didn't have his stash on the premises.

Too, the relationship between Gus and Sugar Ray became apparent. His only conversations with Sugar Ray involved bar matter and it was evident that there was no close tie between them. As Gus was a sloppy and disinterested bartender we decided Sugar Ray was simply a soft touch. It was apparent that Gus was a has-been down on his luck.

We eventually set Gus up for a buy and made the arrest. He

was sent to trial and then to jail. But then we got word that the A.B.C., the state's licensing agency, was in the process of taking Sugar Ray's license away. A license was worth $50,000 basic, without stock or real estate, so it was a tough penalty. Neither Ray nor I felt Sugar Ray was involved and were convinced that Gus had done no business in the bar.

We appeared at the A.B.C. hearing and testified for Robinson.

He knew nothing of this and I'm sure didn't even know we were narcotics agents. We had chatted with him during our surveillance, about boxing and that was all. I never saw him again. But he did keep his license. Yet, he nearly had been a victim of street gossip simply because he was a celebrity.

4

Working Undercover

New York narcotics work has a zest and pace which compares to no other city in the world. In most towns in the United States a few cases a week is considered a standard. Even in cities such as Chicago, San Francisco, or Los Angeles there isn't the exciting turmoil and furor which is the commonplace in New York. There we often had a dozen cases each day, moving and stirring them about like busy cooks over a range. When one would begin to simmer we'd cover it to season while the boiling pan next to it might get the day's major attention. Four or five busts a day weren't unusual.

Yet, even in Manhattan there were dull days when it seemed there wasn't a needle in use. Each agent kept his own record of contacts, gossip, and rumor known as the Z File. For example, I might have the name of a smalltime street peddler who I knew I didn't have enough evidence on to make a case that would hold up in court. Yet, even if I couldn't conduct a legal search, I could hassle the subject and turn what evidence I might find over to the government, knowing that the U.S. Attorney would decline prosecution. But the peddler would know he was in serious trouble. He could usually be turned into an informer. Sometimes this could start a chain reaction of information that would lead us up the ladder to a top source and a big case.

I recall a slow day when Tony Peters, Stu Nadler, and myself had drunk a half dozen cups of coffee, read the papers, and listened to a dull Dodgers game waiting for something to break. Tony started rummaging through his Z File and came up with the name of a suspect. We knew it was a weak situation but, having nothing better to do, we decided to drive out to the address and give it a try.

Now Stu Nadler was a prized companion on such projects. For he was New York's finest door-kicker. As mentioned before, I've always maintained that my old buddy from Atlantic City, Teeny Sheppersen, would win the gold medal for door-kicking if it was one of the Olympic Games. Stu was certainly second best in my experience. In New York where every peddler, and most people in the poor sections of town, had a "police lock," an expert door-kicker is as vital to a narcotics team as a valued placekicker in pro football. Stu was that. Police locks come in many varieties but the most common is an iron bar across the middle of the door suspended on bolted brackets.

When we arrived at the address, a dingy apartment house, we could see a light under the door. We knocked. Silence. We knocked again.

Stu backed to the far side of the hall and made a lunge. He grunted. "Feels like a two-inch round steel bar," he announced with relish. It took a half dozen driving lunges as Tony and I watched with envy and wonder that Stu could hit with such driving power without breaking his shoulder. He didn't take out the door. The bar remained intact. But he broke out the top half.

We looked at one another with triumphant smiles and started our search of the empty room. Then Tony picked up some letters and his face suddenly turned gray. He handed me the letters, all addressed to a couple. We knew immediately we'd hit the wrong apartment.

There was nothing to do but bluff it through, A crowd had gathered in the hallway and were peering in at us.

Tony turned on them in a mock rage. "All right! Get back to your apartments or I'll take you in. Get back fast!"

Assured that we were New York City police, they scurried back and closed their doors. We made a futile effort to put the door back in place, propping the destroyed upper half against the frame, and made our own quick getaway, musing over what the respectable tenants would think when they came home and how they'd explain the incident to their neighbors.

Such misadventures did happen when we'd start out on the weak information our Z Files provided. I remember one dull autumn evening when I decided to take off for Harlem with several leads I had from my own Z File.

In those days a single policeman was safe in Harlem. Even someone with an Irish mug like mine could walk down the sidewalk and no one bothered him, knowing automatically that he was "The Man" and never approaching you. All you had to do was walk fast and never look to the right or left.

I was young and aggressive, and it didn't occur to me to be frightened at the idea of wandering about Harlem alone.

I'd taken several addresses from the file. I went to the first tenement where I had a lead on a woman who was supposedly dealing. While such tips were vague enough in themselves, there were added problems in such attempted busts. For example, in the beaten buildings many apartments had no numbers on the door. That was the situation this particular night. There were no numbers on half the doors. But as I passed one door which should have been the correct number I heard a woman's voice and concluded this was it. I stepped back to the far side of the hall and kicked the door with my right heel. There's a knack to this. You must place the kick exactly next to the doorknob. If you kick above it you can break your ankle and below it you'll break your toe.

The door broke open with a crash. On an old iron bedstead before me a naked couple were in the act of balling under an equally naked lightbulb.

Both leapt up, fear on their faces and the woman began to scream.

"Are you Shirley Jones?" I demanded. She shook her head. A few more questions, after I'd flashed my badge hurriedly so they'd think I was a New York City vice squad officer, and I knew I had the wrong woman. This girl was a whore with her customer.

"Do you know her?" I demanded. She shook her head.

"Okay," I continued, "I'm after her and I'm going to let you go this time."

"Thank you," she replied, but then looked at her client. "But what about my trick? Look what you done to him!"

It was true. The frightened John was hurriedly getting into his clothes and it was clear sex was the last thing in his mind.

I shrugged. "You should have collected first," I replied. She turned on her trick and demanded her money. He was too afraid to pay her, obviously thinking it would be some legal trap which would mean I'd arrest him.

The two of us departed, the whore yelling and cursing as we went down the stairway. We split to our mutual relief.

Other comedies and errors happened constantly in Harlem. We sometimes used an undercover panel truck with two-way mirrors on the sides with signs such as "Plumber" or "Ajax Pest Control." The *modus operandi* was for one agent to drive the truck and park it before the residence under surveillance. The driver, in workman's clothes, would leave but locked inside would be another agent with a camera and radio. With luck, he'd be able to photograph a buy on the stoop and steps of the house, which was a common place for a dealer to peddle and we'd have photos of the actual buy—excellent evidence in court.

One day we parked before a Harlem apartment house to get some photos of a suspect who we wanted to identify. We knew he lived at the address but we had no pictures to identify him. Ted Heisig sat despondently sweating inside the truck with the camera and the driver departed. This was one of the worst assignments we could draw. In the summer a few hours of being locked in the sweatbox could wipe you out. And this was summer.

In a way Ted was lucky. For within fifteen minutes two kids

came out of the doorway with a newspaper and walked directly to the truck. Spreading out the papers they casually scotchtaped the newspaper over the two-way mirror, laughing as they worked.

Ted sat in bewilderment a few moments and then knew he'd been had. He unlocked the truck from the inside and sheepishly walked around to the front seat and drove away while a gang of youngsters merrily yelled, "Fuzz! Fuzz!"

One of the finest agents I worked with in those days was Bill Jackson, a black graduate of Brooklyn University Law School. Bill could have been the prototype for that list of characteristics of a good scout in the Boy Scout Manual. He was one of the finest officers I've ever known, always cheerful, devoted, ready to go out and work with you at three in the morning, dedicated and always thinking, planning ahead. In the four years I spent in New York, Bill made more undercover buys than any agent in the Bureau, or, I suspect, more than any dozen agents collectively. He was superb, born for his role like no agent I've ever met.

His wry humor was singular. One night three or four of us worked out a tactic sitting in a car to make a buy. Bill was to make the buy and then we'd move in and arrest the suspect as Bill departed.

"Okay," Bill agreed. "But first let me go into the office and change my shirt." He was wearing a dark blue buttondown. We looked at one another, puzzled.

"What the hell for? You look all right," one agent asked.

"But it's dark blue."

"What's the difference?" I asked. "You developed a fetish that you have to make a buy in a white shirt?"

"Nope. But as black as I am, you want to be able to see me and know when to move in, don't you," he explained.

In the years to come Bill and I were to work together in Washington, North Carolina, and Los Angeles. Always his subtle wit and planning fascinated me.

I recall a curious case I worked on with Bill. He had bought a couple of ounces of heroin from a cleancut Italian boy called Jimmy.

Something didn't fit. He was certainly no stereotype of a typical peddler. The youth had a steady job and seemed legitimate. Bill tailed him to his home, an apartment on West 79th Street, and checked the mail boxes. There was only one logical name, Mr. and Mrs. James Pappalardi. A fast check with the Motor Vehicle Department's files showed the photo to be our man.

We kept checking Jimmy. He never seemed to go to any source. He'd leave his house, go directly to a meeting with Bill and sell an ounce, then return home. We arranged a warrant. Bill set up a meeting for five o'clock on a Saturday afternoon. At four, Armando Muglia, the partner I was working with at the time, and I went to Jimmy's apartment, assured that he'd at least have the ounce of heroin which Bill had ordered. We knocked on the door and Jimmy answered. We identified ourselves, pushed our way in, and formally placed him under arrest.

I began to search the apartment. It was neat and clean, if second rate, the sort of place a nice, struggling young couple would have in their first years of marriage. It was nothing like the disheveled, filthy stash pads we usually encountered.

I tried to open the door of one room and it was locked.

"Open it," I ordered Jimmy.

He hesitated. "If you don't, I'll break it in," I said.

He got a key from the kitchen cupboard and unlocked the door.

It was a surprise. An air conditioner was humming, there was luxurious furniture, Chinese vases, an expensive Oriental carpet, beautifully papered walls with fine paintings in elaborate frames. It was like stepping from the Bronx to Park Avenue in one step.

There was a large refectory table and a carved chest of drawers, but no bed.

"What is this room?" I asked in amazement.

"It's a room a guy rents off me," Jimmy replied.

"It's a funny kind of room to rent. Where does he sleep?"

Jimmy shrugged. "I don't know where he sleeps. He just rents the room."

I quickly found some mixing paraphernalia, a sieve, some

cellophane envelopes, and two ounce packages of heroin.

Jimmy was visibly shaken.

"What's this all about?" I asked.

He simply looked down at the floor and mumbled.

"Look, kid," I said softly. "You might as well tell me. We're going to take you down and book you and put you in the bucket anyway."

Silence.

"If what I think is going on is going on maybe we can make some kind of a deal and you could walk away from this case," I continued.

Jimmy rapped the table a few times with his fingers. "Can I talk to my wife?"

"Take your time," I said.

They whispered in a corner for a few minutes; then he came back to me. "I'll tell the whole story."

What he told me amazed the whole office. He was paid a hundred a week by a man who used the room. The stranger arrived only once a month, closed and locked the door, stayed a number of hours and departed for another month after paying the next month's rent. He always arrived and departed with a shopping bag, Jimmy explained.

This was more or less what I'd expected. The surprise was that Jimmy knew the man's first name, Herkey. I knew immediately this must be Ercole Ercolano, alias Herkey, who lived on West 78th Street and was on the books as the top nationally listed violator in New York City—which meant the top violator in the U.S. He had been the target for the past three years of every agent in New York but no one had been able to make him. And here it was! Herkey was obviously getting a supply from Europe each month, taking it to Jimmy's apartment to cut it with milk sugar or quinine and then distributing it to his peddlers. He was actually touching the stuff only once a month and briefly and then his lieutenants took over and he was clean.

We booked Jimmy in the Federal House of Detention, taking

him out the following Monday, so he could return to his job as usual.

Herkey had carefully picked Jimmy because he had no connection with the narcotics trade. It was a clean setup in theory. But Herkey didn't know two things: Jimmy had another key to the room and Jimmy was hungry. Some months after Herkey had rented the room Jimmy and his wife unlocked the room out of curiosity and found the heroin packages. Jimmy started taking one pack, then two a month. Soon he was selling three or four ounces a month to a few users—including our agent, Bill Jackson.

We set to work planning a sure trap to catch Herkey. We thought of using Jimmy to make a buy from him. But he complained that he was sure Herkey would refuse and move out. It made sense, of course. We went over the past pattern with Jimmy. It was usual for Herkey to call Jimmy before he arrived, the youth told us, to say that he'd be over in a few hours. But there was no way of knowing what day. Usually, Jimmy said, Herkey would call around six in the evening knowing Jimmy worked until five. It was also the pattern that Jimmy's wife would buy cokes, beer and cold cuts for Herkey's visit each month. Sometimes Herkey would even bring his girlfriend, who would visit with the couple while Herkey locked himself in his room. An hour or so later he'd emerge with his shopping bag, pay Jimmy the rent, and depart. The last such visit had been some two weeks before.

I finally sat down with Jimmy and outlined our plan. "We don't want you to do a damned thing. Just go on as before, act normal, follow your usual schedule. When you get a call, phone me immediately no matter what time of day or night."

Meanwhile, Armando, Stu Nadler, Jimmy Ziegler, and myself set up a 24-hour schedule of tailing Herkey. We soon knew every restaurant he favored, where he sent his laundry, his favorite bars and drinks, and other trivia of his daily life.

The day finally came when Jimmy called. "I got a call from Herkey at work today about like two o'clock. He's coming tonight."

We were ready. I told Jimmy to meet me immediately. I took him to the Assistant U.S. Attorney, Mort O'Brien, and with him we went before the U.S. Commissioner. I assigned Jimmy Pappalardi a new name, one we just made up, Giuseppe Acardi, and had Jimmy swear out an affidavit that he had personal knowledge that there were narcotics in his house on West 179th Street. In effect, he explained in the affidavit that on a specific date he'd seen two ounces of heroin in the apartment and told which room it was in. It was a magnificent legal document. With it I was able to obtain a search warrant for the apartment and I dropped Jimmy off at his apartment and told him to simply play it cool. Then I went directly across the street to an apartment I'd rented the week before with Armando and we settled back with a pair of binoculars in the dark front room ready to spring our dandy trap. But Jimmy had goofed. The Venetian blinds were closed. I sent Armando to phone Jimmy to open them. He did so and told Armando that he'd just had a call from Herkey saying he was going to be a bit late: a few minutes after eight o'clock.

Meanwhile, the other part of our team had been tailing Herkey. He'd been lounging in front of a cigar store, one of his favorite haunts. He stood about for hours. Then a car drove up and Herkey jumped into his own and followed it. Another car pulled up in back of Herkey's while our men followed the three as they circled, went up and down streets, and doubled back. There was a moment of panic. Either he'd made our detail and knew he was being followed or was being doubly cautious. But one thing was apparent. He was going into action.

Back at our stakeout we waited for hours. Ten o'clock. Midnight. We were discouraged, convinced that we'd somehow tipped Herkey during the day and he'd decided not to move. We called Jimmy again. Jimmy told us not to worry. Herkey had never failed to show when he called. So we returned to the dark window, nervous and tired.

At 1:38 A.M. Herkey's blue Oldsmobile pulled up in front of the apartment and Herkey got out carrying his shopping bag. Bingo! He had his girlfriend with him, a chunky peroxide blonde who had a dishpan face that looked like she'd run into a wall while she was still soft. Herkey stood a moment looking up and down the street, up at the lighted apartment, then motioned for the girl to follow him and went up the steps.

We looked at one another and grinned in relief. I started watching with the binoculars as Jimmy opened the door for the couple, they moved about chatting, and Jimmy's wife stood at the drainboard in the kitchen window making sandwiches. They settled down at a table with beer and the sandwiches and there was an animated, laughing conversation going on. We had only a partial view of the table and were getting anxious again as we couldn't see Herkey and suddenly realized he might be in the room cutting his heroin without us knowing it. Then a light in the room went on. We'd arranged a signal for Jimmy to tip us that the cutting had started. Jimmy appeared at the kitchen window and opened and closed the blinds.

We put on our coats, checked our weapons, went down the four flights of stairs and up the four flights to Jimmy's door.

"Shall I kick the door in?" Stu whispered.

We were all anxious and excited.

I shook my head. "Please!" I whispered. "Don't be so crass. When you work a case with me you go first class!" I triumphantly pulled out a key to Jimmy's apartment I'd gotten a week before.

I turned it and we stepped in with drawn guns in a second. Jimmy and his wife were sitting on the couch and Herkey's girl was in a chair holding a bottle of beer with a stunned look on her face. "Cover them," I said. "I'll get Herkey."

I went to the closed door, tried the knob gently, and found it was unlocked. I stepped in. Herkey looked up. He was sitting at the table up to his elbows in heroin, mixing it in a big bowl with milk sugar and quinine.

"Hold it right there," I said, grinning.

He had a moment of shock, then began to make a screaming noise like a woman. "Don't hit me! Don't hit me!" he pleaded. To see a 220-pound thug in a gaudy silk sportshirt sobbing and begging like a hooker was a peculiar sight.

Then I suddenly realized he thought I was another peddler there to heist him.

"Hell, Herkey, behave yourself," I said. "Nobody's going to hit you. Just clean your hands off."

He was wearing rubber gloves up to his elbows and peeled them off his hairy, muscular arms, still watching me with fear.

"Dust all that heroin on the gloves back into the bowl," I ordered. The others came in and we started packaging the stuff. We seized two sieves, a staple machine, a case of glassine envelopes, two scales, five cans of milk sugar, and twenty-five pounds of quinine. The heroin itself came to more than a hundred ounces valued at about $880,000 on the street at the time. All of us felt enormously satisfied as we returned to the office.

But the real fun was still to come.

Herkey got out on $50,000 bail. Mort O'Brien, who was to prosecute, pushed for an early trial and in a matter of a few weeks we were in the courtroom. Each agent testified and it quickly emerged that the defense attorney was going to build his hopes of acquittal on our right to enter the apartment.

I had left the search warrant on the premises, listed in detail everything that we had seized, and done everything above board— or at least, legal.

The defense attorney turned his attention to Giuseppe Acardi. I was called to the stand and a grueling examination started. What right did Acardi have to sign the affidavit? We went through the whole seizure again and I answered each question honestly. Herkey denied knowing any Giuseppe Acardi and then said that he'd asked Jimmy, who said he didn't know a Giuseppe Acardi. The astute lawyer knew there was something wrong but couldn't spring the right question.

Jimmy, of course, was not in the courtroom but back in the witness room waiting to be questioned.

"Who is Giuseppe Acardi?" the attorney demanded.

"Well—he's a man," I replied from the stand.

"I know, but I want to know who this man is."

"Well—just a man," I replied.

"Can you produce Giuseppe Arcardi?" he demanded.

"Yes, I can," I replied. I was enjoying myself enormously.

Finally something snapped in the attorney's mind, like in a parlor word game.

"Is Giuseppe Acardi the true name of the man who signed this affidavit?" he demanded.

"No," I replied happily.

"Well, I want to know his true name."

I hesitated. The judge turned to me. "Come on, Mr. Kelly, you have to answer this attorney."

I still stalled, milking the little drama to the last moment.

"Mr. Kelly," the judge said sternly. "I am ordering you. As a matter of fact, I want to know myself!"

"Very well, Your Honor," I said with a shrug. "Giuseppe Acardi is James Pappalardi!"

There was a momentary shocked silence, then a tremendous uproar in the courtroom. Herkey leapt up in panic. His attorney stood with an expression of amazed confusion.

The judge pounded for order and then stopped the trial.

"Do you mean to tell me that you had a man sign a search warrant for his own apartment?"

"Yes, Your Honor, that's true."

"You said that this man saw two ounces of heroin in this apartment two weeks before the date of the arrest?"

"Yes, Your Honor, that's true."

The judge shook his head. "Well, what were the circumstances? Why didn't you arrest the man?"

"We did, Your Honor," I replied. "We arrested him in possession of those two ounces of heroin."

The judge cradled his chin in his hand for a moment staring intently at me. "Mr. Kelly, this is the most unethical thing that I have ever heard in all my years on the bench. Now I am recessing this trial for ten minutes and I want to see you in my chambers."

"Yes, sir," I said, suddenly realizing that my ego trip was over.

Mort O'Brien started to enter the chambers with me. The judge turned. "Never mind, Mr. O'Brien, I want to talk to Mr. Kelly alone."

God! Maybe he's going to hold me in contempt of court, I thought.

He took off his robe as he motioned me to a chair, then sat down behind his desk. Here it comes, I decided, my stomach knotting up.

"Young man, I want to congratulate you for having more imagination than any of these agents who have come in here! I'm sick and disgusted with police and agents who come in here with stereotype cases. This is genius. It shows a great imagination!"

I am sure I looked bewildered.

"I know the caliber of this man Ercolano, and for you to make an arrest like this is certainly to your credit. You really tried something different and again I congratulate you!"

I thanked him and walked out stunned. Mort now stood up when court was reconvened, objecting to the defense questioning the right of search and seizure and the search warrant. James Pappalardi had obtained the search warrant, Mort contended, and Ercolano had no right to contest it.

The judge ruled in Mort's favor.

There went Ercolano's case. He got on the stand and Mort ripped into him while he talked in circles, afraid to commit perjury. He became so enraged on the stand that he kept glaring at me and putting his fingernail up to his teeth, giving me the Italian curse everytime he saw the judge wasn't looking. I grinned and gave him back the hand in the crook of the elbow with a resounding slap that caused the judge to turn and stare at me, wondering why there was all that laughter in the courtroom.

Ercolano, alias Herkey, got the message. And he also got five years in The Joint.

If Herkey was the bigtime peddler in New York, he was smallfry as compared with Sol Gelb, alias Solly Gordon. Sol is generally credited with being the first entrepreneur to import drugs from Europe on a mass scale. He reportedly set up his own laboratories for heroin in Italy and, when these were closed down, opened new labs in the Marseilles area. He was also the first to go to the Far East and make arrangements for that channel of mass importation. He was not only an imaginative, daring operator, but an elusive, tough, old man. He had a record of eleven arrests dating back to 1913 but only a few minor convictions. He was extremely wealthy, with offices in the Empire State Building and import-export businesses on the east side of Harlem and downtown.

Sol was somewhat of a legend among the agents. We'd constantly pick up rumors of his being the source of smoking opium for show business people and some of the top racketeers. In the 1930s this had been a fashionable pastime with these people but by the early 1950s was dying out.

Sol had only recently hoodwinked us. A relatively new agent, a young Italian, had made a buy of a half kilo of heroin off of Sol. He'd been with us less than a year and everyone was amazed and suspicious of how a newcomer could crack the biggest peddler in America. It seemed that the New York Police Department had a wiretap on a peddler known as Tony Iodine. In due time they found that our agent was calling Iodine and was crooked. While they couldn't verify that our agent was taking cash, he had accepted such things as steaks for his freezer and—of all things—a pedigreed dog, to help Iodine. When the police brought this news to District Supervisor Jim Ryan he was in a rage. Not only did he have a crooked agent but the case we had against Sol automatically went down the tube. What infuriated Ryan was that the agent had spent close to $10,000 for the half kilo and there was now no way of getting it back. That was the entire budget for the month.

Ryan was out to get Sol anyway he could. But he was also despondent. He didn't know how.

In Enforcement Group Two, our outfit, the subject of Sol was a perennial topic. We were extremely closeknit, all friends who went to baseball games together, socialized together, worked together. Our common goal was to arrest dope peddlers and—like a football team—we were competitive, anxious to be known as the best team in the country. We were famous already for one avocation, our payday crap games. In police circles it was a widely known social fixture and every payday agents would wander into our offices from all over town. It was illegal to gamble on government property, of course, but who was ready to destroy a fine old tradition?

I mention this because it was during the idle chitchat after one of our crap games that we decided to go after Sol in an allout effort to put him away. If we ganged up, all using the limits of our imagination and talents, even at the expense of ignoring smallfry peddlers, we concluded, we could get Number One, Sol.

We went to Jim Ryan and asked his permission to stop work on other cases and concentrate completely on Sol Gelb. Ryan listened, mulled it over for a week, and then finally gave his blessing. "If there's anything you need, call me," he said, "but I'm only going to allow you a month on the case." The time limit he imposed just made the prospective chase even more exciting.

"We can do it in three weeks," our spokesman told Ryan.

He laughed ruefully. "Let me tell you something. You want Sol Gelb. You work on Sol Gelb. But people have been trying to get him for thirty years. It's impossible to get Sol Gelb. I don't want to dampen your ardor or beat you down. But the simple truth is that you aren't going to get him ... "

We mapped out our campaign. First, we split into teams. In Group Two, some started pulling his tolls from the telephone company to see who he was calling and others organized a 24-hour surveillance watch.

In a short time we developed some fascinating data. Sol lived in a penthouse at 545 West End Avenue. But he also lived in a coldwater flat at 310 East 56th Street, an apartment at 258 West 17th Street, and, as it later developed, several other addresses. The old rake had a woman stashed in each apartment.

We concluded his wife was in the penthouse and so there'd probably be very little drug action there. So we concentrated on his other lovenests. We rented apartments across from the 56th and 17th street addresses and settled into a routine. Sol drove a tan

Cadillac sedan. Armando and Stu Nadler took turns tailing the Cadillac while I sat on one of the apartments. Then Ray Enright would take over my job and I'd tail the Cadillac. Tom Dugan, who later became the U.S. Marshal of Manhattan, a deputy director of the Peace Corps, and later ran for sheriff of Westchester County and died a few days before the election, was part of the team, as was Norm Mattousi.

We knew everything about Sol by now: where he went, what he ate for breakfast, who he called, what he wore, what his favorite dinner was, what he drank and how much.

Armando, my partner, was spending most of his time on building this background dossier. He was one of the finest researchers in the business and with a single name could build up information that would fill a filing cabinet in a week. Later he was to prepare the Mafia book for the Bureau and was the most instrumental man in building up the details of the Mafia families which were later revealed and verified by Joe Valachi.

One freezing day in February Armando and I sat in our apartment finishing our eight-hour shift across from Sol's place on East 56th Street. As I've said before, stakeout is one of the dreariest jobs in the business. But at least we were grateful we were in a heated room. We'd both talked ourselves out and mutely stared down at the street watching a few shivering people move through the chill sleet. We were grateful when Stu and Ray arrived to take over and were putting on our topcoats when Stu suddenly said, "Hey! There's Solly!"

We all hurried to the window. Sure enough, Sol was coming down the sidewalk. A slight, white-haired man who wore horn-rimmed glasses, he was always handsomely and expensively dressed. Today he was wearing a blue cashmere topcoat and a black homburg, and looked very much the prosperous businessman.

We were all excited because Sol seldom used this apartment.

Any plans to leave were forgotten as the four of us sat back to wait as Sol entered the apartment house.

It was some two hours later when he emerged and started down the street at a hurried pace leaning against the wind. We rushed down the steps and tailed him, two on each side of the street. Where was he going? Where had he parked his car? What urgent business had brought him out in this kind of weather? It was six in the evening and dark by now.

Sol crossed a street and as he reached the curb pulled something from his overcoat pocket and casually arched it like a ball toward a nearby trash can. Stu stopped at the can while we continued to tail Sol to his Cadillac another block away and watched him drive away.

Stu was holding brown wrapping paper wadded into a ball. Inside were several silver colored glassine bags used to peddle heroin and, even by the dim light of the lamppost overhead, we could discern a few traces of powder. We took out a marquis regent—our small glass vial tester agents carry at all times—and dropped a few granules. The sulphuric acid and formaldehyde it contains turned purple immediately.

"Hot damn!" Stu said softly. We all knew what this meant.

Bigtime as he was, Sol was still handling his drugs directly and if we caught him at the right moment we'd have our case! In fact, we could have arrested Sol right then if we had wanted to risk it. We had evidence—even though it was less than a half gram. Too, it meant several other things to us. This was the apartment he was using as his stash and probably his lab.

We called everyone on the team that night to tell them of our find. By the next day we were able to obtain a search warrant based on the minute evidence we'd found in the trash can. We also made arrangements for warrants for the other apartments and reorganized ourselves into teams to hit the three pads at the same time. Our plan was that whoever saw Sol come out of the apartment the next time would hit him immediately and the other teams would go into immediate action searching all the apartments simultaneously.

It was perhaps a week later when the call came from Tom Dugan and Norm Mattousi. Sol had just gone into the 56th Street stash apartment. The Group leader started calling all the teams, alerting them to get ready to move.

Before we arrived at the address, Tom had placed himself on the third floor and Norm on the second of Sol's apartment house. Sol stepped out of the door of his apartment and Tom let him get halfway down the steps. Then Norm and Tom both stepped out and Sol was trapped. "He just stared down at me and the cigar he was smoking fell out of his mouth," Norm said later. "I knew he knew immediately who I was—and that he was holding."

There was one and a half kilo—about three pounds—of heroin in each pocket of Sol's cashmere coat. Norm and Tom took the packs. They led Sol back to his apartment door and took his keys. When we arrived a moment later, the five of us went in. There were all the facilities of a lab: scales, sieves, milk sugar and mannite and quinine. We also found four and a half more pounds of heroin, forty ounces of smoking opium, fifteen pounds of crude opium and a .38 revolver with the serial numbers filed off. Finally, there was a check-certifying machine which showed Sol was buying cocaine in South America.

Meanwhile, the other team, Stu Nadler and Ray Enright, hit the other apartment on West 17th Street and arrested a woman, Joan Kauffman. She was dressed in a gingham apron like a homey housewife but was cooking crude opium down to smoking opium on the kitchen range. By the time we arrived with Sol, Stu and Ray had uncovered 1100 ounces of smoking opium, three and a half pounds of heroin, a heroin tableting machine and opium smoking gear.

We were jumping for joy over our grand coup. I recall riding downtown in the back seat next to the gloomy Sol. He turned to me. "Hey, kid, you like Florida?"

I was puzzled. "I've never been there. But I'd like to go," I replied.

He reached into the inside pocket of his coat and pulled out an envelope. "Well, kid, here's a round-trip ticket. I guess I won't be needing it now . . . "

The total seizure of Sol's stash came to a value of $2,175,500.

Harry Anslinger, the commissioner, flew up from Washington and called a meeting of all the agents. We'd brought in some New York police at the tail-end of the West End Avenue apartment to see they got some credit, too, although they had nothing to do with it. Anslinger and Police Commissioner Francis Adams made a public ritual of the affair, shaking hands with all of us. It was the largest seizure since narcotics came under international control in 1921, Anslinger announced. In fact, the record of the smoking opium still stands today as the biggest seizure in U.S. history. As for Jim Ryan, he was delighted to eat crow and admit we'd done the impossible, busting Sol after years of effort. As we cleaned up the case against Sol other touches emerged. Sol was a student of narcotics, he had a complete library on pharmacy. Too, we found out that Sol was bringing in some of the drugs from Italy in cans of olive oil. Sol had discovered an ingenious way to do this. The waterproof bags of heroin were secured loosely at the top and bottom by rubber bands inside the cans. If an inspector put a stick or tester into the can and accidentally hit one of the bags it would simply move about with the stick and the unsuspecting inspector would find nothing but a tester dripping with olive oil.

They put Sol away for five years.

If there was a deep sense of loyalty and camaraderie in the New York office there were also tragedies and conflicts which were to affect us all as the years passed.

I recall particularly the finest undercover agent I ever knew, Tony Zirili. Of Italian heritage, he worked scores of cases both in the U.S. and Europe before he was destroyed by the Bureau. Today, I still come across magazine stories and see television shows which I know were the true adventures of Tony, who specialized in working only on the biggest undercover cases, usually involving the Mafia.

Tony's appearance was ideal for the role he played. Small, wiry and athletic, he had a swarthy, dark skin and his hairline grew down almost to his eyebrows. The result was an eternal fierce and angry look which was in direct conflict to the real Tony, who had a gentle, kind demeanor which made him beloved to all who knew him. But he was also a magnificent actor and—as an Italian gambler, the character he usually played—he could turn into a different person.

It was this role which was to lead to Tony's tragedy. The Bureau would not reimburse agents for gambling losses while working a case. Tony was often mingling with top Italian gangsters and it was inevitable that he'd be invited to baccarat games. He had no choice, he had to play if he was to maintain his cover effectively. One day he told me despondently, "I've lost so damned much money I don't know how to make it up."

He complained to the Bureau. "I can't do this anymore," he told his supervisors. "There's no way that I can possibly afford to play for the stakes these hoods I'm after throw around. What do I do?"

The Bureau decided the best way was to bend but not break the rules. "Make it up another way, Tony," was the word he received from his bosses. "Say you're out with four top gangsters and lose in a game. Charge up that you took them to dinner and don't be afraid to put down big figures. Ask for $125 reimbursement for dinner if you've lost it gambling and we'll take care of it."

Tony shrugged. "Okay, if that's the way you want it."

I knew that Tony had lost a lot of money and felt sorry for him. He was a devoted family man and kept worrying that he was depriving his children in his uncomfortable tasks at the Bureau.

Tony went with Howard Chappell to Chicago where they worked undercover on a variety of big cases which led them later to Steubenville, Ohio and Cicero, Illinois. When he returned he told me that he was ready to quit. He'd lost so much money that there was no way to make it up on expense vouchers. Now one might suspect that he was shaking down, complaining about his losses, but not mentioning his winnings. Or that he was a compulsive gambler. This, I know, wasn't the case. At our weekly crap games in the office Tony showed complete disinterest and never joined in. And I knew by the way he lived that if he'd made any big kills at the baccarat games he would have used some of the money to buy clothes and goodies for his kids.

Soon after his Chicago foray he was ordered to New Orleans to make a case on two men who were supposedly bigtime dealers. Actually, they were our own narcotics agents and their assignment was to investigate Tony. They kept a careful tally on the money he spent, stalling him and telling him they were going to sell him a big supply of heroin while he entertained them. Tony didn't make the case, of course, but put in a big expense account, far over what he had actually spent to get back some of the money he'd lost in Chicago as he'd been instructed to do. The two investigators turned in their report and Tony was casually fired. The Bureau shrugged off his explanations.

It shocked all of us. Here was a man who had given so much of himself, was deeply in debt and had even taken out a bank loan to juggle his personal expenses against those gambling losses—completely destroyed by bureaucratic ineptness.

An added fillip was to come soon after when one of the agents—then the agent-in-charge for New Orleans—who'd ruined Tony was forced to resign when the New Orleans police arrested him in a public men's room going down on a youth. The other was also fired when the Bureau discovered he was actually involved in narcotics sales. I know I'm not alone. When the U.S. Commissioner of Narcotics, Harry Anslinger, autographed his last book, "The Murderers", to Tony, he wrote: "To Tony, the greatest narcotics agent of them all." Tony died a few years ago, a victim of his own innocence about the devious ways of bureaucrats.

I recall one flamboyant case I worked with Tony. It all started when Henry Giordano, who was later to work his way up to Deputy Commissioner of the Bureau and then succeed Anslinger as Commissioner, was working a case in Canada involving two brothers, George and John Mallock, who were known as two of the most wanted men in North America. Giordano had met with them and set up a deal to buy heroin. He made the buy and it looked like they were trapped, but they escaped before the Royal Canadian Mounted Police could make the arrest. John was to be machine-gunned down later in Mexico City. George simply disappeared although agents picked up reports that he was in the U.S.

Tony came to me one day and explained that he was working an undercover case and his contact had confided to him that his source of supply was a Canadian, George Mollard. "From his description, he could be George Mallock," Tony observed. "Let's team up and see if we can nail him to the wall."

I checked out the wanted poster of Mallock and found there was a warrant out in Vancouver for selling narcotics and conspiracy to sell narcotics. He was listed as one of the five most wanted men in Canada, with a record for breaking and entering, theft, auto theft, shop breaking, possession of dangerous weapons, unlawfully wounding, and intent to do grievous body harm. In large type the poster noted: "Fugitive is considered dangerous and probably armed. Caution should be used when apprehending."

I showed Tony the poster and he nodded ruefully. "My suspect tells me he always carries two guns," he said.

Tony went to work on his contact and set up a meeting with George at an East Side bar for three one afternoon, supposedly to make a big buy. As Tony was known, I picked up from there with another agent, Weldon Parks.

We arrived at the bar about two and entered separately. Weldon took a stool in the middle and I sat down near the entrance. Both of us were wearing work clothes, looking like truck drivers and warehousemen.

At 2:45 a small, stocky man, five-foot six and weighing about 160 with faded blue eyes and light brown hair going bald came in. I knew instantly it was Mallock but turned away to order a fresh beer.

He went to the far end of the bar, took a stool with his back to the wall, and ordered a whiskey sour. As we were the only three customers in the place he looked us over carefully as he sipped his drink.

The problem now was how to arrest him without a shooting incident. I puzzled over the problem for five minutes then made my move.

I could sense Weldon's surprise and panic when I suddenly got up and started for the far end of the bar. Mallock tensed, eying me suspiciously and I sauntered toward him, then reached in my pocket for a dime and put it into the juke box nearby. Then I turned and went back to my stool, seemingly oblivious to both Mallock's and Weldon's concern. Mallock turned back again, watching both me and the door.

I finished my beer, ordered another, and then got up and strolled to the jukebox again when the number was finished. Again, Mallock turned to watch me suspiciously. Again, I nonchalantly put a dime in the jukebox and went back to my stool.

When the number had finished I got up once again and strolled to the jukebox, selected a number, and dropped a dime. This time when I turned around Mallock hadn't turned around to watch me.

I pulled my gun out, grabbed him by the coat collar, and jammed him hard against the wall, putting my gun against the back of his head. "Move, Mallock, and I'll blow your Goddamned head off," I said.

Weldon rushed up and we stuck Mallock up against the wall. He had two guns, sure enough, which we pulled from his shoulder holster and a back pocket.

After officially placing him under arrest we took him to the office, fingerprinted and photographed him, and telephoned the Royal Canadian Mounted Police at Ottawa. They told us they'd send a RCMP plane down the next day.

We checked Mallock into the Federal House of Detention on West Street where they strip-searched him, put him through a metal detector test as they do for skyjacking today, and placed him in a cell. Two RCMP officers picked him up and returned him to Canada. Two days later I was called by a Sergeant Price. "Jack, I hate to needle you," he explained. "But remember when you swore that you'd searched Mallock and said he didn't have anything?"

"Come on, Sergeant," I replied. "They even put him through a metal detector and strip searched him. He couldn't have had anything on him."

"We know Mallock better, I guess," the Sergeant laughed.

"We not only searched him, we took his clothes and tore them apart and then his shoes. In the sole of one shoe he had two hack saw blades and in the other we found a hundred dollar bill!"

I had by now settled into the routine and companionship of New York and was content to stay on forever.

Someone in the personnel section of the Bureau is trained in ESP to understand all that. For word came that I had been assigned to Greensboro, North Carolina. It was to be a new kind of life in the world of narcotics enforcement.

5

Drugstore Narc

I've often wondered what is inside a guy to make him a good cop. In many ways it's like the military, a subtle mixture of alchemy that goes beyond all the superficial bromides about "duty" and "honor."

There is the uniform, the sense of being a part of something unique and respectable, pride, the curiousity and, of course, often the excitement of not knowing what each new day will hold. Your very isolation from the rest of the citizenry imposes its own society and mores for good or bad. Even though you don't like to admit it you enjoy the curious prestige of your job. It's often out of proportion but it's also real. Prominent businessmen, doctors, even lawyers give you undue attention and listen to your anecdotes because they attach some mystique and glamour to your chores. There's the marvelous sense of camaraderie of the squad room, the gagging and practical jokes and bullshitting and real concern for one another's personal problems. Finally, although not many of us will like to admit it, there's the feeling of absolute power. You know you are The Man. The citizen sees you as a symbol of authority which can alter his life at a whim. We have frightening power to discipline and command and to demand from a full-grown, sup-

81

posedly free adult an immediate subservience similar to the relationship of a child and a parent. Quite naturally, such power usually only leads to fear and, hence, resentment on the part of the public. I can only chuckle when I read of those public relations programs by various police departments which emerge from time to time to make the modern policeman a lovable and concerned symbol of some sort to the citizenry. It will never work. During any given year of duty he will be called upon to be a minister, a doctor, a lawyer, a marriage counselor, a child guidance expert and, of course, a disciplined military figure. But to seriously ask to be loved is more than we can expect.

I mention all this because when I was transferred to Greensboro, North Carolina in August, 1954 I discovered immediately the importance of camaraderie in police work. I had always been surrounded by other officers in a tightknit, minuscule group with our own interests and concerns. Suddenly, I was in a small office with only a few associates and felt alone and isolated from the world. Yet, I was to discover it was to be among the five happiest years of my life.

I immediately found a radical change in work patterns. Rather than five or six big cases a week, I was lucky to make a case a month. Too, in New York heroin was the major commodity. In North Carolina such drugstore narcotics as morphine, Pantapon, Demerol and other legitimate, manufactured drugs were the thing. The addicts' sources were quacks, addicted doctors, and drugstore burglars.

My territory included parts of Virginia and South Carolina and all of North Carolina. It involved endless travel and hard digging for each case—in contrast to New York, where prospective cases could overwhelm me. Too, I ran into a curious paradox. I had to learn to work with honest cops. It took time for me to overcome the cynicism and skepticism I had developed over the years. I had always paused when it came to asking the local police to cooperate. Now I was able to work with professional police, such as the South Carolina Law Enforcement Division, who, when I was undercover, I could depend upon for every assistance.

Shortly after I arrived I ran into one of the most unique problems of my career. Bill Atkinson, the Agent-in-Charge in Greensboro, was an odd duck who'd been there some 32 years. I couldn't quite make him out.

One night Paul Calhoun, the Chief of Police, called me at home and said he had a serious problem. Bill Atkinson had been caught stealing steaks from a supermarket!

"There's some mixup in identity or something," I said. I was still new enough that I must admit I suspected it was probably a frame of some sort by local cops—if it really was Bill.

Unfortunately, it was no mistake. Ludicrous as it sounded, Bill had a longtime reputation as a shoplifter in Greensboro with a particular yen for good steaks. His technique was well known, as later investigation showed. He'd strike up a conversation with a clerk at the counter about baseball or local news, then go back to the meat counter and order steaks and maybe a pound of hamburger. When he went to the check stand he'd pay for the hamburger but have the steaks hidden inside his coat or under his belt. He had already been barred from several supermarkets in town, but not arrested.

He'd been caught by a clerk in Ralph's, where he'd pulled his standard trick. It had been a slack period and the clerk had checked him out, then wandered back to chat with the butcher, remarking that Bill was a goof about who was going to win some upcoming baseball game. The butcher shook his head. "It's those damned steaks. He spends so much on steaks it's a wonder he doesn't turn into one." Immediately the two compared notes and decided what Bill had probably done. The owner was furious. He wanted Bill arrested the next time whether he was the town's Federal Narcotics agent or not. They nabbed him a few days later with ten dollars worth of steak in his pocket. He claimed forgetfulness.

Ralph was adamant. "Get out of my store and don't come back," he ordered. Then he started brooding about it and called the Police Department, wanting to swear out a warrant. The Chief of Police had started investigating and found Bill Atkinson had a reputation as a steak thief all over town.

"Please don't do anything yet, Paul," I asked. "Let me talk to Greenie first." Greenie was my boss, the District Supervisor. The chief agreed.

I called Greenie in Baltimore, who was very excitable anyway. He went into a panic, raging and swearing. He told me he would call the assistant commissioner to see how to handle it. The next day he arrived and demanded Atkinson's retirement. A week later I had my first job as Agent-in-Charge, thanks to bovine kleptomania!

Even while I had an assigned area I often ranged far afield. One informer came to me one day and told me he had an Italian source in Washington, D.C. This had an immediate lure for me as it could lead to possible Mafia contacts. My informer was scared to death of the man, however, and refused to go with me to the city to make contact. The best he would do was introduce the two of us on the phone. "Bill," his dealer, did sound rough enough on the phone to explain why the informer was afraid.

We arranged to meet at a hamburger stand on K street a few days later, after I explained I was staying at the Ambassador a few blocks away and he picked the meeting place.

Bill was swarthy and thin-lipped and had as cruel a pair of eyes as I've ever seen. He had called my room at three in the afternoon and set a five o'clock meeting.

After a few minutes of talk I knew things weren't going to go right. He didn't trust the set-up, he obviously didn't like me, and he was suspicious because I was white but had been introduced on the phone by a black. We talked about a deal but I got nowhere. Finally, he finished his third cup of coffee and stood up. "I'll see you tomorrow, but not here," he announced. "I just don't like this."

"How about my place?" I asked. He shook his head. "No dice," he growled.

"Hell, let's meet someplace and have a drink," I countered. "I don't like these one-armed joints."

He paused.

"Look, I know a little Italian joint on 13th Street," I went on. "It's got great food."

"What's the name of it?"

"The Vineyard."

"I've seen it. Okay."

He obviously liked the idea, as the place was on his turf. We arranged to meet there the next day at five. That night I told Roy Morrison, the Agent-in-Charge of the Washington, D.C. field office, about the deal. He was skeptical. "You got some guy we've never heard of and all you're going on is the word of the informer. It doesn't sound like much." Roy indicated I could go ahead but not to expect him to assign cover.

I then went to see Vince Iorio, who owns the Vineyard and is an old friend, and told him I planned to use his place to make a deal. A uniformed cop I knew was there, Jack Perry, and he volunteered to give me some sort of cover in mufti. "I'll be in the bar if you need me."

Bill was prompt and nervous, and he carefully checked out the other customers before we went to a back table. "Look, I want to tell you something. I'm not the boss of this outfit. I just work for it."

"Okay. So you work with somebody. I guess everyone works with somebody."

"Yeah. But this is a broad and this is big time stuff. I don't know if you can handle enough to interest us."

I tried to reassure him. "There's a shortage of heroin down there. I can always use all I can get. All we have down there is drugstore stuff."

"How much can you take?" he asked, his eyes shifting nervously to a couple who had just entered.

"How about five ounces?"

"Well, that's not bad . . . "

"And I'd like to work it up to where I can get ten ounces a week," I added.

He nodded, pleased. "I'm going outside. She's waiting around the corner. You come out and meet us in five minutes."

I nodded, ordering another martini.

"She wants to look you over. If you look okay she'll talk with you. No, make it fifteen minutes, then come to the bar around the corner. Not five, then come on out," he said, getting up. He went out the door. I hurried to where Jack sat. "Follow him and see where he goes."

Jack was back in a few moments. "He went into a bar around the corner all right."

"When I go in this guy may come out," I explained. "Try to get his license number. If he gets in a car tail him or something! The way this son of a bitch is playing it I can end up making a buy and not know who the hell I am buying from. So do what you can." I was concerned with a volunteer, untrained harness cop trying to cover me, but I knew he'd do his best.

I went to the bar and saw Bill in a rear booth in the dark interior. He was alone although the figures of four of five women who were largely indistinguishable in the gloom were sitting at the bar.

I ordered a drink. "What now?"

Bill's mean eyes studied the fly-specked window. "We'll know pretty soon. If she comes over she'll talk. If she doesn't in ten minutes, you can get lost—the deal's off . . ." To see a tough hood like Bill seemingly frightened of some woman seemed comic. I glanced at the women, my eyes now adjusted to the dark, trying to guess which one was the boss. They all had their backs to us. It was useless.

"How do I get in touch with you if we set this up?" I asked.

Bill shifted nervously. "No way, not unless she okays it."

Just then a beautiful blonde who was wearing a mink jacket picked up her white gloves and, it appeared, started toward the door. Then she stopped, turned and came over and sat down next to Bill.

My God, I thought, this is the connection! Bill gestured with his head. "Jack, Barbara," he announced as a cursory introduction.

She was a brittle and tough operator. Skipping amenities, she barraged me with questions. How much could I handle? What would I pay? Who had I dealt with before? It was a tough grilling and she knew her racket. She seemed satisfied with my price finally and agreed on five ounces.

"Meet me at eight tomorrow night at the Maryland Club," she said.

I started to argue. There was something odd! I'd been there the night before with Jack Perry. Coincidence? I didn't want to get into a trap of some sort.

She stood up with finality. "Be there at eight and have $1500," she said. "Otherwise, no deal."

I went out, leaving them in the booth and signaling Jack to follow up. I returned to the Vineyard to wait for Jack. An hour later he came in. They'd gone to an auto in a parking lot and he'd gotten the license number. We checked it out. It was registered to a William Green. It didn't fit. If Bill was named Green, my name was Giuseppe. I told Jack about the plan to meet at the Maryland Club. He was puzzled, too. The night before, we'd had some drinks and I'd met a friend of Jack's who turned out to be the standup comic billed as the "Glass Head." We'd gone into the main room after meeting this pleasant, personable fellow for a drink at the bar. He immediately turned on me and started attacking my clothes, my hair, everything about me. I was startled. It was funny even though I was the butt of the joke. Later, he came back to our table, sat down meekly, and apologized and explained that it was just his act. His name was Don Rickles.

We were both concerned not only about the choice for the buy, but "Glass Head." If Rickles said hello to me I could blow the whole deal. We drove out that night to explain our problem to Rickles. He was off. We were even more concerned now. We decided Jack could arrive early and cool it with Don before Barbara arrived.

The next day I met with Roy Morrison to give him a progress report. He listened, then put it on the line. "I want to put someone else on this, Jack. You're way down in Greensboro and can never handle this right. I want someone here to pick it up."

I had to admit he was right.

"What about Bill Jackson?" he suggested. Bill, my old crony, had recently been transferred to Baltimore from New York.

"No one better," I agreed. "But let me make this one buy tonight or they're likely to get suspicious."

Roy arranged for me to draw $2500 from the Official Advance Funds, known to agents as OAF, and I set out for Club Maryland, hoping Jack Perry had gotten there in time to see Rickles.

When I arrived I spotted several agents outside, sent by Morrison to cover me. Rickles was in the middle of his act and immediately spotted me. "Come on, dummy! Quit wandering around and sit down." I felt goose pimples, praying that he wasn't going to pick up on me. But Jack Perry had apparently gotten to him as he veered off, making terrible faces, and started attacking someone else.

I found Barbara and Bill at a back table. I started to order a drink but Barbara interrupted. "Do you have the money?" I said I did. "Hand it to Bill," she ordered crisply. I did. He quickly counted it under the table, nodding to her.

"Go with Bill," she said.

"But I haven't even had a drink."

"You don't need one."

I sighed, got to my feet, and started out with Bill, spotting Perry in a corner. Rickles started hollering as we passed him. "Where you going, dummy? You come in, wreck my act, now you leave without even buying a drink. Cheapskate!" Everyone laughed as we went out. We found Bill's car and he took a paper bag with five glassine bags from the trunk. I asked Bill for his phone number for future buys and then went immediately to a taxi and left, going to the Vineyard where Morrison was waiting, gave him the evidence and Bill's phone number. We arranged to move Bill Jackson into the act.

The rest was a wrapup. I called Bill and told him I wanted to work out something on a regular basis and couldn't drive up from Greensboro every week. He objected, but the next week I brought Bill Jackson with me. Meanwhile, other agents had checked out Barbara. It was all startling. Barbara Floyd was the secretary of Senator Herbert Lehman of New York! We couldn't believe it, and of course, the senator was in a jet-propelled tizzy when we told him.

He was due for re-election and foresaw chaos coming out of the unhappy situation. But Bill Jackson was to establish it beyond doubt, even making a buy from her in the Senate Office Building. When the case was all wrapped up, which involved quite a ring, I picked up a cheap scandal magazine on a newsstand one day. The cover blurb read "Undercover Purchase in Senate Office Building." The article praised an agent, Walter Fialkewicz, as the hero of the whole big bust. I accosted him later, asking why Bill Jackson wasn't even mentioned. He explained that the writer had come to the Bureau for information and the assistant commissioner had assigned Walter the task of explaining it all. Somehow, the writer had made Walter the superhero. He was embarrassed by the whole incident, but I've never let him forget it. So go the newspaper tales of narcotics chasing.

Such odd sojourns seemed to happen when I was stationed in Greensboro. One day an army officer, Captain John Detar, from Fort Bragg, home of the 82nd Airborne Division Paratrooper Batallion, called at my office. A huge number of first aid kits with morphine surettes had been stolen. Would I come to Fort Bragg and discuss the problem with the commanding officer? I agreed.

After one meeting we worked out a plan. I would go undercover and settle in with the troops. I had a crew cut, was issued a complete Army identification and uniforms, and became overnight Master Sergeant Gene Black, a career regular.

I decided to ease myself in slowly. In a bar in Fayetteville, North Carolina, near the base, I started drinking beer with an ex-soldier, Art Flannagan. The next day I told him I'd like to get some pot. He had a contact, a private in the 98th Field Artillery, he said. We met with the kid, who was named Benny, a day later and I bought a bag of marijuana for $75. I left that night for Greensboro, elated that I'd made such fast inroads into the drug-using circles of Fort Bragg.

My feeling of accomplishment didn't last long. I sent my buy on to the Baltimore lab and a day later the chemist called me. I'd bought a bagful of oregano! I felt like a star sucker. I hadn't even bothered to look at the stuff. "Send it back as soon as possible," I asked. He shipped it back by air mail. Ordinarily we sent drugs by registered mail but as we were shipping nothing but spaghetti seasoning, he didn't bother.

As I was getting ready to go back to Fort Bragg, one of the agents in the office, Dick Patch, asked if I'd deliver a gun to Captain Detar. I had my own gun in my right shoulder holster so I stuck the other under my belt on the left side.

I drove directly to Benny's house near the post where he lived with his wife. He answered the door.

"You son of a bitch," I yelled, shoving him against the wall.

He was flustered and frightened. "What the hell's the matter with you?" he gasped, as I pulled back my fist. "I forgot about this stuff. Until last night." I threw the bag of oregano to the porch floor. "I tried some of this with a buddy. You took me ... "

He started laughing.

"I don't think it's so Goddamned funny. I want my money back."

Benny just giggled. "Why should I? Who are you going to report me to? Without facing a rap yourself?"

"Come up with the money," I said angrily.

"Give me a reason," he replied.

"I'll give you two reasons," I said, opening my coat.

Benny stared a second. "Just a minute, give me a minute," he said, quickly going into the house. He was back immediately with a bag of real marijuana, apologizing and muttering that it was all a gag.

Benny spread word of the encounter in no time and soon I was known as the tough pothead with money to spend all over Fort Bragg. I started hanging around the Sergeants Club making buys from different soldiers. Repeatedly, I kept asking for hard stuff, heroin or morphine. No one seemed to know or to be able to fix me up with a source.

Yet, we knew it was around town and that civilians were getting it. Why was it so hard to find on the base? The serial numbers of the missing surettes had been recorded and the Bureau was feeding reports back to me showing the morphine was showing up all over the country. More than that, it wasn't just a problem of drug peddling. First aid kits going to Korea were being discovered repeatedly with no morphine surettes.

Then I ran into a new trouble. A guy named Richard Lester came up to me in a bar one day.

"I want to talk with you," he said. We went out into the alley.

"I hear you're The Man," he said.

"Who told you that?"

"People. You been buying all over the area. And Benny tells me when he first met you your name was Jack. Now it's Gene. We know there's an agent named Jack Kelly operating around here."

"Screw off," I blustered. "My name's Gene Black. Here's my ID."

"Anyone can have a fake ID. You answer the description of Kelly. Gray hair, freckles, Irish mug . . . "

I shrugged. "Look, Lester. Don't you see why Benny said that? He told me not to buy from you. That you peddle junk and he has the good stuff right out of Mexico."

Lester cursed. "That little bastard! I get my stuff right out of El Paso from Guzmann. I know what that little son of a bitch is doing now!" He gestured with his head, "Come on with me, I'll show you . . . "

We went down a side street in Fayetteville to a pool hall where a fat sergeant was shooting eightball with some other soldiers. Lester called him aside. "This is Sergeant Guzmann," he said as an introduction. "Tell him where you get our stuff, Guzmann."

Guzmann must have been sure I was clean if Lester was so casual. "Right out of El Paso. Who's complaining, anyway?"

"Benny is. He's bum-rapping us around town," Lester grumbled.

I made a buy of a hundred sticks from Guzmann at fifty cents a stick and made a case against him. Yet, I was worried. If word got out that I was indeed The Man, I knew I had to arrange a cover in case I had to split. I called Greenie, who sent Bill Jackson to join me. Bill, who'd been working another military base in Virginia, had all the right identification and moved in easily.

But we were still getting nowhere on our mission—finding the source of the stolen morphine. Then, as so often happens, an accidental break came when we made a routine case—against a woman. Bill and I had heard she was moving cocaine and went to make a buy.

She was a red-haired hustler who lived in a bungalow court and turned tricks for soldiers. Dealing was a sideline. After we'd named a few of the dealers at Fort Bragg she agreed to sell us some cocaine. Almost as an aside as she handed it to us she mentioned that she had some morphine surettes if we were interested.

I turned to Bill. "Shall we give it a try? Ever use the stuff?"

Bill shrugged. "What's to lose?" She went into another room to get a box of five which we asked for and, after a hurried whispered conference, we decided to bust her right there. When she returned we arrested her and started shaking down the apartment.

We found 44 boxes of the surettes, all half-grain morphine.

She'd never been busted before on a drug rap and was scared to death. We convinced her that if she'd talk we'd bring it to the attention of the judge and do what we could. She copped out immediately, naming two army sergeants as her source. Both were attached to the medical division of the 82nd Airborne.

We arranged for her to introduce us and easily made a buy. In the cleanup with arrest warrants we picked up fourteen soldiers from whom we'd bought marijuana and the two sergeants with the morphine. Both were career soldiers with years of service. They'd moved into the drug business because, like most 30-year men, they understood the abilities of the military to foul itself up in red tape. The Army some time before had issued an order to change from half-grain morphine surettes to quarter-grain. The obsolete half-grain surettes were ordered to be destroyed and, with the paperwork completed, everyone forgot about the matter. The two sergeants had simply stored away the half-grain issue, stamped the right forms and had a massive supply of drugs to sell across the country.

The soldiers were all tried in Federal Court, rather than by courts-martial.

Greensboro was to offer one of the most unique cases I've ever encountered, and it was in yet another sphere. It all started with a call at home one night from Harry Anslinger, the director of the Bureau. I was stunned. A call from the director was comparable to a call from the President; he was an omnipotent name like the Wizard of Oz. He was brusque and got immediately to the heart of his message. "I want you to go to Bluefield, West Virginia, and meet a man there, Sheriff Perry Dye. I've just had a call from the senior United States Senator from West Virginia. He says there are addicts from five states coming into Bluefield. There's a doctor there peddling to anyone and everyone. Go find out what it's all about. Let me know through Greenie. I told the senator I'd call him as soon as I had something. . ."

The next morning I was trying to find a way to get to Bluefield, a hamlet in the central part of the state. The best way seemed to be a plane to Roanoke and then to Princeton where the sheriff was located. It was snowing, and a hairy ride, but the sheriff was waiting for me. He was besieged, he explained to me over coffee in his small office, with burglaries, robberies and other crimes he'd never seen in this hill village before.

"I've got to have somewhere to start—an informer or someone who knows what's happening," I said.

Sheriff Dye leaned back in his creaking chair. "Hell, man. I got me a man in jail right here, Tom Patterson, who probably knows more than anybody . . . "

I was less sanguine than the sheriff. If I talked to Patterson and got nowhere, he'd be able to finger me to everyone in town when he got out. But I decided to take the chance.

The sheriff got up. "It's about time for me to give him his medicine anyway," he announced. He pulled a large brown bottle from his desk. "He's supposed to have one of these tablets every four hours. He had the bottle on him when I arrested him."

"What are they for?" I asked.

The sheriff shrugged. "High blood pressure, I think he said."

I asked for the bottle and looked at the label. They were quarter-grain morphine tablets!

It was my turn to shrug, realizing that the sheriff had no idea that he'd been keeping an addict supplied while he was in jail.

Tom Patterson was an aging, bald little man who freely told me he'd been an addict for more than 40 years. I was to find out later that he shot up in the jugular vein. This happened when I had to call a doctor for him and Patterson motioned toward the jugular. The doctor couldn't do it, so Patterson took the hypo and did it himself. The first addict to shoot up in such a vital spot I've ever met.

At that first meeting in his cell I roughed him up. I told him I was going to put his ass in jail permanently unless he leveled and he'd never have anything stronger than a cup of coffee. He was in on a burglary charge and I explained that I could probably get him off on that if he'd work with me. If not, I pointed out, he'd be up against West Virginia law, which we both knew was harsh.

It didn't take him long to crack, particularly when he knew he wasn't going to get anymore of his tablets in jail. "I'll do what you want, but I haven't any money," he said.

"I'll make your expenses if you do what I tell you," I said.

"Okay. Everything in this town comes from Doctor Horton," he said. "He's the only source."

"Who's he?"

"He's been here forever. He's about 75 years old. All you have to do is ask him for something and he'll give it to you."

"What does he charge?" I asked, figuring it was a case of a quack clipping the addicts for everything he could.

"Five dollars, maybe ten, for a prescription. And if you don't have any money he'll take radios, spark plugs, pen and pencil sets, alarm clocks. Once I paid him by fixing the fence at his house . . . "

I was shaken. This certainly wasn't a routine narcotics case with a crooked doctor.

"How long has this been going on?" I asked.

"I've been buying about the past five years."

"How about the others who buy from him?"

Patterson chuckled. "They come from a hundred miles around. Most of them are shoplifters and they bring anything they have."

I couldn't believe an operation on this scale could have gone on for so long without a clue. I asked Perry Dye what he estimated the shoplifting take was in the county. "About $25,000 a month," he replied. "That's why folks hereabouts are concerned." My God, I thought, about time!

"When could we do something with the doctor?" I asked Patterson.

He looked puzzled. "Why, right now, I guess."

"What do you mean, right now," I said. "It's about six in the afternoon."

"Doc will see you anytime. No problem."

"You mean we can score tonight?"

"Sure. No problem."

I arranged to take Patterson into my own custody and we drove the few miles to Bluefield. I registered in the Matz Hotel and changed to a sweater and work pants and then went with Patterson to the doctor's office. It was nearly seven o'clock but Doc Horton, a kindly appearing old man, came out to meet us in a white smock.

"Hi, Doc, can I get a shot of Dolophine?" asked Patterson as if he were in a market asking for a can of soup.

"Sure, Pat, come on in," Dr. Horton said happily. I couldn't believe it. I followed them in while the doctor administered the shot, then turned to me. "You want one, too?" he asked politely.

I shook my head. "Not now. But I'd like a prescription for some later."

"Sure," he said, writing out one for more Dolophine, which I took later to the Princeton Pharmacy and had filled to complete the violation and mailed off to the U.S. Chemist in Baltimore, a policy agents follow even if it is a legitimate drug, as this was.

As we started toward the door, Dr. Horton gave Patterson a friendly nudge and cackled. "You know, Pat, you ought to quit this doping. It's no good for anyone."

I knew now I was in an Alice in Wonderland dream and I guess my face showed it. "Don't you think so, son?" the doctor said, turning to me.

"Yeah, that's right," I managed to reply.

"Great idea. How?" Patterson asked.

The doctor gave his patient a stern look. "Eat more, you've got to eat more."

As we drove away I felt completely confused. We'd been in town less than ten minutes and I'd already made the case that had the U.S. Senator in a furor. "Is there anyone else in town?" I asked Patterson. "Does everyone—all those shoplifters who've come here—get their stuff from Dr. Horton?"

Patterson meditated a moment. "No," he said reflectively. "There are a few more sources in town. But *they* all get their stuff from Dr. Horton. He just gives them prescriptions and they go fill them and then peddle the stuff on their own. Some of them travel around the state moving their supplies."

"Do you think we could get into them?" I asked.

He yawned. "I doubt it. You're too healthy looking. I think they'd turn you down. You don't look like an addict. I was really surprised when Doc offered you a fix . . . "

I was puzzled. "Why?"

"Because Doc Horton doesn't ordinarily give fixes unless he thinks folks need one. He just wants to help people . . . doesn't like to see them hurting, you know."

I didn't know at all, but wanted to clean up the ring if there was any way to do it. "What about a jockey?" I asked. "What about a little, skinny jockey who could say he was down here from the racetrack at Charleston? Do you think those other guys would sell to him?"

"Maybe, if he was real skinny and sick looking," Patterson allowed, pursing his lips in thought. "But where you going to get a guy like that?"

"Let me take care of that," I said. "I'll see you tomorrow." I dropped him off at the hotel to report to Greenie.

"Can you send me Walter Morris right away," I asked. Walter

was an agent who weighed about 110 pounds and stood five-foot
three. He was stationed in Baltimore. Meanwhile, Greenie said he'd
check out Dr. Horton's order forms filed in our district office. When
a physician orders narcotics he uses a triplicate form. He keeps one,
one goes to the wholesale house, and we receive a copy. We are able
in this way to keep check on how much narcotics a physician is
ordering. Greenie found out that Dr. Horton was ordering a
staggering amount, not only from one wholesale house, but from a
number of them throughout the country.

The case was really already broken by now. Walter arrived
posing as a jockey, and worked with Patterson. I found an addict-
peddler, Jack Kidd, and built a series of cases involving other addict-peddlers—all of whom operated with Dr. Horton as the
fountainhead—and we rounded them up in one major sweep.

The old man—who I have always been convinced really
believed he was simply helping suffering mankind—went to court
pleading insanity. Various psychiatrists testified, Dr. James Hirt of
Roanoke claiming Dr. Horton suffered from a chronic brain disease,
government doctors saying that he was sane. Judge Ben Moore
ruled that he was sane and the case went to trial. He was found
guilty but the judge was able to bypass a mandatory sentence and
give him probation as well as stripping him of his license to practice
medicine.

I was glad to see this old man, who'd performed a service to his
community for more than fifty years—questionable as a part of that
service was—go free. As for Jack Kidd, the addict-peddler I picked
up as part of the operation, he came to a more tragic end, dying in
jail the day I arrested him. It was listed as a heart attack but the
attending physician told me that he believed Kidd had used narcotics for so many years that he simply died when he didn't have his
drug. So ended the case. But it wasn't all unhappy. Walter Morris,
the diminutive agent, married a waitress at the Matz Hotel as a
result and later was stationed in Roanoke.

Shortly after I returned to Greensboro I came across an informer who told me of a massive marijuana operation going on in

Martinsville, Virginia. He claimed the entrepreneurs, all black, were shipping throughout the southern part of the U.S. It sounded exciting and I called Greenie to see if Bill Jackson could be assigned with me to the chase for a time. But Bill was busy on his own and Tony Johnson, a black agent from New York, was sent in. He went with the informer to Virginia and was back within a few days bearing four sealed tin cans and a wide smile.

"What the hell's that?" I asked.

"You wouldn't believe it, man! But they're supposed to be filled with marijuana. I paid $100 for them. They better be something."

We sent a secretary to a grocery store for a can opener and sat staring at the cans wondering what new wonders of merchandising the drug trade would think of next. We opened them and they were indeed filled with marijuana. The operation, it seemed, not only grew and cured its own plants but packaged them with a home canning machine and shipped them by railway express and even the U.S. mail on a direct order basis.

Long after I left Greensboro I was to find several interesting results of my days there. First, I discovered why Bill Green, that strange swarthy Italian, had such an unusual name for an Italian. Bill Jackson told me. "Man, he was colored," Jackson explained. "He tried that Italian bit on me. But he couldn't fool a brother!" Bill told me later of the lovely blonde secretary to Senator Lehman. The Senator, it seemed, had raised all kinds of hell with the Bureau, being particularly incensed at the publicity the case created, and claimed he'd fired the girl five days before we arrested her. If that made him happy, the Bureau decided, why not?

6

Detroit Fat Cats

Occasionally, a simple case can burgeon into a wild chase which leads into myriad bypaths. One evening I bought 422 quarter-grain Dilaudid tablets, a derivative of morphine, from a youth in a Greensboro poolhall. He had a contact at a drugstore who supplied him, he said.

It wasn't much, but I called Bill Jackson in to work with me and by the time the fun was over we had six defendants right in Greensboro. One of them was my informer, who was to become convinced I was a God of some sort before it was all over. Further, he was to work for me again and again in the years to come in such places as Washington, D.C., Texas, and Colorado. He was one of the two or three addicts I've ever known who actually kicked his habit.

My elevation to godhead came about when I explained to the U.S. Attorney that this boy, Al, worked for me. I was sure his case would be dismissed. At the time lawyers felt that there was nothing to do with mandatory cases but dismiss them.

He appeared before Federal Judge Johnson J. Hayes, a wonderful old jurist with a reputation for being strict but fair. The U.S. Attorney, meanwhile, had told me not to worry, that my man

99

should simply enter a guilty plea and he'd take care of him. I told my informer what I'd been instructed.

The time came for sentencing. Judge Hayes gave him ten years! I thought Al was going to faint and I, too, was in a state of shock.

I waited until court was over and went in to see the judge, telling him what the man had done for the Bureau and how the U.S. Attorney had promised to intercede for me.

The judge shook his head. "He said nothing to me. I know how you people in narcotics need informers and how it's worthwhile to trade a small fish for a shark."

"It's not only that, Judge," I went on. "He's out of the traffic and has quit using. He's found a new life."

The judge nodded. "Tell him not to worry. Send him back tomorrow."

The next day Al stood before the judge. "I understand I made an error by automatically making this man guilty when he's not guilty. He can withdraw his plea if he wishes."

I nudged Al and he nodded. "Not guilty is right."

"I dismiss the case."

From then on my informer thought I could move mountains. He thought the only way to repay me was to find peddlers.

"I got you a pot peddler," Al called one day. "A guy called 'Fat Cat' on the street but he calls himself Tito."

"What the hell's Tito?" I asked.

"Fancy for Theodore."

"Or seeing he isn't called Theodore," I chuckled.

We made the contact. Fat Cat was a chuckling, happy, fat black with a laugh like a bellow. I bought a hundred sticks of pot at a dollar each. I was a bit reluctant as buying marijuana was considered trivia even then in the Bureau.

"Know where I can get some H?" I asked as I paid off Fat Cat.

"I got a contact in Detroit—but we ain't in Detroit, are we!" he replied, roaring at his wild humor.

"Let me know if you can set it up," I said. He nodded, chuckling.

A few days later I asked Al to call him and tell him we needed more marijuana cigarettes. We met in a restaurant. Fat Cat was one of those "cupacoffee-and-pie" men, I discovered as I watched him knock off three slices of Banana Cream Delight while he gabbed on and on.

"My brother's a big man in Detroit—a wheel, get it!" he explained, roaring with merriment.

"Why don't we take a trip," I suggested.

"Christ! I'd love to," he said, his shining face beaming.

"Or maybe you can get your brother down here," I added.

"No, no," he said quickly. "It would be a hell of a lot better to go there. I'll call my brother and get back to you." Tito, alias Fat Cat, badly wanted a free vacation.

The next day he called. "My brother says he won't come down here. But he's interested. He says it could be four to six months before he could get to Greensboro. He wants I should go along to Detroit with you. That's what my brother says."

I replied that I'd think about it but that I wanted a big buy if we went. I ran a make on Fat Cat's phone number and had them check out the number he called in Detroit. It was indeed his brother and his brother was under suspicion as a major peddler and had a long record.

A few days later we made the arrangements and I set out with Al and the beaming, laughing Fat Cat. I wasn't that happy. I've always felt that having an unwitting informer with you is one of the most awkward combinations there is. If you have a real informer you can work things out. He can take the point and run interference for you. You can talk over any and every situation and know what your next move will be. But when you have a potential defendant, you are telling him a story and he's selling your story to the other defendant and it can all blow up at any moment.

We were driving a government Cadillac. It was a lavish car we'd taken from a big peddler. The theory of such a legal seizure is that if you deprive a peddler of his car you help destroy his ability to peddle. It's true. I've had cases where a man would plead guilty and go to trial with his car, which is actually treated as a defendant. If it is found guilty, it's turned over to the Bureau. In the old Bureau every car was a seized car. Today, they still seize them but the laws have been modified and the present agency has a budget for autos. In our days when we spotted a peddler with a beautiful new convertible, he didn't know it but he was begging for arrest as we looked upon the idea of stacking the Bureau with expensive autos as both a game and legal booty.

When we arrived in Detroit, we all moved into a colored hotel although the agents in the office had a reservation for me at the Pick Hotel.

We settled in and I told my companions I had to go see a girl. Al covered splendidly with Fat Cat, accusing and kidding me of being a cocksman. I went to the Pick and met the local agents. The man assigned to work with me in Detroit was Phil Smith, now head of special projects for the present Bureau, a capable, straight agent. It was a closeknit group in the Detroit office. Nearly all were graduates of Michigan State police science school and they mixed socially like our group in Enforcement Group Two had in New York.

Phil and I worked out the details. He and two others were going to cover me "loose," meaning a casual surveillance which wouldn't give my contact any hint that something was amiss if he was checking me out before we met.

We had a couple drinks and I went to bed, exhausted from the trip.

The meeting was set when I picked up Fat Cat and Al. We drove to Fat Cat's brother's apartment, a lavish spread filled with gaudy, kinky furniture and a half dozen equally gaudy, kinky girls as well as three or four men in the flashy garb of the pimp.

Jimmy Morman, Fat Cat's brother, was glib with that superficial, suave style of a successful black man in The Life. He was running a string of girls as well as dealing, it was clear.

A casual grilling began. "Do you know Willie Carson at Winston-Salem?" he asked.

"Sure, I know Willie."

"Red Smith?"

"Sure!"

The other men joined in asking me of one black gangster after another in North Carolina and Virginia. I knew the names. Most were in prostitution although some dealt in bootlegging white lightning, the lethal booze which blacks call "splo," a derivative of "explosive" and an apt nickname.

The names came on and on. I claimed to know them all. It was a stupid thing to do, and a moment later I knew it. Morman handed me a photo of a group of men. "Which one is Red Smith?" he asked softly.

Al saved my ass, pushing next to me. "Hell, there's ol' Red right there!" he yelled. "And there's Jim and that's Kracky . . . "

It worked in a confused way. But the day wasn't over yet. We sat down at a long coffee table and I started discussing the buy. Jim held up a huge hand with two diamond rings flashing.

"Hold it, man. I ain't said I deal in heroin. I ain't said I'm going to deal with you. I don't know you . . . "

I tried to bluster. "What the hell is this? I drove all the way up here. Your brother's with me! He knows me."

Fat Cat chortled. "Yeah, yeah! I know Jack a long time . . . Jack's good people. Top fuckin' operator! He got a lot of things going down there. He's a big man down there."

"Yeah," said Jim with an indulgent sneer. "And I know you, brother dear."

I always made it a policy to pose as a hood in a general way with as few specifics as possible. I tried to leave the impression that I was a pimp and drug dealer and avoided details. Details can always snag you later and the people in the trade are suspicious of anyone who tells too much about himself as it marks him as an amateur or fake. The rule is, stay vague and let them draw their own conclusions from passing references. I also found gambling a curious touch. In the drug world, there is, for some reason, an awe of gamblers.

Such a posture leaves room for an emergency and one was to come up in the next move. One thing you never do is pose as an addict. The reasons are many. If you claim to be an addict and the people with you are, you have addict-peddlers on your hands. They are always desperate smallfry and that isn't the kind of case worth wasting time on. Further, such a pose can put you in a position where you're forced to use drugs and no case is worth that. Also, of course, operators have no use for addicts if they are serious dealers.

Now they tried a new angle. I was sitting next to a cat in a bright orange velvet coat called Icky D. Next to him was Morman's girl and others ranged along the long coffee table. Morman grinned during a break in the talk and pulled out some sticks of marijuana. I knew immediately what was next so I casually pulled out a pack of cigarettes and lit one, trying to appear not to notice the pot.

Everyone was handed a stick. I took one and lit it, holding it in my right hand while my own cigarette was in my left. I'd nonchalantly take a drag from the joint, blowing out the tobacco smoke. I talked as rapidly as I could to divert attention. No one seemed to notice and I finally ground out my cigarette and slipped the roach into a pocket.

Morman and three others were half high with the talk all focused around dealing, The Man, and drug prices. Morman suddenly got up and went into the kitchen, coming back a moment later with a box of Mother's Oats. He handed it to me. "Got a hundred dollars, you can have it," he said.

I looked inside. It was filled with marijuana. I nodded and counted off a hundred from my flash roll. Morman grinned, his two gold teeth shining, and stuffed the money in his flowered shirt pocket.

"Okay," he announced. "It's snortin' time."

He pulled a saucer with white powder from the drawer and started passing the heroin around. But first he tore the end from a paper match box and dipped into the heroin himself, taking a deep pull in his right nostril. His eyes seemed to pop out as he shook his head, coughed, and sneezed with an ecstatic grin.

I watched as it moved toward me, Icky D taking a snort, then the girl. This is another good case blown, I thought, as I knew I wasn't going to take a pull of the stuff and started thinking how to get out of the apartment. I reached down to my leg holster and snaked my gun out, holding it under the table.

I watched Al take a snort and it pissed me off, tense as I was. He hadn't touched H for some six months and I'd developed an avuncular pride in seeing him kick the habit. Now, nervous as I was, I thought he'd be back on it again.

The saucer came to me. In desperation I made one of the most ludicrous moves in my career. In movies and television there is always the scene in drug dramas when some buyer or cop takes a bit of heroin on his fingertip and tastes it and announces "it's heroin all right" or "it's fifty percent pure." No agent ever does such a thing. First, you can't tell if it's heroin that way. Too, you could get yourself a nice taste of strychnine if someone knows you are an agent.

But I had just done it! I took a bit on my tongue and said, "Christ, that's good stuff—real good stuff . . . "

Morman's face turned stony as his smile disappeared.

"Wait a minute. Ain't you going to snort none?"

I shook my head. "Hell no. I didn't come here to party. I came to do business. I don't like this. Your brother said you were a good businessman. You kind of surprise me."

Morman laughed again. "Okay, okay, Jack. I like your style and I'll take care of you."

I relaxed a bit, trying to get my gun back into the leg holster but was unable. I sat until everyone's head was turned and then managed to slip it into my pants pocket quickly.

Morman got up and motioned to me and I followed him into the kitchen. He opened a cupboard and pulled out a can marked "flour." Stretching a woman's silk stocking over the top of another can, he began to mix heroin and milk sugar, working it through the silk with his forefinger. "How many spoonfuls you want? I'm not cutting it much cause I like you."

This threw me. I had never heard the term and thought it was another trap to see if I was The Man.

"What the hell you talking about? I never heard of spoons," I replied.

He stopped the mixing. "Man, where you been? I don't understand you." Later, I was to find that heroin was sold in the

Detroit area by the teaspoonful, but I didn't know it then.

"I ain't interested," I said, trying to sound all business. "I only buy by the ounce."

He relaxed. "Okay, okay. Look, I'm a little short now. Next time you come to Detroit I'll take care of you righteous. Right now all I can let you have is about two ounces."

"I'll take it."

He went on sifting, making the mixture fluffy and giving it bulk, then stapled the mixture in two glassine bags. He took my box of Mother's Oats and dumped it into a brown bag with the two bags of heroin and neatly rolled the top. "There you are, man! Anyone see you, they figure you got some nice groceries there."

I gave him $1000 for the heroin and we shook hands, the deal completed. He gave me his phone number.

"Next time you come up here, Jack I'll show you a time. You like white girls or black girls?"

I shrugged. "I like all girls."

He grinned. "Okay, man. The next time you come I'll meet you at the airport and have you set up with two girls, a white one and a black one. I'll show you a time. I'll pick you up at the airport and have you registered at the Algiers Motel. You ever hear of that?"

"I don't know Detroit," I said.

"Well, man, we'll have a time. And I'll have more supply for you."

"That sounds great, pal." Years later the Algiers Motel was to be a *cause célèbre* when there was a shootout there. At the time, it meant nothing to me.

I collected Al and Fat Cat and we left, driving them to the hotel. Fat Cat was puzzled when I told him I had a chore to do and that we'd leave in the morning. "What you going to do with that stuff?" he asked.

"Hell, you don't think I'm going to carry it around, do you? I'm going to mail it back. I'm going to the post office right now."

Fat Cat seemed mollified. I let them out and drove to the Pick Hotel where Phil Smith was waiting. He looked over the buy.

"Congratulations, Jack. You are the first white man to work undercover in the Detroit area in fifteen years."

I was amazed. "How come?"

Phil smiled ruefully. "Ever since the race riots back in 1946 whites don't even go into that area anymore."

I met with Walter Panich, the Enforcement Assistant, and told him of the apartment. Phil and Walter puzzled over Icky D being there as he was a top peddler in his own right. They concluded maybe some alliance was in the works to swap stuff. I officially handed over the evidence, told them I'd file my reports to them from North Carolina, and left the next morning for home.

A month later I called Phil. I suggested we crank up the case again and get Morman. "Good idea. And why don't you bring Fat Cat with you and we'll wrap him up at the same time." I agreed. A few days later, Al, Fat Cat, and I arrived in Detroit, registered just as before and I went to the Pick to meet with the local agents. I told them I'd like to work alone.

"Why not?" replied Phil. "Just let us know if you need us to back you up."

I asked Fat Cat to set up a meeting with his brother. He came back to report Morman didn't want to meet at his apartment for some reason. "He wants to get together at Icky D's place."

I didn't panic over this, but did contact Phil for a cover. "By the way," he added after agreeing to cover me, "Morman's got a beautiful new Oldsmobile he just picked up a day or so ago."

I chuckled. "That's nice. Maybe I'll be able to pick up a new Olds for your office."

Phil laughed.

I went over to Icky D's in a taxi, figuring that if we did go anywhere we'd be in Morman's car, which the cover could spot easily and, if we made the case, we could tie up the car.

It was a ground-floor duplex, a soot-covered brick building in the belly of the black district. I hadn't felt uneasy in the area until Phil had told me of the aftermath of the race riots. Now I did.

Icky D let me in. Morman hadn't arrived. I had scarcely sat

down when Icky D, in his own idea of being a host, said, "Come on man, let's blow some pot."

"Look, Icky D," I replied. "I'm not that big on pot to start with. But I hate blowing it when I'm working. If fuzzes me up and I don't want to get my money screwed up. I don't want to get busted either. It's a long way home to North Carolina. But if you want to give me some I'll take it back and blow it when I'm ready to go to bed."

He was apparently shocked at my lack of sense of camaraderie but did hand me a silver package with some pot in it. "There's a little sample," he said with a grumble.

I took it, knowing I now had Icky D as a defendant. Just then Jimmy came in. He seemed hostile and went immediately to the bay window. We all looked out. A two-toned beige and gold Olds 90 with a vinyl top was in front. He went over and sat down, lighting up a thin cigar and glaring at me.

I waited. "Look, Jack, you aren't kidding us!"

"What do you mean kidding you?"

"We know there's something wrong with you."

I looked confused.

"We watched you. There you were smoking a cigarette and you take a joint and don't hit it once, faking us with cigarette smoke. Then you pinch the roach. I saw you. Then when you tasted the saucer of my stuff! Man, you aren't kidding us. The thing that confuses me is that The Man wouldn't be that stupid. But there's something wrong."

I felt like an ass, being told I couldn't be a narc because I was too dumb. Well, I figured here we go again. I crossed my left leg over my right as I had my gun in my left sock. I easily put my hand over the gun, figuring how I could take them if I had to move fast.

I decided to bluff it through. "Morman, you're full of shit." He glared at me silently.

"What kind of an asshole do you think I am?" I continued. "Do you think I'm going to snort and blow pot when I'm up here on a righteous money deal trying to make a good connection? I want to set up a supply line and I'm not going to screw it up partying. I came here for business—that's what I can't make you understand. How about that, Icky D?"

I took him by surprise. He paused a moment, then went on to explain to Morman how I'd just turned down a joint and said the same thing.

Morman studied the points of his shiny patent leather shoes. "Why didn't you tell us that the last time?"

"I did, man. I know you meant well. I didn't want to hurt your feelings."

He threw a hand up in a grandiose gesture. "Okay, let's forget it. How did you like the stuff I sold you last time?"

The agents in Detroit had tested the stuff and found it only 20-25 percent pure and while it was better than ordinary street stuff it was nothing great.

I made my next move, raising hell about the quality. "It was so lousy I couldn't even cut it. If I had cut it any more my people just wouldn't have bought it. It was pure shit. I got a reputation to think about. My people down there are used to straight drugstore morphine. Unless I get quality stuff they'll stick with morphine while I'm trying to create a new market. Unless I can make them want H more than morphine they'll stick with what they're used to."

He nodded. "Yeah, yeah, I see what you mean. But I thought that was pretty good stuff."

Icky D spoke up and I was surprised at his frankness. "I got better stuff than he has."

"You do?"

Morman got up, his eyes blazing. "Who you dealing with, me or him?"

I paused. "Why don't I deal with both of you? Why not? I know you're good friends." I lit a cigarette. "Why don't I take an ounce from each of you and test them. Whoever's got the best stuff from now on is the man I deal with for that load. You can work out the rest between yourselves."

They both thought a bit then Morman spoke up. "Okay. But you sure got to take more than that. Two ounces each."

"Okay, but look, this is just a sample. If this stuff is good I'll be back in a week and take ten ounces of the best."

They whispered a bit. "Okay, that doesn't sound like too bad a deal."

Morman got up. "Well, I got to go get my man and get the stuff."

Icky D went to call his contact. He was back in a moment. "My man can't come over," he said.

Morman snorted. "See, that's the kind of man he's got. Can't come over. My man will come over!" He started for the phone, then turned. "You got the money, stud? He'll be here with two ounces in five minutes." I got up and counted out a thousand on the mantlepiece. He made the call.

Morman went to the bay window and, within a few minutes, announced, "Here he is." I stepped over and saw a brown Pontiac which had just stopped in the middle of the street. Morman ran out. I saw him grab a package from the driver and hand him some money. But then he did something odd. I expected him to come back to the duplex. Instead, he went to his car and got in as the Pontiac drove off, the tires screeching.

"What the hell is he doing in his car?" I asked Icky D.

"Yeah, man, well I don't rightly know. Maybe he wants to deal with you in the car so he can be ready to run or something . . ."

Then Morman honked and motioned to me in the window. I scooped up my money and went down. When I opened the door I decided why he'd done it. He simply wanted to show off his new car. I started raving about it while he grinned, noting that it only had 428 miles on it.

He handed me the pack. "See, man, I deliver. Now the next time don't jazz me. Call me and I'll have the stuff for you at my pad."

I opened the bag. There were two glassine bags, each with an ounce of heroin. "Okay, from now on," I replied. "What do I do now?"

"Go on back. You set yourself for two ounces from Icky D and I guess you want it. But it won't be quality like mine."

I got out. "Maybe I'll see you around. Al and Fat Cat want to stay a day or so."

Morman shrugged. "Maybe. But I may have to make a run. I got business down in Wilmington, Delaware."

Icky D was waiting. "Did you make your buy?" I nodded.

"All right. He's a nice boy. But his stuff ain't like mine. Now we'll go see my man." We got into his new Dodge and drove around the streets for some half hour, finally pulling up behind a blue Cadillac on a side street. Icky D took my money and was back in a moment with two glassine bags. "Where do you want to go?" he asked, his manner abrupt.

"Just drop me off at the first taxi stand." I'd been watching and saw no hint of any cover. But when I got back to the hotel in the taxi they pulled up behind me. It had been a beautiful covering job all the way. They knew who the driver of the Pontiac was, one Fred McCoy, and they'd already checked out the driver of the Cadillac, a Ned Scott, who was in their files, too. It turned out great. We had three defendants and three nice new cars all in one day's work. I gathered with the Detroit agents that night and we celebrated.

Next morning I was awakened by Al. "I think I really got a good one."

I was still fuzzy from the previous night's festivities. "What you mean?" I stuttered.

"I told Fat Cat that the pot his brother sold you wasn't any good and if he could find a good connection with quality stuff you'd give him some of it. He says he's got one named Walter."

"Great! Where are you now?" I asked.

"At a pay phone. Fat Cat's waiting in my room."

"Stall. It will take a little while to draw some money. How much can he get us?"

"He said any amount," Al replied.

"I'll have to get the other agents and money lined up. Keep Fat Cat there."

I went to the office. We'd originally planned on arresting Jim

Morman and his crew right away. Now Panich and his staff suggested we hold off. The plan was that I'd call Morman in a few days and ask him to meet me at the airport and bring ten ounces, explaining that I'd pay him right away and leave immediately. Then I'd call Icky D and the others to also meet me at the airport at different times.

Then I told them about Walter. They'd never heard of him as he was another of the Black Belt dealers. "What do you want to do?" asked Panich.

"I want to play out the string. I want to make Walter and find out what he's got," I said.

"Okay. What are you figuring on buying?"

"Well, I don't know," I said. "What about five hundred dollars?"

"With five hundred in Detroit you're only going to get about three pounds. It runs around $150 a pound right now." I drew five hundred and we set up cover and I drove back to the colored hotel.

I parked in a vacant lot across the street, which gave the six agents in three cars clear access to see everything, and went up to see Al and Fat Cat.

Fat Cat was bouncing with excitement, sweat streaming from his round, smiling face. "Walter is on his way! On his way! Here!"

"How soon?" I asked.

"Fifteen minutes! Walter will be here in fifteen minutes!"

"I'm going down to my room. You bring him down when he gets here." I wanted to show Walter that I did have a room in the colored hotel and was for real.

It was nearly a half hour later when Al, Fat Cat, a very light-skinned Negro, Walter, and a pretty, dark-skinned girl arrived. Fat Cat introduced me as Jack McGuire from North Carolina. Walter made no effort to hide his caution. He checked the curtains, looked under the bed, ran his hand down the lamps looking for bugs. It looked like it could go on all day.

"What the hell you looking for, man?" I finally demanded.

"You can't be too careful when you're dealing with white

studs," he said slowly as if he was reciting a catechism.

I leaned back on the bed. "Have a field day," I said with a gesture.

Walter loosened his flashy overcoat and dropped his hat on a table. "I don't read this. Fat Cat's brother deals. How come you want another connection?"

"Simple," I said, taking my own time lighting my pipe. "I bought a pound off him and it was shit. It was nowhere, man. We got all the homegrown stuff we want down there now. What we want is some good Mexican or Texas pot—something I can sell."

"My stuff comes straight from Mexico to me," he boasted quickly.

"What do you get for it?"

"How much do you think you can handle?" Now greed had taken over and his fears were forgotten.

"I figure on coming up here once a month," I said expansively. "I'd like to pick up say ten, twenty pounds each time. I'm scoring H from Jimmy and Icky D. No reason you can't be my pot man."

"Good, man, good." He seemed lulled by the mention of the others.

"Where's your stuff?" I asked.

"Man, I ain't bringing no stuff here. You come get it."

I nodded. "Glad to."

"I'll take you over to my pad and you can pick up and I'll bring you back to the hotel. How that sound?"

Downstairs I looked for my cover and could see no one. But I was sure they were there somewhere. Walter and his girl and I started across the wide boulevard to the vacant lot where his car was parked too, a shiny new blue and gray Oldsmobile. I eyed it, feeling like I was an auto supplier for the Detroit office. I spent time admiring it outside so the agents would be sure to see.

Walter settled behind the wheel. "Just in case we got a tail let's have a little ride," he grinned. For a half hour we circled about while I tried to appear nonchalant. Finally, Walter announced, "Here's my street." I glanced up at the sign: "Joseph Campeau St." As we went up the brick steps to the three-story ancient building covered with frayed asbestos siding, I noted the address number.

Walter called at a door and a towering, unshaven man in a black turtleneck sweater stepped out, glancing at me suspiciously. "This is my brother, Alex," he said.

Alex sniffed and turned to Walter. "I got to talk with you. We've got a problem. Come on in the kitchen."

Walter pulled his girl over. "Mary, you take Jack up to the front room and put on a tape for him." It seemed a non-sequitur sort of request. But when we'd settled before the big stereo I found out why. Walter apparently fancied himself as a showman of some sort. He'd made his own tapes and introduced the songs, commenting on them as both master-of-ceremonies and critic and then the music would come in, picked up from another machine. "Well now folks, we got a little number by Ray Charles. Listen to the way Ray handles this . . . " If it was Duke Ellington he'd advise "listen to the Duke hit those ivories and catch the trombone in the background." He had his own corny one-man disc jockey show and his own captured audience.

It was a large room with many chairs along the sides and the middle had been cleared for what seemed to be a dance floor.

I was a bit puzzled by this "home", as Walter had called it, and was still looking around when Mary excused herself and disappeared.

I was still wondering when a tiny dude in a garish yellow plaid jacket and yellow billed cap came in gandy-dancing, did a few shuffle steps on the floor and glided over to me, reaching out his hand. "Heello, honkey maaan! I'm Calvin the Cutup, Calvin the Rip. Hit five!"

I tried to shake hands and got a friendly slap as Calvin pulled out a stick of pot and lit up. I watched his loose gestures with fascination. Calvin reminded me of a marionette hung on strings. He flung himself into a chair and started blowing that stick of pot as I'd never seen before, fast, quick puffs which were immediately exhaled as if he was showing off his affluence by not bothering to get the full kick from a deep, slow draw.

Mary came back in with another beautiful black girl in a purple sequined dress cut so low her navel showed. Oddball clothes for the afternoon, I thought. She sat down next to Calvin, lighting a stick from her purse and the two of them leaned back losing themselves in Walter's tapes. Two more girls in slacks arrived. One wandered off, the other began slowly dancing by herself, her mascaraed eyes closed and a look of ecstasy on her face.

I got up and went over to Mary, who was idly thumbing through a frayed copy of *True Confessions*. "Where the hell is Walter?" I asked gruffly.

She looked up and smiled benignly. "I don't know. Better go ask Alex." She motioned toward the kitchen in the rear. Alex was sitting at a kitchen table wearing a foolish apron with the lettering "I'M FRIED!" munching on a cold pike sandwich.

"Where the hell's Walter?" I demanded.

"Man, Walter, he gone on a delivery. Sit down and eat a bit."

I heard more cries and laughs from the front room and knew more people had arrived. I was tense, feeling things weren't shaping up.

"I came up here to get some shit, not to party," I replied. "I want to get my stuff and get my ass out of here."

Alex shrugged, taking a massive chomp of his sandwich. "Walter, he gone, I tell you. Relax. Go in and ball one of them nice chicks out there . . . you too good to associate with us niggers?"

I saw I'd better back off. "Naw," I said easily. "It's not that at all. I don't mind partying, it's just I don't play when I'm working. You got a pot party going out there in the front room. This whole Goddamned place can get busted and me along with it. That ain't what I came for."

"Walter, he be back right soon." Alex closed his eyes and munched contentedly away.

I wandered back to the party. Some 30 people were there by now. One girl was bare-assed, bumping and grinding to the music. Another chick got up and walked over to her and started fondling the dancer's breasts, pulling her to the floor as the others laughed and guffawed. A girl moved up to me and reached down and grabbed at my penis. "Want to play, stud?" I pulled away and she added fetchingly, "Free . . . "

I sat down, getting more nervous at the way this was all going. Mary came over and dropped to my lap. "Don't you want to get laid, honey?" she purred. "Walter wouldn't mind if you ball me."

"I just want to get my stuff and get the hell out, Mary."

She giggled. "We got a good party going and you want to split. We gonna have a big gangfuck and you talking business. Come on, Baby."

In a far corner a fight broke out, there was a brief flurry of fists, and the two guys were separated, one reeling off yelling he was going to "cut your dirty heart out." Mary giggled. "Lemme get you some wine, Jack," she said, pulling herself up.

She went to a table where the pot smokers were gathered with wine glasses, wetting down their parched, dry throats from the pot smoking. I looked at Calvin. He was sitting alone, facing the wall and angrily talking to himself, complaining about some past-due money owed him. A robust kid in a heavy knit sweater walked over to me, a glass of Rhine wine in his hand. "Man, where'd you get those threads!" he said ecstatically as he fingered the material of my lapel. I pushed his hand away. "Come on, man, will you get the hell out of here," I growled.

"I just want to know where you got them threads," he said in a hurt tone.

"I bought them downtown," I snapped.

He wandered off. "Downtown. He bought them downtown. Got to remember that. Downtown."

I looked around. The two dikes were on the dance floor and still at it. Calvin was shouting to himself louder than ever. Two girls had a guy in a far corner laughing as one went down on him. Several other couples were spread about making it on the floor.

I've got to get out of here fast, I thought. The only white man in the place and it's only going to take a spark and I'll be in deep trouble. I went back through the pot-smoke-hazy room toward the kitchen again

I couldn't help but think of that old saw about marijuana making one only want to lean back and listen to cool music. Here was every kind of wild action from near mayhem to Calvin's flipping out alone and no one was using anything but marijuana.

Walter was in the kitchen having a cup of coffee.

"What the hell is this?" I demanded. "I came for a buy."

He was all apologies. "I just had some fast business. I'll make it up to you. I'm going to give you a good score, a real, good score. How much you figuring on buying?"

"About three pounds, I figured."

"That would be $450. I'll tell you what. I'll give you four pounds for $500. How's that?"

"That's fine. But what the hell time is it? It must be nine or so already. Where can I get a cab?"

Walter held up his two hands in a gesture of supplication. "No, no way, man. I'm going to take you. I'll drive you." He handed me a bag already prepared with five pounds.

"Come on, Jack," he said and we went down the back stairs to his car. As we rode toward the hotel I couldn't help but thinking again of the ways I'd seen the pot affecting different people that night. I am no scientist but it was clear to me marijuana affects no two people in the same way. More than that, as I am convinced, I didn't buy the theory that marijuana is no worse than booze. It's a hell of a lot worse and twice as unpredictable. A user loses his sense of time and his sense of distance. He's a menace at the wheel of a car more than any drunk. A man can have a drink and handle an auto. A man who has a stick of pot may, or may not. The most important thing of all is that most people don't drink to get drunk. But they blow pot only to get high.

At the door of the hotel I got out and chatted briefly with Walter. He gave me his phone number and I agreed to call him when I was due back next so he could have a load ready for me.

I went up to my room, then to Al and Fat Cat's. No one was there. I went back down to my car and turned on the lights. When I did I heard a little honk. I pulled out and drove a few blocks and stopped. Phil Smith got out of the car behind me and climbed in with me and we drove on toward the Pick Hotel.

I complimented him on the great job of tailing me. He started to laugh.

"I've got to cop out to you and tell you the truth. We never saw you."

"You must have seen me when I came out and got into that two-toned Olds," I gasped.

"Nope," he laughed. "This is the first time we've seen you since you went into the hotel. Where the hell you been?"

I was glad I didn't know until now. I had been worried enough at that party and, if I'd have known I was all alone, I'd have really shit. I told him the whole story and showed him the bag of marijuana.

When we went into the hotel I handed him the bag. "You take this. I've got to get a beer. I'm so damned dry I can hardly breathe." I went into the bar and a few minutes later the other agents joined me at the table. We sat chatting and drinking. I noticed they kept eyeing me in a peculiar way and was puzzled as I told them all about the wild party. "My God," I went on, "You could have cut that smoke with a knife! That's why I had to have a beer, my throat's so dry . . . "

They all started laughing. "What the hell's so funny," I asked indignantly. "You guys are acting awfully funny."

"You smell like a marijuana field, that's what's funny," Phil said. "And you're high whether you realize it or not." I sniffed my tweed coat sleeve. It reeked. It took three cleanings to get rid of the odor.

I went up to bed. At about four Al called. "How'd you make out, Mr. Kelly?" I was numb.

"Great."

"I just want to tell you Fat Cat and I made another connection tonight. We can score some heroin."

I tried to sound enthused. "You really can?"

Al's voice was jubilant. "Yeah, tomorrow!" He gave me the two suspects' names.

"Great—we'll talk about it," I muttered, thinking that narcotics cops may be able to save themselves from their enemies but what can you do about your friends as I dozed off again.

The next morning I felt a little more like facing life again. I went to the office, initialed and dated the evidence, and helped process it to go to the chemist.

"I think I may have a couple more," I told Phil, giving him the two names Al had mentioned before.

"I know one of those guys," he replied. "Let me look in the files." A moment later he was back. "We know both of them," he said. He looked at me oddly. "You know, you're making more cases around here than we have for a long time."

"Yeah," I agreed. "I'm enjoying it."

"I guess you are."

Just then Walt Panich came in. "Jack, Mr. Ellis wants to see you."

I was pleased with myself and thought now the District Supervisor is going to tell me what a good job I'm doing, too.

Ellis motioned me to a chair.

"The boys tell me you've done a good job," he began.

"Thanks."

"You made some good cases and got some people."

I nodded. "I got another one cooking today," I said, trying to sound modest.

He paused. "What did you come here for?" he asked softly.

I looked up. "What do you mean?"

"Didn't you come here to make Jimmy Morman?"

"Sure," I agreed.

"And all these other people. They're just icing on the cake?"

"Yeah," I said puzzled. "I guess so."

"Well, don't you feel you've accomplished enough? What you came for?" His voice was flat.

"I'm afraid I don't follow you," I replied.

"Do I have to draw you a blueprint? You're making this office look bad. Why the hell don't you go back to North Carolina?"

I was stunned. The idea hadn't occurred to me. "If that is what you want," I said.

"That's exactly what I want. You did a good job and I'm pleased with what you did. But I think you've carried it too far. Go back and put some North Carolina peddlers in jail."

I walked out and told Walter and Phil what had been said. "I'm going to get my men and take off." I called Al and Fat Cat and told them to pack. They objected, my two kookie informers, one who didn't even know he was. But we left within an hour.

A month later I called Morman and ordered ten ounces of heroin, then Icky D and ordered the same, telling them I'd be in town to pick it up on Wednesday. Then I called Walter and ordered 25 pounds of marijuana.

Then I called Phil Smith and Walter Panich. They pleaded with me to come to Detroit and relax with them a bit. But I was bitter. "No. You guys make the cases and let me know what happens."

They got them all and made the seizures and called me. That night I went out with Bill Jackson and with the State Bureau of Investigation and we arrested twelve defendants that Bill had bought from in the weeks since I returned. One of them was Fat Cat.

7

Infighting

In December, 1958, I was in my Greensboro office trying to catch up on the endless glut of paperwork and looking forward to a Christmas leave of ten days when Henry Giordano, the deputy commissioner, called from Washington, D.C. "You've done a fine job in Greensboro," he said, "but I think it's now time for you to move on. I have a spot for you. It's a tough job but a good office and I think you deserve it."

There was a long pause. "I want you to go to Houston as Agent-in-Charge."

I was pleased. "Fine! When do I go."

"We'll give you about a month. How about figuring February 2?"

After the holidays I cleaned up the final details and flew to Houston, eager to move up from a three-man to a ten-man office. Meanwhile, my wife stayed on in Greensboro to sell the house. Within a month she'd found a buyer and I'd bought a house in Houston and I flew back to get the family. To illustrate the financial state of the Bureau at the time, I had to pay my own way back, load the family of six in a station wagon, and drive two nights and three days back to Houston. When I submitted my expense voucher I was told I could not collect per diem because I'd already reported to Houston. The Bureau gave me only the six cents a mile for gas.

I hadn't told my wife but my early enthusiasm for the Houston assignment had ended abruptly when I arrived. I could look forward to nothing but trouble and crisis, it seemed.

It had all started even before I left Greensboro. Mr. Giordano had called me late in January. "Listen, Jack, I just want you to know that the Bureau will back you up when you get down there."

Such a remark bewildered me. "That's nice," I replied, wondering who the Bureau was going to back me up against.

"I just want you to know that the District Supervisor in Dallas, Ernie Gentry, isn't the easiest man to get along with and you may have problems. But don't let him browbeat you and don't let him tear you apart."

The name Gentry meant nothing to me. "What do you mean?" I asked.

"Well, we've had the biggest turnover in the country in that office in the last year. He's run off a couple Agents-in-Charge and some others haven't been able to stand up to him. We've had three Agents-in-Charge there in Houston in the past year, two of them in the last six months. We just want you to know that we're in back of you. You do a good job down there and we'll stand behind you. . ."

I was nonplussed, wondering why the Bureau would keep a man with such a record in charge. I started calling friends in the Bureau after this ominous bit of news and by the time I left for Houston I knew I had troubles. Gentry had a wide reputation as a tryant and disagreeable martinet. More than that, it seemed, he was bitter. He had been District Supervisor in California and Commissioner Anslinger had pulled the rug out, transferring Gentry to Houston from San Francisco and rewarding the legendary George White with the California post.

It was all quite understandable. George White was in the true sense a living legend. The movie, *To the Ends of the Earth*, had dealt with his exploits fighting the drug traffic around the world, particularly in Turkey. He was the friend of world leaders, the major politicians of the country, and within the Bureau, other agents viewed him as a god-like figure. He was the first agent to go overseas and was the Bureau's only celebrity—with the exception of Harry Anslinger himself. More than that, San Francisco was his home.

Such elements aside, there was another reason for the transfer. Gentry was of the old school. He beat down any suggestions, was unimaginative to the point of bleak despair, and fought off anything which seemed an innovation or might involve added work. Typically, under Gentry the Bureau office in Los Angeles consisted of just two men. Today, there are over 200 men and, if the budget allowed, the office could use 100 more.

So I walked into the Houston office with some major concerns that were soon justified. In a few days I found out what had happened to those other previous Agents-in-Charge. Not only was Gentry's petty tyranny one reason but the doings of George White himself had created an unbearable situation. I had heard rumbles of White's recent antics in Texas but had no idea of the chaos he'd caused. He'd arrived in Houston when the District Office was still covering Texas, Mississippi, and Louisiana. There had been rumors of strange doings in the Houston Police Department and White had been dispatched by the Bureau to find out what it was all about. White had more than done his job. By the time the dust had cleared he'd turned up the fact that the Chief of Police was an addict, that the police were actively engaged in the narcotics traffic, that the sergeant of the Narcotics Squad was addicted and stealing drugs, that a lieutenant of the Narcotics Squad had either blown his brains out or someone had done it for him right in the Narcotics squad room of the police station, that a search warrant had been obtained to search an Inspector's locker and investigators had found a kilo of heroin.

The Police Department was in disgrace, the city in an uproar, and there were new headlines every day. City fathers and the police blamed the entire scandal on the muckraking tactics of George White. The Bureau had moved District Headquarters to Dallas to escape. And now I was the Agent-in-Charge in Houston!

It didn't take me long to find how I stood with Gentry. He came down to Houston from Dallas the first week I was there, brusquely introduced himself and called me into my office, closing the door. "Look, Kelly, I want to tell you something and I want to get it straight right from the start. I didn't want you in this office. I didn't ask for you. I don't even know you, so you certainly aren't my choice for Agent-in-Charge."

I had to admire his candor. "Well, I'm sorry," I said. "I don't know anything about all that. All I know is that the Bureau sent me here."

He nodded suspiciously. "Yeah, I want to know who sent you. I'm the District Supervisor and I should be the one who selects the Agent-in-Charge for Houston. I never have seen orders like yours before. They say to report here as Agent-in-Charge. They should say just to report to me and then I select who is the boss."

"I told you, Mr. Gentry, I'm sorry about that. But I don't know anything about it. All I know is that Mr. Giordano called me and told me I was taking over here."

He got up. "Well, all right. You're here. But just remember, I don't want you." It was a real Welcome Wagon visit. After he'd departed I sat staring out the window. My God, I thought, what have I gotten myself into? The District Supervisor doesn't even know me but is out to get me. The Police Department is out to get the Bureau anyway it can. And I'm in the middle!

Our woes with the local police were already a day-to-day crisis. If they found we had an informer they'd arrest him on some trumped-up charge. They also threatened any dope peddler in town with a bust if he cooperated with us in any way. Without informers we couldn't move and with police following our agents we couldn't even start building any cases.

The final ironic touch to this "promotion" was that it had been handled in the Bureau as a lateral transfer, meaning that with the increased responsibility and larger office, I got no raise in pay. Such a raise had to come through Gentry and he'd made it quite clear that he was only interested in destroying me as soon as possible.

I brooded over my unhappy lot for several weeks, then decided that if I was going down the drain I'd at least do it with some drama. I called in one of my best agents, Jesse Bautista, who knew the local narcotics scene better than anyone.

"Jesse, I want you to take me over to the Police Department and introduce me to the head of the Narcotics Squad."

Jesse shook his head. "Harry Cole is the Captain over there and he's a real hardnose. He wouldn't give you the time of day."

"I don't give a Goddamn. We can't go on like this. I don't give a shit what happened before. I'm not responsible for what George White did to Houston. I have to change things. Call them up and make an appointment."

Jesse shook his head ruefully. "Forget, it, Jack. You're being naive. We call up and he'll never give us an appointment. He'll always be busy. Don't you see he doesn't want to talk to us and he doesn't want to get along with us. You want to get along with him. Any cop seen talking with us is up for grabs in the Department. . . ."

"Then we'll just go over there and walk into his office."

I got up. Jesse, shaking his head, followed. We walked into the Narcotics Squad room and the Captain's office led off it. A few policemen were sitting around. I'd warned Jesse that I didn't want to be introduced to anyone until I'd met the Captain. But they all knew who we were. They just stared at us. I felt like a sideshow freak on display the way they studied my suit and shirt and tie. They were all wearing cowboy boots and ten-gallon hats and old shirts.

Jesse nodded to them. "Is the captain in?"

One of them finally answered. "Yeah, he's in there," was the surly reply.

Jesse opened the door. "Can I speak to you a minute, Captain?"

There was a muffled reply and I followed Jesse in.

Jesse introduced me and Cole did shake hands, then leaned back and asked coldly, "What can I do for you?"

I told him I was the new Agent-in-Charge and that I felt I'd better come over and see him, considering everything.

"Well, what about it. What do you want?" he asked icily.

I decided all I could do was try. "I want to get this mess straightened out. I don't know anything about what happened here in the past and it has nothing to do with me. I want you to know I'm an ex-policeman and did six and half years in a department. I know what it is to be a cop and my sympathy lies with the police always. Now I happen to be a federal agent and I've got a job to do and you've got a job to do. It's always been my feeling that we have to work together. This is one hell of a fight against the narcotics trade at best. It's a damned tough job out on the streets and if we fight each other the only one who benefits is the peddler. We've got to get along. You don't have to like me but as law enforcement officers we've got to work together. I want you to know that if any of my men bust some of your informers it won't be on purpose. It will be unwitting if there's any kind of double-cross. None of my men are going to screw around with your cases. If they do they are going to answer to me and if I can get them suspended or fired, I will . . ."

Harry Cole leaned back and crossed his arms, studying me for a long moment. "You know, I think you're on the level."

"Your damned right I'm on the level," I said. "I'm a cop the same as you are and all I want to do is a good job. I've got enough problems protecting my own ass from that Gentry in Dallas without worrying about the police."

Harry Cole suddenly broke into wild laughter, putting his head on his desk as he roared. I knew I'd won. Everyone in law enforcement who knew Gentry knew what I was up against.

He stood up. "Let's really shake hands." I left feeling I'd made an ally. I had. Harry Cole was straight with me forever after. He called his men in and introduced them one by one. Before I left he took me aside. "I want you to know something—what you said about letting you know if your men foul up my men in any way. The same applies on this end. If my guys do anything I'll level with you. I know they've done things in the past and we felt we were justified.

Let's just start from here. Just one thing. If that Goddamned George White comes to town, why, screw him—all bets are off. Keep him out here!"

I nodded, although he must have known I would have no say on such a matter.

So began my four-year stint in Houston. Among the first policemen I met were Buster Hightower, a stocky, powerful guy with a foghorn voice, and a Mexican-American, Mike Chavez, two of the finest officers I have ever known, both of whom became close friends in the many cases we were to work together.

But my woes with Gentry were just beginning. As the agents who worked in my office began to trust me they tipped me off to the tricks and foibles of Gentry: how to watch my daily reports and daily activities and expenses so that every minute detail was recorded. How to always keep a record of car mileage as Gentry was so picayune he'd assign agents from Dallas to tail us and try to find if we were falsifying our mileage.

It didn't take long to discover, for example, that Gentry had assigned a Dallas agent to tail me, that he was pulling my toll calls to see who I was talking with in the Bureau. He was convinced, I found out, that I was reporting on him to someone in Washington, D.C. Once I felt reasonably secure about his tactics I invented little things to make him panic. For example, when I was sure he had a record of every phone call I'd made to the Bureau I would casually mention that I'd been talking with Mr. Giordano that morning when I knew he had no record of such a call. He would go into a tizzy, I knew, wondering how many other calls I'd made which he didn't know of.

Meanwhile, I became increasingly frustrated over running a large office with the same rating, Grade Eleven, that I'd had in Greensboro. I should have automatically become a Grade Twelve upon being assigned to Houston. The reason I hadn't was that Gentry had to put in for it and simply wouldn't do so. I knew I was permanently stopped from a raise as long as I stayed in Houston.

Maybe it was my success at bravado with the police that

caused me to take an even bolder step. I did the unmentionable. I sat down and wrote a letter directly to Commissioner Anslinger asking for a raise! I simply said that I thought I deserved it, citing cases and my job and pointing out that several of Gentry's favorites had been promoted over me running much smaller offices.

It was a daring and desperate move. I heard nothing from the Commissioner. Then I got a paycheck with more money and a formal notice telling me I'd been promoted to GS-12.

By the next day Gentry, who'd received a dupe of the notice, was in Houston. I had seen him nasty, surly and mean. But never had I seen him truly angry. It was sheer delight.

"I understand you wrote the Commissioner directly," he shouted.

"That's right."

Just to needle him, I told him basically what I'd said in the letter. He could only sputter in rage.

Then I became the voice of sweet reason. "I just want to point out to you that you think writing the Commissioner is terrible. I don't hear the Commissioner complaining. He hasn't said a word and furthermore I got my GS-12. I sure wouldn't have gotten it from you."

The die, as they say in Latin, was cast. I took heat daily. In a way it was nice to be so in the open in the hate we had for one another. For example, I could take all the heat off my men. I'd tried to improve the low morale and to form an office that functioned as our group had in New York, a pleasant team working together and interested in helping one another. Now, if one of my men fouled up I moved in and took the blame. Two of my men made a case of using an informer in San Antonio, and this encroached on one of Gentry's favorite agents, Jack Frost. Gentry was in a rage and told me he was going to have them fired immediately. I stopped him cold by saying I had ordered them into the area.

It left him helpless. Because he had built his case to believe that I had a secret, powerful ally somewhere in the Bureau. If he got me, I know he thought, someone would get him.

8

Marijuana for Gentry

In our running feud Gentry developed a talent for sarcasm that was inspirational at times.

One morning he called with an affable tone in his voice that disturbed me.

"The Royal Canadian Mounted Police has asked the Bureau to supply it with a hundred pounds of marijuana. They want to run tests in Canada so they can determine what is and isn't Mexican marijuana," he explained. He went on to point out that this actually was a United Nations request. The Bureau had alerted him, he said, to see what could be done. "Actually, I'm just going through the formalities of telling you this," he said loftily. "I don't expect your office to come up with such an amount. I know we'll have to depend on Jack Frost down in San Antonio. He'll come up with it." Frost, as Gentry's pet, was once described by Gentry as "like a son to me."

I thanked him for the information and hung up, feeling that he was a bit off form trying to rile me.

A few hours later Jesse Bautista came in, an expression of delight on his brown face. "I think I've got something going." He went on to explain he'd come across an informer who'd introduced him to a man who claimed to have a big marijuana connection in

129

Mexico. A big load was coming over today, the man said.

"Great. How many men do you need?"

Jesse looked down at the floor. "There's a complicaton. You know how things are here in Texas. They want an Anglo buyer."

I knew what he meant. The Mexican-Americans in Texas have been held down as inferiors for so long that even many of them accept the discrimination as valid. It's ingrained and inbred, I suppose, all the way back to the Alamo. I'd been shocked when I first arrived in Texas but now accepted it as a reality of our working conditions. The idea that a Mexican would have enough money for a big buy just couldn't be sold to a dealer, Anglo or Mexican.

"What the hell, how about a nice Irish boy!"

"I hoped you'd say that," Jesse replied. "With that gray hair you look like an old bastard who would have all the money in the world."

Jesse looked at his watch. It was 10:45 in the morning. "We're due at the hotel at noon. But we're going to have to put together some kind of flash roll." It was standard, you show the dealer the money and just wait for delivery. When the narcotics arrive you make the arrest and the money never changes hands.

But we had a problem. We didn't have the kind of money in the office to flash for a big buy, even a Michigan roll, which is a hundred dollar bill on a stack of ones. The entire Bureau at the time had a budget of about $3 million as compared with today's budget of about $70 million. Yet with it, although we had less than 2 percent of all the Federal enforcement agencies, we put 15 percent of the people in Federal prison with only 300 agents.

I judged that we'd be expected to come up with something that looked like $50,000 for a big load. We began scrounging, borrowing some money from the Houston Police Department. When we were through we were quite proud. It was an impressive-looking bundle.

We went to the hotel. I waited in the car until Jesse came out and motioned me in. He introduced me to Miguel, a plump man of 30 or so in a worn leather jacket, blue workshirt, and dirty levis. Miguel explained over a tequila that he lived in Richmond, a small town 30 miles from Houston. I did my best to be an expansive bigtimer, flashing a roll and ordering repeated rounds of drinks. I knew Miguel was impressed.

After an hour Miguel politely stood up. "It's time to get over to Richmond," he announced. "The truck is due soon."

"Truck? What kind of truck?" I asked.

He described it as a big flatbed. I shrugged. We arranged to meet Miguel at a bar and left.

As we started out I was still puzzled. "What kind of load do they have to need a truck— and a flatbed besides?"

Jesse leaned back in the Cadillac. "He's talking about a hundred."

"A hundred pounds!"

"No," Jesse corrected. "A hundred kilos."

I shook my head. "Whatever—you just don't drive across the border with a hundred kilos of weed."

"Yeah, I know. But he says they're doing it."

It made me nervous and cautious, smacking of some kind of heist. The flash roll suddenly felt very heavy in my coat pocket.

Miguel wasn't at the bar where we'd arranged to meet. We sat nursing warm beer for an hour, then two. I was getting more and more apprehensive. Finally, I told Jesse to stick around and went down the street, making sure I wasn't being watched or tailed, then ducked into the Richmond police station. I knew the chief, Bailey Anderson, a young man the Bureau had worked with before. He agreed to assign a few men for surveillance and to make his jail available if we made a bust. Then I called our office in Houston and asked for two men to come down and cover us from the outside of the bar. I felt easier when I returned. A few minutes later Miguel arrived.

"Señor, my man is in town. He is here. The time has come to show the money. Not only this, one of the people is coming to see the money." He told us to follow him. We went out and followed Miguel in his car to a dirt road outside of town, keeping our guns handy as it all smelled of a blatant ripoff.

But if it was an ambush it was a poor one. We stopped beside an ancient paneled truck. An old Mexican with a week's growth of gray beard and a tattered straw hat sat alone behind the wheel. He spoke no English.

Jesse, who spoke Castilian Spanish but could also understand the Tex Mex slang they spoke in the area, talked with him. He had come from Mexico that morning, he said, and had the stuff with him but wanted to see the money.

For safety I'd dropped it in the trunk of the car and locked it up when we left the bar. Now I went and opened up, taking out the roll which had a hundred dollar bill on the outside and was secure with thick rubber bands. I knew it was impressive, and looked like at least $50,000.

The old man stared at it with bloodshot eyes and then mumbled to Jesse.

"He wants to count it," Jesse announced.

"Tell him to go to hell," I said. Miguel started laughing and I turned on him. "Just what the shit is this? You got us out here and we don't even know you. Who the hell do you think you are? You're seeing the money now and that's all you're seeing of it until the deal goes through. We've wasted the whole Goddamned day on you."

I walked back to the car, disdainfully tossed the roll in the trunk and went and got behind the wheel, gesturing for Jesse to come. Jesse chatted a bit more, then joined me and we drove off. He started laughing. "My God, you scared the hell out of them. They thought you were going to leave and take the money with you and that the deal had fallen through. Now everything is set except we got one more problem. We're to meet Miguel back at the bar. But not until nine tonight."

"Screw it," I said, still angry. "We've wasted the whole day and we still don't know if they have any stuff."

"Wait a minute," Jesse replied, pulling a brown bag from his jacket. He opened it and it was filled with beautiful manicured marijuana. It was an awesome sight. A kilo brick of marijuana when pressed is usually full of stems, seeds and assorted trash. When you sieve a kilo brick down, you have maybe a quarter pound of manicured marijuana. But here was a kilo, maybe two pounds, of carefully manicured stuff. I was impressed. "God, a hundred kilos of that is worth wasting some time for," I muttered in agreement.

We went back to the local police department and filled in Bailey and the others on what had happened. We still didn't know where we were going to go, of course, or who we'd contact. But we arranged to post men around with the idea that they simply might drive up to the bar with the load and we could make the arrest.

By nine, Jesse and I had finished a dinner of filet mignon which had the sweet taste of horse and strolled down to the Metaxa tavern.

Miguel was toying with a warm beer. "Ah, señors! I've been looking for you."

"Where's that friend of yours?" I demanded. "I want to wrap this up."

"Oh, Señor. I am going to take you to him."

"You mean he isn't here," I said angrily.

"No, Señor, regretfully. He don't come here. We have to go to him." Miguel smiled apologetically.

There was nothing else to do. "Okay. Where do we go this time?"

Miguel made a little gesture with his forefinger. "I tell you what I'm going to do, Señor! You will follow me out on this road and you will see a big truck, what you call a trailer truck, and it will be parked on the side of the road and have its lights on. Now, Señor, when we pass the truck I will blow my horn twice. That is the signal for you to stop. I will keep on going because I do not want to be in the area when this transaction is occurring." He smiled pleasantly.

"Wait! We pull over and get the stuff there?"

"*Si, Señor.*"

I shook my head. "I don't like this. It's dark. It's out on a country road. I don't know my way around here."

"It is not that bad, Señor. What is wrong?"

I stared at him. "Are you off your rocker? I'm carrying fifty thousand dollars around in the dark out in the cactus patches and you ask what is wrong!"

"But there is no problem, Señor. You do not give the money until you get the stuff. I personally guarantee you that all is fine. Mexicans are very honest, Señor."

He got up. "Where the hell are you going now?" I asked.

"I am going to continue on my way, Señor. If you want we could see one another again but there is no need for me to do that. Only if you enjoy my company, Señor."

I had to laugh. "Okay, okay, Miguel. But what are you getting out of this?"

"I will be taken care of out of the fifty thousand dollars," he said softly.

I looked at Jesse, who shrugged, amused by the whole conservation. "All right, Miguel. We'll follow you."

We went out of the bar with Miguel. I was tense. I didn't think one of the local cops stationed outside would make a premature bust with the three of us together and burn things up, but I wasn't sure. All was peaceful. We started following Miguel out of town and in the rearview mirror I could see my two agents trailing us. We went a couple of miles out on the highway, then Miguel turned onto a secondary road. "Well, here it comes," I told Jesse, "better get our guns on the seat and be ready."

He nodded. "Looks that way. And I'm worried about those guys in back following us."

We made the turn and so did the two agents, Lou Cerda and Jay Daily, behind us.

Then Miguel made a second turn, onto a rutted, twisting dirt road. There was nothing to do but follow him and to make it worse, he was moving at some 50 miles per hour. "I hope to Christ Lou and Jay don't make this turn," I said. There was no traffic on the secondary road. If they followed now it would be a sure giveaway that we were being tailed. They kept going and I saw them stop and turn the lights off as as we wound down the road. I thought perhaps they planned to try to follow us with their lights off and hoped they didn't as I was sure they'd crash and burn.

The road twisted and turned for some five miles. Then suddenly we were back on the highway! I realized that Miguel had flim-flammed us to shake any tail he might have suspected. In the distance we could see the lights of Richmond.

We went about three miles and then Miguel honked twice. Ahead we could see the big trailer-rigged truck with its lights on. Miguel, as he'd said, kept going on at full speed.

Stopping, we got out and walked back toward the truck. We each held our arms down with our guns tucked up our sleeves. Three men got out of the cab and stood beside the headlights.

"Señor, maybe you better follow us," one said.

"Quit the horseshit," I replied. "We've just finished following Miguel over half of Texas."

I recognized the old man we'd met earlier now. He was whispering to one of the others. "He's telling them you are the big boss, the Jeffe," Jesse said.

"Just ask them where the hell the stuff is," I told Jesse.

One of the men replied in English. "Señor, we have to make sure you are alone. It is not far from here."

He got into the cab with the others. "Follow us." We let them pass us and started following them through the darkness.

Two miles and he turned onto a side road again. We went about a mile down this side road, then the truck stopped. The lights went off. "This is it. If we are going to get heisted, it's now," I said. Jesse nodded, leaving our lights on. We got out, hiding our guns as we had before and walked toward them. The two young men disap-peared into the darkness and a moment later came back, dragging a heavy canvas bag which looked like a U. S. Mail bag. It was some six feet long and as they opened the clasp, brown sealed bags tumbled out. Jesse split one open. It was the manicured marijuana, as promised. "Okay," I said.

We moved back toward our car, supposedly to get the money. "Shall we bust them now?" Jesse whispered.

All my fears were gone. I felt full of derring-do and good humor. "Hell, no. Let's get them to load it into our car first. That will save us the effort later!"

They loaded one canvas bag in the back seat and then went back to get the other, which they loaded into the trunk, totaling out as the hundred kilos.

"Let's get them around in front of the lights so they can see our guns," I whispered to Jesse. I turned to them. "Come on, I'll pay you off in the light so you can count it." Jesse repeated it in Spanish.

They lined up like boys awaiting a candy ration and we pulled our guns. Jesse yelled in Spanish, "We're federal agents. If you move you'll be dead." We shook them down. Jesse took a .45 off of each of them and found a shotgun in the cab.

We handcuffed the three of them together and then wondered how to get them back. Finally, we decided to lock the Cadillac with the marijuana and Jesse climbed into the cab. I put the three prisoners on the flatbed and got back with them holding a gun on them during the rocky ride into town.

We took them to jail, where Bailey Anderson had Miguel, who had been picked up and arrested when found with a pound of marijuana in his car. Lou and Jay appeared while we went back to get the Cadillac. We eventually lost that dandy flatbed because we couldn't prove they really ever had the marijuana on it.

It was past one in the morning when I got home, exhausted and filthy. My wife told me Gentry had been trying to reach me every hour all evening. I called him.

He was raging. "You haven't been in the office all day! Who the hell do you think you are? I want you to report every time you have to leave the office for anything, do you hear!" He shouted and screamed for perhaps three minutes. I let him wear down.

When he seemed about through I spoke up. "I've been out on a case. It took a long time. . ."

He launched into a new tirade about shiftless civic servants and wasting taxpayer money. Again I waited.

When he was worn out again I recited the day's haul, three Mexican nationals and one Mexican-American arrested and some marijuana. It didn't pacify him. "I still want to know where you are when you are out of the office," he grumbled.

Just before I hung up I dropped my little *bon mot.* "Oh, by the way! That big load of marijuana for the Mounted Police you wanted. I forgot to tell you how much we got. About a hundred kilos. You can tell Washington I took care of it for you on the same day. . ."

There was only a frustrated sputtering on the other end of the line before Gentry hung up.

9

Miss Kerry

One thing about sitting around a police squad room: you can pick up more bullshit than in the Chicago stockyards. Every cop has a home remedy for corns, bunions, and allied occupational diseases. Some joker has his own home-brewed formula for a grease to keep holster leather pliable and another can spin a fine tale of the corpse of a wino he found with an inch of beard that had grown after death. Superstition and personal vanities and prejudices even make for better police work sometimes. I recall one plainclothesman—a dude who spent half of every paycheck on clothes—when we were strolling down the Boardwalk in Atlantic City one day. He spotted a kid in expensive clothes and shook him down. We found six sticks of pot.

"What made you suspect him?" I asked.

"Didn't you notice that fifty-dollar suede jacket?" my companion replied. "It was two sizes too big. I knew that if he bought it himself it would have fit. It had to be stolen."

I mention all this because a squad room old wives' tale was to lead to one of the biggest cases I ever made.

I was sitting in the Houston office one bright spring morning nursing a magnificent martini hangover which I'd acquired celebrating another agent's promotion the night before.

I recalled a grizzled old sergeant's claim in New York that the one sure cure for the great American ailment was a platter of egg fu yung at a Chinese restaurant on Division Street. At noon I set out to find the equivalent in Houston.

As I sat sipping green tea and awaiting my double order I casually studied the dozen or so elderly Orientals reading Chinese newspapers and gossiping. Idly, I wondered how many of them smoked opium. To most Occidentals the idea of a dark, hazy opium den smacks of such hoary Hearstian nonsense as The Yellow Peril, Fu Manchu, and devious whiteslavers kidnapping innocent society girls. But I was aware enough of the Chinese penchant for a relaxing pipe of "yen shi" to be convinced that at least half of the elders sitting with me that day were occasional users. The fact that Houston was such a large port made it likely that opium was being brought in regularly. When I returned to the office, my hangover abated if not completely gone, I asked the other agents if any work had ever been done on opium. Nothing, was the reply.

I knew something about the Chinese customs with opium. In New York I'd gone out with Jimmy Ziegler, an agent whose pride and joy was a frisky gray Weimaraner known as Detective Dog Flo. Today, there's a lot of publicity about these dogs, which are trained to smell out narcotics or explosives on planes. Actually, it's old hat. Flo and other such dogs were busily at work more than twenty years ago.

Our operation was simplicity itself. Jimmy and I would take Flo of an evening to Chinatown and go to the top floor of one of the dilapidated eight-story tenements where two or three families of Chinese would be crammed into every bleak apartment. The odor of exotic Chinese spices permeated everything and along the decaying dingy walls were the graffiti from decades of whores with notations for the next hustler on prices customers would pay or descriptions of vice cops.

Jimmy carried a ball of opium wrapped in a cloth in a coat pocket. Flo would smell it and we'd then unleash her. She'd run from door to door sniffing. We'd work our way down floor by floor until she'd start to scratch and whine at a door. We'd knock and, if there was no reply, we'd break in.

We had been forced to quit for a curious reason. On more than one occasion we'd kick in the door only to find a puzzled Chinese family sitting at the dinner table staring at us, leaving us with the proverbial egg fu yung on our faces. Flo would look mildly ashamed, we'd apologize and back out in embarrassment.

Eventually, we found the reason for this. If someone smoked opium in a given apartment in January the heady, sickening smell would linger in the rooms until June even though the tenants had departed and been replaced with new renters. "To hell with it," I'd finally told the crest fallen Jimmy, "I'm not going to end up in trouble because Flo can't tell fresh opium odor from the old. She doesn't know what she's doing." I had continued to work some other cases against Chinese opium smokers with my partner, Ray Enright, but snubbed Flo.

I decided to make opium investigation in Houston a hobby for slow days, much as we'd ruffled through the Z File in New York for action when things were quiet. Within a few months I'd seen enough in Houston's Chinatown to pinpoint one shop as worth watching. It was a plain storefront with drawn white venetian blinds in the building of the On Leong Association and, even though it seemed to be no legitimate business enterprise, a steady line of Chinese would go to the bolted door, knock, and be admitted. I guessed what was going on, a constant mah-jongg game. And I knew that where there's Chinese gambling the happy winners often celebrate later with a pipe of opium.

A word about these family associations or, as they were once called, tongs. An Occidental can't appreciate the influence they have on the estimated 150,000 Chinese in the U.S. who belong. They take care of employment, medical problems, act as benefactor and protector, lend money to start in business and, when needed, discipline members who misbehave. Many are business tongs such as the Chinese Hand Laundry Association and the Chinese-

American Restaurants Association. The days of violent feuding with highbinders and hatchetmen are long past. But tongs still regularly bypass our courts in passing out punishment to troublesome members.

Family associations are based upon relationship by blood or marriage. All people named Lee, for example, are considered members of the family and called "cousin." There may be several million Lees but they assume a common ancestor thousands of years ago. Women who marry outside their own associations become a member of their husband's group but continue to maintain friendly ties with their own kin.

Some tongs may involve more than one family. The Gee How Oak Tin Association is made up of the Chan, Woo and Yeun families, for example, all claiming a common ancestor.

Anyone who thinks such ties are flimsy is mistaken. An insult to one Lee is considered an insult to several thousand other Lees across the nation. One Lee's problem is all Lees' problem. That's why traditional proprieties are vital. A father who doesn't seem to be raising his children correctly is cautioned by the association's elders. If he doesn't shape up he's disciplined. This usually takes the form of boycott, socially and in business, until he mends his ways. Tong leaders also act as arbiters in civil disputes. If a member agrees to accept the tong's decision and then changes his mind he may be treated as an outcast, the ultimate humiliation. It's common lore among police that Chinese crime and conflicts are almost non-existent. That isn't so. It's just that such matters are settled quietly without anyone in the Occidental world knowing.

When I was sure of the On Leong operation I went to Captain Harry Cole of the Houston Police Department.

I told Harry, a big, towering officer with black curly hair who looked like a pro fullback, about what I'd seen. "How about raiding the game?" I asked.

Harry eyed me with cold disdain. "You're a Goddamned fool," he snarled. "We don't know their language. We don't know how to play mah-jongg or even how much they bet. We couldn't even prove they are gambling. The case would never hold up in court. It's a waste of time."

"Look, Harry," I pleaded. "I just want to know who's gambling and get their names and run makes on them. Do you know any of these Chinese?"

Harry shrugged. "No, and I don't give a shit. We don't have any trouble with them. I know that."

"Sure! That's just it," I argued. "They have their own criminals who break the law but they handle it all themselves. They do their own thing because we don't know their language or their customs. I'd like to get all those gamblers photographed and fingerprinted and see just who we have in town."

Harry reluctantly agreed. "I'll call the gambling squad and see what they think," he grumbled.

The next day he phoned me. "They'll do it. But only with the understanding that you stay out of it."

I agreed with alacrity. It was just what I wanted—for the Chinese to think it was strictly a gambling raid so their suspicions wouldn't be aroused.

A little after one in the morning the following night the squad of five officers broke in the door and rounded up 52 excited, chattering gamblers and their mah-jongg games and domino sets. They took them to the station, mugged and fingerprinted them and a few hours later released them for lack of evidence, even giving them back their gaming gear. From the group, they held two: a fugitive from New York state and a frightened little chop suey cook who was in the U.S. illegally. His name was Eng Bok Heng and, like many Chinese, he'd jumped ship to evade the strict immigration laws. I studied the copies of 52 photos and decided Eng was as good a place as any to start my investigation. It has been my experience that the most frightened people you can find are those who fear being deported. Most will turn informer. I asked the Houston police to release Eng to me.

Eng Bok Heng was a frail, pock-marked man wearing frayed white pants and a dirty sweater. He had a tic which would have given him the appearance of being tense and nervous even under less trying pressure.

The day he sat in my office anxiously rubbing the arm of an office chair he seemed ready to break down before I said a word. I decided to try a bit of Chinese gambling of my own.

"You smoke yen shi, don't you," I said.

He slipped into the common Oriental trick of seeming unable to understand my English. But it was clear that he did and my announcement had obviously shattered any self-confidence he might still have had.

"Just every six month, maybe once a year," he replied feebly.

I went on to explain what was ahead for him. He couldn't be deported back to China because a federal law does not allow deportation to a Communist country. But papers were already being drawn up asking Hong Kong to accept him, I told him. Maybe, I suggested, if he'd cooperate with me and tell me all he knew about narcotics I could help him.

He sat back, the tic on his sallow face flicking again and again. I knew what he was thinking. If he didn't talk he faced poverty in a strange city back in the Far East. If he did? Banishment or even death in the netherworld of the Chinese community.

"Of course, there's no reason anyone will know you told me," I added softly.

He talked. He explained how opium was being brought into Houston regularly by Chinese seamen and trans-shipped to New York, Los Angeles, and San Francisco. The West Coast, he explained, was being bypassed because of the strict searches by Customs, which, by the time the ships got to Houston, were hastier and more relaxed. The local customers were, of course, the older Chinese. He went on to give me names of users and one center of activity, Ah Gee, a little store in downtown Chinatown.

The following Sunday afternoon I took my two daughters, Ann and Eileen, and drove to Chinatown, parking the Cadillac sedan across from Ah Gee. My plan was to sit on it and, to divert suspicion, I had the girls lounging in the back seat reading comic books and playing ball on the sidewalk. I knew there was no danger.

It was a tiny building with peeling, weathered white paint. The front display window contained a few fly-specked Chinese dolls, lanterns, and fans, a vague effort to give the impression that it was a novelty shop of some sort. But the interesting feature was a massive, rusty fan some five feet in diameter that had been built into a rear wall. Sitting in the hot summer sun, I watched a dozen or so older Chinese hobble up, rap on the door, and enter.

I'd chosen Sunday for my surveillance for a simple reason. Most elderly Chinese work as laundrymen, cooks, or waiters and Sunday is their day to frolic with an opium pipe.

Soon, the massive fan began slowly to rotate. I assumed it had been installed to clear out the pungent opium stench. I drove away elated, convinced that I had a fix on my first Houston opium bust.

During the coming week I made plans for the raid. I called in Jay Daily, Lou Cerda, and Jesse Bautista from our own office and, because of local laws, asked Buster Hightower and Jay Strickland of the Houston Police Department to join us.

We settled back in the car that humid afternoon, smoking and chatting until we'd counted nine Chinese who had come to the door and knocked. Then the fan began slowly to rotate and we concluded the pipes were lit.

We didn't bother to knock. The worn door gave way with two lunges.

The action was so fast that Ah Gee was still squatting beside his burner cooking opium staring up at us in amazement. His customers were stretched out on the dirty straw pallets on the cement floor, their heads resting on hard, black leather headpillows about the size of telephones. There were a few gasps of shock. Then everyone began to chatter wildly as we pulled them to their feet and confiscated the pipes and opium. This proved to be a bit of a disappointment as Ah Gee had only enough opium on hand to take care of his clients for that day. But we were pleased; it was the first opium seizure in Houston in years.

A few days later I was sitting in my plain office on the top floor of the ten-story building on Rusk Street that served as our headquarters when I was interrupted in my monotonous paperwork by a call from Eng Bok Heng.

He explained excitedly that a Chinese businessman, a friend who was trying to help Eng bring his wife over from China, wanted to talk to me. Eng was now sort of an ally as I'd helped to kill the effort to deport him to Hong Kong. "He knows about opium and hates it," Eng announced.

I was skeptical. Knowing the insular restrictions of Chinese society and Eng's own background, I just couldn't envision a Chinese do-gooder on a white horse out to help a narc officer for the public good.

I was wrong. Events that followed that hurried phone call were to lead to the biggest break I ever got in chasing opium.

Suey, as I shall call him for his protection—he is still a close friend—was indeed an influential businessman with five going enterprises.

Our first encounter was at the bar of his restaurant where he sat sipping from a water tumbler of straight whisky, Sunnybrook. In the years since I seldom have seen him without the tumbler of Sunnybrook, dressed always in black slacks, a white shirt and tan windbreaker. He had, also, somehow adopted a mannerism of the Texas plains and swaggered about in a bow-legged walk like a Chinese cowboy. A tiny man, weighing perhaps 100 pounds, he is aggressive and stern, ordering everyone around like a martinet.

He curtly motioned Eng and myself to adjoining stools and, without asking what we wanted, ordered us each a bottle of beer. We shook hands and then Suey, about 45 with shiny, black hair combed in an old-fashioned pompadour, sat staring at me with that passive, enigmatic look of the Chinese. As he silently scrutinized me sipping steadily from the ludicrous big glass of straight Sunnybrook, there was no way to tell what he might be thinking.

I decided it was his move to bring up the subject of opium. He didn't, just making small talk about the heat, fishing at Sugarland,

and sports. When we'd finished our beer he stood up in a gesture of dismissal.

"I have no more time to talk," he announced. I felt that he'd decided against me. But then Eng started out the restaurant door and Suey touched me lightly on the arm. "Come back tomorrow for lunch," he ordered, motioning his head toward the departing Eng. I nodded, realizing he didn't want to talk in front of my companion.

The next noon he was at his barstool with the ubiquitous tumbler of whisky. He greeted me happily and this time asked what I'd like to drink. I ordered a martini and then he led me to a rear booth.

Already spread out and steaming before us was an elaborate meal of a dozen dishes. I sat down while a smiling woman in a black silk pajama suit hurried over bearing a massive plate of egg rolls.

"This is Mama, my wife," Suey announced. Bowing, she softly acknowledged the introduction in Chinese and faded away.

Suey began to eat, taking only a bowl of white rice but gesturing for me to have at it. Quickly finishing the rice and turning back to his Sunnybrook, he began to talk rapidly, becoming more expansive as he went on.

Opium was the curse of his people, he said, and he wanted to do what he could to rid Houston of it. But he must be cautious. As he went on in general terms to denounce narcotics I saw a familiar pattern emerging from his talk. He was a thwarted cop of sorts and vicariously craved the excitement which he thought went with my job. I'd known many an informer with the same cops-and-robbers syndrome and, unless they got too frisky and officious, they were usually helpful aides. Later, when Suey and I became fast friends, I was to be amused by this stance. When we'd go fishing at Sugarland he'd chat about narcotics doings like a seasoned old-timer. Once, when we were with a black agent and stopped at a bar for Suey's hourly ration of whisky the bartender refused to serve us because the agent was colored. "I'm colored, too," howled Suey, rolling up the sleeve of his white shirt, going on to imply that the three of us could wipe out half of Texas with our political power. We got the drinks.

I was sure this time that he was going to tell me something useful after his tirade. But when I had finished lunch he stood up as abruptly as before.

"I'll be in touch with you," he said briskly.

Again, I felt let down. I'd expected something more and the possibility of his contacting me sometime in the hazy future was hardly exciting.

But two days later he called and asked me to meet him at the bar. He had by now worked out his own concept of my name, which he was to call me ever after. "Hello, Miss Kerry," he greeted me, shaking hands briskly.

He led me to the back booth. "Have you ever heard of Ing Hok?" he inquired. I shook my head.

Suey went on to explain that Ing Hok, a local businessman, bought opium regularly from Chinese seamen for his own use. "I know he has some and is going to lay down tonight. He was talking about it at a mah-jongg game this afternoon."

I took the address. That night I took Buster Hightower, a short, muscular officer built like a fireplug who rattled the chandeliers wherever he went with his foghorn voice, and Jesse Bautista from my office. We arrived at Ing Hok's house about nine. It was a pleasant neat bungalow but with an incongruity. Old blankets had been hung over the front windows. Certainly Ing Hok was not so impoverished that he couldn't afford curtains. They had been hung up as a screen against nosy visitors and to prevent the odor from seeping out.

We knocked. There was no answer. We knocked again. Then Ing Hok opened the door after a long delay. The sickening odor of opium hit us like a spray of urine.

We pushed our way in, the smell being reasonable grounds for a search. Ing Hok stood expressionless, pretending that he couldn't understand English.

We went to a back room where a pallet had been spread. There was a headrest with an opium smoking lamp and pipe beside it. Also on the floor were several copper containers the size of tobacco cans with Chinese figures engraved on them. These were the common opium containers known as Five Taeltins.

We started shaking down the house to see if there was more opium about.

Buster emerged from a dark closet with an expression of stunned confusion on his face. In his hand he held what looked at first to be a club of some sort.

"Suffering Christ! Look at this!" he growled, dropping the object with distaste on a table.

We all stared at it in disbelief. It seemed to be a ten-inch sculpture of a penis, brown and dried.

"What the hell is it?" I asked, staring at the realistic hole on the uncircumsized head.

Ing Hok's brown, angry face was sullen.

"What is it?" I demanded again.

"That's a plick," he grumbled.

"A real plick?" I asked.

"Yes."

"Where in hell did you get it?" growled Buster incredulously.

"I sent away to Hong Kong . . . "

"What do you do with it?" I asked.

"I eat it."

"My God!" gasped Buster.

Ing Hok looked at us defensively. "Velly good for you! You chew it and it make you velly strong!"

Dismayed, we put it in a bag with the other evidence and started for headquarters.

I was later to find from conversations with other Chinese that this is not an uncommon medicinal object. The legend is that it will make you potent and you'll have massive erections. It's still in alcohol in the jar in the Houston office, a cherished memento of that dilly raid. I've wondered how the Chinese smuggled those penises through Customs.

I discovered later that Suey had simply been testing me with his disclosures about Ing Hok. He wanted to see if I would make the arrest, if there would be publicity, if there would be any kickback on him as an informant. It was all handled in a routine way with little public notice. Ing Hok went to jail for possession and the matter was over. Suey knew now that he could work with me safely.

A few weeks later, on a chilly night in November, 1960, I came home to find the phone jangling repeatedly. Suey sounded excited for the first time since we'd met.

"Miss Kerry! Come to the bar right way. There's a man here who has offered to sell me a pound of raw opium. I'll keep him here as long as I can but I'm afraid he'll walk out any minute." Suey went on to explain that he didn't know what nationality the man was. "He speaks English funny and looks like an Indian or something," he said vaguely.

"I'll be right there," I said. As it was a half hour drive from home to Suey's restaurant, I dialed the police station, which was only five minutes away. Jay Strickland, H.M. Grey, and E.J. Stringfellow, three officers I knew well, were on duty. I described briefly what Suey had told me. "Will you get over there and tail the guy if he leaves the restaurant?" I asked. Then I called Jay Daily, an agent, to meet me there and took off.

I arrived about midnight. Suey was standing at the door pointing. "He left and started down that way—some cops are following him," Suey said excitedly.

I ran down the deserted street but could see no one. I slowed to a walk so I could look down intersections. Five blocks from the bar I found Jay Daily.

"What's going on?" I gasped.

Jay nodded toward the nearby bus station. "He's just going in," he said calmly. He pointed to a squat, swarthy man in tan pants and denim jacket across the street.

We followed him into the station and watched as he went to a locker and took out a pea coat and started toward a bus going to Beaumont.

I wondered for a moment whether to tail him or arrest him immediately. There was no time to ponder. We had to nab him and just hope he had the opium on him. We grabbed him just as he put his foot on the first step of the bus.

We found the pound of raw opium in a back pocket. He feigned that he could speak no English, gabbling in a language none of us could recognize. But then his identification showed him to be one Said Ahmad, age 40, a seaman from Pakistan aboard a British cargo liner, the *M.V. Elmbank,* which we found later was on a regular voyage to Australia.

He refused to talk, only shrugging and shaking his head to our questions. I called an old friend, Customs-Agent-in-Charge Al Scharf, who had spent most of his life on the border, and arranged for him to assign two of his men to go with us to Beaumont where the ship was docked. Customs agents have the sole authority to search a vessel for contraband.

We called at the captain's quarters and asked to inspect Said Ahmad's bunk. Under the bunk we found a sea-chest and, using the keys we'd taken from Ahmad, opened it to find 24 pounds of raw opium which would have a value of about $50,000 when refined. We found out later he had bought it in Calcutta for $1,500.

It was Said's first voyage and in our later talks when he admitted to a primitive knowledge of English, he told us the tales he'd heard from other sailors about how one could become rich in just one trip smuggling opium.

Too, we found he was a user of a rather unusual sort, an opium eater. In jail he became desperately ill and went through withdrawal.

Said got five years in prison and then was deported back to Pakistan. It was our first big opium case in Texas. We were all enormously pleased. Al Scharf boasted that it was the first opium seizure in the 25 years he'd worked as a customs man in Texas. Little did we know that a bigger surprise was in the offing.

I was still working on the case several days later in the office. It had created a major international stir. The United Nations wanted

more details. The Ambassador of Pakistan called and wanted to
know everything as Said Ahmad was a citizen. India wanted all the
specifics because Said claimed he'd bought the opium there. I was
still trying to catch up with the tedious paperwork involved when
Suey called me.

I assumed he wanted to talk about Said and started telling him
how swamped I was.

"No, no, Miss Kerry! I want to talk to you about something
else. Maybe another case . . . "

I forgot about the reports. Suey was too hot an informant to
ignore. "I'll be down to the bar right away," I said.

I arrived about three o'clock and Suey was sitting in the back
booth.

He hurriedly explained that there was a ship in port carrying a
load of opium. "It has a Chinese crew and I've invited some of them
here for dinner tonight."

"How do you know this?" I asked.

"Never mind, never mind."

"You are sure these men are involved?"

"I'll know more tonight."

"Do you want me to be here?" I asked.

"No, no. I'll handle it. I'll fill you in, Miss Kerry."

I was cautious. I appreciated Suey's enthusiasm. But I was
afraid he might foul up our opportunity.

"What if I come with Jess Bautista and we just have a beer at
the bar? Just to see them. You never know what's going to happen
in the future and we should get a look at them."

Suey reluctantly agreed. "But I'm not going to look at you or
speak to you."

We did more than that. We were in a booth having dinner when
eight seamen arrived chattering happily. All wore expensive shore
clothes, well-cut dark suits, white shirts and topcoats, looking more
like business executives than deckhands.

Suey had ordered one of his usual lavish dinners and, as always,
ate a bowl of plain rice and sipped his Sunnybrook while carrying on

an animated conversation in Chinese with the man next to him, who seemed to be the leader.

Jesse and I tried as best we could to memorize the faces, then departed before they'd finished the meal. I went home and about one o'clock Suey called. He was excited and agitated.

"I tried to buy some opium but they claim the whole cargo is going to one man, an American Chinese, in Houston."

"How much is it?" I asked.

"Many, many pounds. And not raw opium—smoking opium."

Now I was as excited as Suey. "What do we do? How do we get it?" I demanded.

Suey suddenly went Oriental. "Patience, you must have patience," he said calmly. "I'll find out what I can."

For two days we paced and worried about the big opportunity.

I made arrangements. I went to Al Scharf and he assigned two customs agents, seasoned old-timers.

Meanwhile, Suey had told us the name of the ship, the S.S. *Utrecht*, a Dutch cargo vessel which had come from Singapore, touched at Hong Kong, and was going on to circle the U.S. and then go to England.

Then Suey's call came. "Tonight! Tonight they are going to bring it off the ship. But I can't find who they are going to deliver it to. I think he may not even be from Houston. But you should be able to get them."

We were ready. A few hours later, by five o'clock that afternoon, the docks were manned with seventeen narcotics and customs agents disguised as workmen and longshoremen. One of the customs agents and I stayed back from the exits hidden behind crates. It was December and already dark but we didn't want to give a clue the ship was being watched. We didn't know exactly what we were waiting for. Maybe just a movement off the ship of some sort. We knew that if they were bringing off as many pounds as anticipated they just couldn't move it like a kilo of heroin so we'd warned the agents to look for any and everything.

All was silent until about nine o'clock. Then a lone figure, one

Chinese seaman dressed nattily in a dark business suit, came down the gangplank.

He strolled about, walking almost to the gate, then returning to board the ship again, then coming back down the gangplank to walk along the dock still again. Then returning to the ship once more.

"What shall we do?" whispered my companion.

I shrugged, pulling my topcoat collar up to ward off the damp chill. The looming hulk of the dark shop seemed deserted. We both were worried that perhaps we'd arrived too late, that the smuggling operation had perhaps gone through sometime earlier in the afternoon.

The man emerged and came down the gangplank once again. This time he walked hurriedly and directly to the dock's telephone booth. We heard him order a taxi. Then, in the blackness we made out the shapes of more men who had come on deck, possibly six or eight. We'd instructed the agents to grab them on our signal but we still didn't know what the hell was going on.

Now the men filed silently down the gangplank and started toward the gate. A taxi had pulled up. We signaled to Jay Daily to grab the lone man and the taxi driver. Then we jumped up and grabbed the group of Chinese when they were about fifty feet from the ship.

We searched them and found nothing. I started going over their identification, trying to recognize any of them that we'd seen in the restaurant. Suey had told us the big man he'd been talking with at the dinner was the ship's boatswain and his name was Hom. Ominously, Suey had added that he was a Fookinese. This means little to Occidentals, but a great deal to Chinese-Americans. Most U.S. Chinese are Cantonese or Mandarin. They fear the looming Fookinese from Fuchow, China. They're known as cut throats and vicious fighters and the Cantonese avoid them whenever possible. "Be careful of them all—very careful—and particularly Hom, the leader," Suey had warned.

But we could recognize none of the men we'd taken into custody.

We had to let them go. They returned to the ship but came back down the gangplank defiantly a few minutes later and said they were on their way to Chinatown for a drink.

We were annoyed and despondent. I immediately called Suey and told him what had happened and that we had blown the arrest.

"Do you think they will be suspicious of me?" he asked.

"No, why should they?" I replied. "We let them think it was a routine customs check during the entire search."

I could hear Suey sigh in relief. "Fine! I'll meet with them when they arrive for a drink and try to find out what happened."

I asked him to again describe Hom to me. But I still couldn't tell if he'd been one of the men on the dock. It was a depressing moment. I knew that the ship was to sail in the morning as Suey had explained that Hom had told him he planned to hold off taking the opium ashore until the last night. I went home to bed, got up at daylight and drove down to watch the ship up anchor.

I had just arrived at the office when Suey called. "Come over right away," he said.

He was waiting at the door of the bar and led me to a booth in the rear. "You were fooled," he said. "That first man was a decoy. He was to get a taxi and they were to come out. Then, when he'd departed in the first taxi they were planning to call another. They were to split up and some would return to the ship to bring off the opium." We had exposed ourselves and the opium was still aboard.

But the exciting good news was that the ship was going to dock at New Orleans. Suey explained that the people who had planned to buy the opium were going to drive over there and pick it up.

The seamen, we hoped, were still convinced that our foul-up on the dock was a routine customs check.

I called Gentry in Dallas to tell him of our plans. He was nonchalant about the expedition. "I'll send Jack Frost over to take care of it. You can forget it."

I was furious. "My ass, you will!" I exploded. "You're not pulling something like this out from under me! You've screwed me every way I turned. If there's any seizure in New Orleans, I'm going to make it! This is my case from the start to the finish and I'll raise so Goddamned much hell that the heat will burn you from Washington."

He backed down. "Well, all right. Go ahead. But I'm not going to allow you to go over there before the ship docks—and I'm going to send Frost with you."

I knew it was a device to save face. "That's okay," I grumbled and slammed down the phone.

I felt that having Frost along would allow me to cheat a little on Gentry. Customs had notified me that the ship was to dock two days before Christmas. So three days before Christmas I arrived in New Orleans.

I sat on the ship right from the beginning. We had a fine, young, aggressive agent in New Orleans, Doug Chandler, who had worked for me in Houston before being transferred there. We set to work together and found out, among other things, that no one of the crew was to be allowed off ship until five o'clock that afternoon.

About three in the afternoon a taxi pulled up near the ship and two Chinese, one burly, the other as whispy and dried as a litchi nut, got out. Both were beautifully dressed. They went to the gate, asked for the *Utrecht* and explained they had some friends aboard they wished to visit.

The guard motioned them through the gate and they started for the ship. A seaman met them on deck and soon they were in an animated conversation with five of the seamen, shaking hands, laughing, and gesturing.

After ten minutes of conversation they shook hands again and came down the gangplank. Three of us followed their taxi to a motel in downtown New Orleans, convinced they were part of the operation. The register showed the room they entered was signed for by one Loo Bong and wife. The hulking fellow had another room. Loo Bong (or as we later nicknamed him, Bing Bong) had registered only as being from New York City. Outside was an auto with New York plates. We called our New Orleans office for a fast check on the plates and soon had word back that Loo Bong owned a large restaurant in Chinatown in New York, was well known as a businessman but had no reputation or record as an opium dealer.

We called for more agents to sit on the motel and follow Bing Bong if he emerged and hurried back to the ship.

At five that afternoon the seaman Bing Bong had first met on deck came down the gangplank and got a cab. Two agents followed him and radioed back that he'd gone to the motel. He spent about an hour in Bing Bong's room, then took a taxi back to the ship.

We speculated. Did he go to pick up the money? Or perhaps just to see that Loo Bong had the flashroll? Or to settle the opium takeoff schedule?

Meanwhile, no one had left the ship since the liberty bell had sounded. We were puzzled but could only stand by waiting for something to happen.

It was 8:12 A.M. when two Chinese came down the gangplank and hailed a cab. As before, we could see other men on deck. They seemed to be waiting to get off just as they had in Houston. This time we were cautious. We let the two decoys go their way. Others straggled down after the two men until there were a dozen or so seamen gathered around the cab. Five of them then went back up the gangplank. One returned moments later and got in the cab with the two decoys and drove away. We put a radio car on their tail and continued to wait. Then, in this quaint game of Chinese checkers, four more seamen came off the ship. A taxi, apparently ordered previously, suddenly arrived and drove onto the dock. They got in. "Hit them!" I yelled.

Our agents, who had been moving crates or sitting in lifts and trucks, rushed toward the four startled Chinese in the cab from a dozen different angles. The driver sat with his mouth hanging open. I yanked the first sputtering seaman from the cab and slammed him against the side, ordering him to put his hands on the roof.

We lined them up with their butts facing us and began the shakedown. They had no weapons and no large packages. I had a moment of panic.

"Turn around," I shouted to the seaman I was hassling.

The Chinese acted as if he didn't understand. I wheeled him around by the shoulder and motioned for him to open his coat.

He stared back, baleful and silent.

I yanked his coat open sending a button rolling down the dock.

Around his neck hung a rope, the ends reaching to his stomach like a yoke. Tied to each end was a small bag! I knew immediately we had made our case. I opened the first bag. It was filled with rich, pungent smoking opium just as Suey had promised.

Ordering the other agents to take them into custody, three of us leapt into a car and wheeled off for the motel, anxious to collect Bing Bong before something could go wrong.

We didn't bother to knock, hitting the motel room door with a crash. Bing Bong, his huge companion, and one of the Chinese were sitting before the television set.

In seconds we'd found more ropes with opium bags attached and Bing Bong surrendered a leather satchel with $50,000 in cash.

The raid was over.

It turned out that the big pal was a Fookinese, a cook in Loo Bong's restaurant and he'd originally set up the arrangements with the other Fookinese aboard ship for Bing Bong to make the buy.

We had some 76 pounds when it was all over, although we only took 52 pounds on the initial raid. And we had a total of nine defendants, two American-Chinese and the seamen, some from Singapore, some from Hong Kong.

But we were still puzzled. Where was Hom, the ringleader who had been at Suey's dinner? Jess and I had cursed ourselves in Houston that we couldn't recognize him among the seamen. It seemed to prove that old gag that all Chinese look alike to an Occidental.

To add to our bewilderment, Customs officials hired a Chinese interpreter who had spent hours with the seamen and reported that he could find out nothing.

I decided to try myself. I spent several hours with the men, one by one, trying to communicate by gestures, pidgin English, and the few words of Cantonese I knew. I finally narrowed the suspects down to three, convinced one of them was Hom.

Then I called Suey and told him of my dilemma.

He laughed happily. "Do you know what you're talking about? You're talking about family names. You can't identify them that way. I'm talking about ship names. Chinese seamen always use different names on a ship!"

I returned to question them again. "What is your ship name?" I demanded of each. They all gave me different names than they had before.

Then the boatswain stepped up. "Bill Hom," he replied easily to my question. I had found the ringleader.

Why hadn't the interpreter been able to find this out? I discovered he was a Cantonese. Besides not being able to understand their dialect he was scared stiff of the Fookinese.

All of them were convicted and went to jail. The foreign Chinese were deported after they'd finished their sentences. It was the largest single seizure of smoking opium ever made in the U.S. up until that time. And all because I'd decided to remedy a hangover with a dish of egg fu yung!

As for Suey, we remain fast friends. Once I visited him for a family dinner in Houston. He sat beaming with his tumbler of Sunnybrook, wearing new black trousers and an open-neck white shirt as his grown family of sons, daughters, and others laughed and chatted. I mentioned to them what their father had done several years before to assist me.

They wouldn't believe it. "You mean, the old man? He did that! Come on, you're putting us on . . . "

Suey just giggled and nodded. "Miss Kerry brags too much," he said modestly.

There were, of course, those inevitable critics who accused us of persecuting a lot of old Chinese who were causing no harm to anyone. I've heard that argument too many times before. From the same middle class liberal parents who couldn't understand why we "harassed" a lot of poor Puerto Rican kids and musicians for smoking pot. Until their own kids later became users, that is.

There are, of course, always complicated political and social ramifications to such problems. But I contend you don't have to be a veterinarian, or understand the evolutionary development of the horse or be an expert steeple-chaser to be a streetsweeper and clean up the shit. The same applies to the narcotics trade.

10

Boys Town

Where the endless feud between Customs and the Bureau of Narcotics began is shrouded in time. It was filled with bitter hatred and dirty, secret infighting and went on as relentlessly as always until July 1, 1973 when BNDD and the Customs Agency Service merged to become the Drug Enforcement Administration. It surfaced in the newspapers from time to time but leaders preferred that as little as possible be said about it. Obviously, it worked only to the advantage of smugglers and assorted hoods. But, as I say, it was like one of those mountain family feuds which can't be traced to any specific incident. Nincompoops in both the Bureau and Customs thought some disloyalty was involved if they helped one another. I was never more aware of this than I was when I moved to Houston. Gentry was, of course, a leading advocate of non-cooperation. He'd even try to order us to screw up a case if Customs was involved. We weren't allowed to give them any information. We were to do anything we could to harass and annoy them.

This was contrary to everything I'd learned. I did get turned around a couple of times trying to work with them and some of the people fooled me. But I was determined it was going to work if for no other reason than it would annoy Gentry so much. I began to make friends with Customs people such as Fred Rodey, Al Scharf, Fred Patton, Jack Givens, and Jack Salter, a former Bureau agent who had become a Customs agent. The case with the Chinese proved how helpful and knowledgeable they could be and how ready they were to work together if given a chance.

Along the border they had all the expertise and we should have been working as a team. We might have been able to claim superior knowledge concerning the interior, even in the foreign field, but not along the Mexican Border. Here they know the people, the moods, the street talk, what is moving. For twelve years I worked with them whenever I could in a voluntary, friendly exchange. But it was still a lonely uphill fight for agents of goodwill on either side.

I mention all this because it connects with Cotton Tomlin, a Houston peddler, who was the frustration of every city, state, and federal narcotics officer in town. He was a lanky, dull-looking fellow with light blond hair, a redneck sort of rake with the girls. But he was crafty, shrewd, and had a memory for faces which would have made him a prize insurance salesman. He preferred heroin.

They questioned informers about Cotton. They hustled Cotton. They searched Cotton. Nothing worked. The main reason was simply that Cotton knew every agent and cop and their friends in town. The day came that Buster Hightower stopped by the office. With his bellowing voice he explained that he had an informer who could put someone in with Cotton. The catch was that Cotton knew everyone who could make a bust.

"Wait a minute," I said. "He doesn't know me except probably by name. I've never been with you when you tossed Cotton."

Buster nodded. "By God, I think you're right."

We called a council of war with the police narcotics squad and went over every possibility. They agreed I was probably the only guy Cotton didn't know. Buster introduced me to the informer, a pimply-faced kid named Jimmy, and we set up a meeting to visit Cotton. I took the name of Gene Black.

It was a rickety, aging house with a broken screen. Jimmy held it open and pounded a long time on the door. Finally, it opened. Cotton, bare-assed naked, looked sleepily at us.

"This here is Gene," Jimmy said.

Cotton yawned. "Yeah. What you want?"

"I'd like to score about a half ounce," I said.

"Jimmy, you vouch for him?"

"Sure."

Cotton looked me over again. "Wait here," he said, closing the door. I heard him talking and a girl giggle.

He came back in a moment and handed me the half ounce, took the money and slammed the door shut.

I couldn't believe it. I was stunned as I went to the car and drove back to the office and told the other agents what the city's Super Peddler had done. We concluded that I must have just caught Cotton at a perfect time while he was still fuzzy and half asleep. But it seemed foolish to break him on such a small buy. We decided I should cultivate him and try to develop something big. I wanted to talk with him and see if he could lead me to something better. A few days later I stopped by his house again.

"Hi, Cotton, you remember me. I'm Gene."

"Nah. I don't remember you. Never seen ya."

I smiled. "Come on, Cotton. I bought a half ounce with Jimmy the other day."

"Oh, yeah. What you want?"

"An ounce."

He paused. "I got an ounce I can let you have for three fifty."

"Okay."

"But I ain't got it here," he continued. "We'll have to go get it. I'll tell you what. Take a walk, come back in fifteen, twenty minutes."

I walked around the neighborhood, then called the Police Department switchboard and told the operator to tell the guys on the narcotics squad that things would be slightly delayed. I'd arranged a tail just in case.

Cotton was waiting for me. "Where's your car?" I told him it was down the block.

"Okay. We'll take mine." We got into a pickup. "Where's the money?" he asked. I paid him the $350.

We started driving out of town. I tried to make some light talk. Cotton seemed more interested in sucking his teeth and bitching about the pickup, explaining he was having his "real" car fixed. "You got the best stuff in town, Cotton," I said.

He gave me a dumb, toothy grin. "Man, I got the only stuff in town! The only stuff worth buying. I got a connection that just won't quit."

"Yeah, I can tell."

Cotton grew expansive. "My man's in Nuevo Laredo and I can score anything I want. Just tell me. I'll get it."

We were some ten miles out of town driving along a desolate country road. Cotton suddenly pulled up. He pointed. "Okay, Gene. You see that third telephone pole down there? Right at the foot of it you'll find your stuff."

"I don't get it. What do you mean?"

He gave that shit-eating grin again. "This is where you get out, that's what I mean."

"Why the hell didn't you tell me? I could have brought my own car."

"I don't know you. I don't know if I can trust you."

I bristled. "Hell, you already sold to me. If you think I'm The Man or something you've already been had."

He nodded. "That may be, I've been looking for a tail and I don't see any. But I got to be careful. You want the stuff, it's the third telephone pole down. Otherwise, I give you your money and take you back. No hard feelings."

"Okay, Cotton, okay," I grumbled and got out, walked to the pole and at the base of it picked up a glassine bag containing an ounce of heroin. I watched Cotton disappear over a rise a mile away. I was sure he wasn't coming back.

Then Jesse Bautista, who'd been tailing us, appeared from the other direction. He slowed down, opened the rear door and I jumped in, stretching out in the back seat just in case. I had made another buy. But the big news was his connection in Nuevo Laredo.

When we got back to town everyone collected in the Police Department squad room to discuss the Mexican connection. It's often amazing what comes out of such a brainstorming session. One agent remembers a bit of gossip, another an incident, a third a tie between a street peddler and a user. Out of it sometimes a tapestry can be woven which shows a pattern to start working a case. This was such a meeting, with everyone contributing a bit of lore or opinion. It broke down to one Octavio Barbareno, a bigtime violator who ran a sleazy bar, the Aztec, in the red-light district of Nuevo Laredo. How the two dealers tied together was still vague, however. We decided it was time to bust Cotton and find out from him what we could. I ordered some heroin from Cotton a few days later and took him in while he ranted about my dishonesty at not admitting I was The Man.

It was a useless move, as we were to find out. Cotton was already on parole. If he was convicted he would do ten years and automatically do the three he had coming from his old sentence. There was nothing we could offer as bait and he knew it. All he'd say was, "Get me out and I'll introduce you to my connection." But we put it together anyway. We subpoenaed his toll call record and found he'd called the Aztec Bar ten times in the last month. We knew Barbareno had to be the source.

I called Gentry and told him what we had and that I wanted to go down and get Barbareno. Naturally, he was against it. "I think we ought to send a Spanish agent," he said.

"That would be the worst thing," I argued. "Cotton is going to be the introduction. Everyone knows he's Anglo and all of his customers were Anglos. Barbareno would know there was something wrong if a Spanish agent showed up."

Gentry grunted. "Well, if you go you are going to have to take Jack Frost because it's his territory. And I want Bo Taylor to be down there, too." So that was it. Bo was Gentry's assistant, Jack was his pet, and neither was a friend of mine. But I had to agree.

We knew we'd be operating under difficulties. At the time we weren't allowed to be armed and had to be assisted by the Mexican Federal Judicial Police. This was arranged, two agents were to be sent from Mexico City to rendezvous with us at a hotel in Laredo. The Mex Feds, as they were called, were always eager for such assignments as it gave them a chance to get to the States to buy U.S. goods.

Mexican laws created more problems. A purchaser was just as guilty as a seller of drugs under their laws so their agents do not buy narcotics. They have to catch a person in possession. The only way we could work it was to set someone up for a delivery and when they appeared the Mex Feds would bust them. Then we had to disappear rapidly as the Mexican government was not admitting at that time that U.S. agents were working in Mexico. Today, there are three offices in Mexico staffed with our agents and we have excellent liaison with the Mexican government. At the time the hush-hush cooperation worked on the basis that if any of us were exposed and there was publicity we were identified as U.S. gangsters who escaped.

I tried to bring Customs into the case. I knew they were in Nuevo Laredo every day and had a file on Octavio Barbareno. Gentry, of course, refused. "We won't even let them know we're working down there," he ordered. "It's none of their business." To argue against such granite prejudice was useless, I knew.

I met Frost and Bo Taylor in Laredo in a hotel and the two Mex Feds, Mario Martinez and Rafael Garcia Tello, who was the nephew of the chief of all federal police in Mexico, joined us. Both, it turned out, had come from Monterrey, not Mexico City. Little did I know that Tello was going to save my life that night!

We went over the plan. I was to go to the Aztec Bar and meet Octavio, using Cotton's name as an introduction. Frost was to cover me in the car. If I could make a deal I was to bring Octavio to a street just outside the red-light district and the Mexican agents would arrest him. Frost would be with me and Bo would cover from another car.

We agreed that I'd enter the bar at exactly 10 P.M. that night and everyone would be in place at that time. The two Mexican agents explained they wanted to shop in Laredo but would be in position on time. To ask for any other cover was foolish. In a red-light district in Mexico any kind of car good enough to use in a chase would by its luxury become a focal point of attention immediately. Boys come to offer to "protect" it; streetwalkers, peddlers, and idlers collect around it.

As for the whorehouse area itself—always known as "Boys Town" in any town in Mexico—it's always the roughest section, where trouble can come out of any black alley.

About nine-thirty we drove across the bridge—the border—into Nuevo Laredo and I left Frost in the car and went into the Aztec Bar. It was a typical, dingy, poorly lit dive with a gutter of running water beneath the bar for spitting or peeing if you were of a mind. Some 20 men and four or five whores with black, greasy, high brilliantine hairdos, lowcut blouses, and tight skirts were at the bar. Everything slowed down and the talking stopped when I entered. A gringo in such an offbeat joint always meant either fast money or bad trouble.

I ordered a rum and coke and sipped it slowly until the banter resumed. Then I called over the bartender. "Where can I find Octavio?"

He made a few vague swipes at imaginary spots on the bartop just as they do in movies. "What do you want him for, Señor?"

"I'll tell him what I want him for, not you."

The bartender sighed, shook his head despondently, annoyed at my bad manners. "Well, I'll tell you, Señor, I'll find out if he wants to talk with you."

I watched him saunter to the far end of the bar and whisper to a lean, grey-haired man of about fifty who was wearing gaudy, cheap cowboy clothes and a cowboy hat. He was swarthy, pock-marked, and weather-beaten and had eyes like black marbles. He turned to another fat man beside him and said something. The fat man, in frayed khaki pants and a dirty, fringed leather jacket waddled to the front door, looked out, stared at Frost in my car in front, looked over the license plates, and then went back to the cowboy and whispered something.

The gray-haired man hooked his finger at me, motioning me to join him. I shook hands. "I'm Gene Black from Houston."

"Octavio. What can I do for you?"

"I'm a friend of Cotton Tomlin's."

"Oh yes. I know Cotton. Blonde hair, tall fellow." Octavio seemed bored. "So what can I do for you?"

"Did you know Cotton was busted?"

He sighed sadly. "I knew something was wrong. I have not heard from him."

"Yeah," I continued. "He got busted and he asked me to take over his business for him to raise money to get him out of jail."

"That's very good."

"He sent me down to get some stuff."

"How much stuff do you want?"

I paused. "I guess a couple of ounces."

"A couple of ounces. You came all the way from Houston, Señor, for a couple of ounces?"

"About five," I replied quickly. "You realize I don't know how much you sold Cotton. He's in the bucket and I can't talk to him. I'm just feeling my way."

"Señor, I understand. I will sell you your five ounces. Do you have the money?"

I pulled out my bankroll. He scarcely glanced at it. "You will pay me when you get the heroin."

I was pleased. I was afraid he'd want the money in front, which would have upset Gentry no end.

Octavio ordered another round. I watched him toss off the shot of tequila with no salt or lemon, wondering what was happening next. He motioned to the fat man who'd moved to a nearby table. "Gordo, I want you to meet Gene," he said. Gordo looked for all the world like a comic Pancho Villa. He had three or four days' growth of beard, black uncut curly hair and needed only some bandoliers over his shoulders and a mangy horse.

He bowed ostentatiously. "Si, Señor, I am El Gordo."

"Fine," I replied. I didn't find out until later that it meant The Fat Man. The two chatted briefly in Spanish and El Gordo motioned grandly toward the door. "Come, Señor, we will go to our car."

I got behind the wheel, Frost got in back, and Gordo started directing me through the rutted dirt streets of Boys Town. We seemed to be driving aimlessly and finally I asked, "Where the hell are we going?"

Gordo smiled. "Wait, Señor, you will see. How do you propose to handle this deal?"

I smiled. "That's no problem at all. You give me the stuff, I give you the money."

"That is very good. That is very good business, Señor."

He directed me to drive west. We went out of Boys Town for some five miles along a lonely dirt road and then Gordo told me to stop. "Just park here," he said. In a few minutes a dusty brown Ford coupe came up beside us. "Ah! That is Octavio. Everything is all right. You wait here." He got out and waddled off toward the Ford.

I turned to Frost. "Look, why don't you get in the front seat and let him get in back so we'll have him hemmed in?" He did. When Gordo came back Frost ushered him into the back of our two-door sedan and then Octavio surprised us by coming to our car, too.

"Señor, Gordo has the merchandise and if there is anything more you want just come to the Aztec."

On the drive back Gordo pulled five condoms filled with heroin from his pocket. "Here is your merchandise," he announced. I pulled to the side of the road and took the rubber band off one. The stuff was brown, as most Mexican heroin is. It meant it was crudely processed with a lot of impurities left in. In Europe, where the German chemists handle the manufacturing, and even in the Far East, the heroin is white. Too, the odor of acetic acid was strong. I wondered if it was made right in Nuevo Laredo.

I handed it back and nodded. "That's fine, just fine."

Gordo looked puzzled. "Well, Señor, take it."

I started the car. "Let me fill you in Gordo. You must know I'm not going to take this stuff across the border. I have a 'mule' to do that." A "mule" is a standard employee on the border, the man who takes it across for the big dealers who never touch it. "I don't want to even take possession of it. You give it to him when we get there."

"But, Señor, what about the money?"

"I'll pay you when we take it, as I promised. And there'll be some extra money for all your trouble."

"Oh, fine. I like that very much."

We drove in silence to the street where we were to meet the Mexican agents. They weren't there. I saw Bo Taylor's car where it should be, but no agents. I drove around the block, then again. Frost tried to keep a conversation going with Gordo to distract him. But he was becoming more and more frightened. "Wait a minute, what are you doing? Where is your mule? What is this?" Gordo's eyes were bulging with fear.

"He's just a little late," I said.

"I do not like this, Señor."

I appealed to reason. "Look, Gordo, what the hell can I do? What are you afraid of? No one can bust you. If we were American Federales what could we do? Nothing. Sit back and relax?"

We drove around Boys Town for a half hour circling past the rendezvous again and again. I wanted to kill those damned Mexican agents. Later we were to find out that they were buying topcoats in Laredo and had simply forgotten about the time. Several times Gordo asked me to stop the car. "Let me out, Señor," he yelled.

It was close to two hours later when I came by the corner for the last time. The agents were there, sitting in the car contentedly. I pulled up in front of them.

"Let me signal for my man to come and get the stuff and I'll give you the money," I said, motioning toward Bo sitting in front in his car.

I turned on the headlights and blinked them. Nothing. I tried again.

"What is wrong? Let me out," Gordo began to shout.

I began pushing the brake up and down, knowing the taillights would flash and that might attract the Federales' attention. Gordo noticed it. "Give me my money and I'll give you the stuff—and let me out," he pleaded.

I decided on a desperate ploy. "Okay," I said to Frost, "Let Gordo get out."

Frost stepped out and started signaling to the Federales. Gordo saw it and went crazy, pushing the seat down, fighting to get out. I tried to wrestle him back but he pushed past me and tumbled to the street. Then he had his own surprise. He pulled a .45 automatic from his belt and cried, "Señor, I am going to kill you!"

I was sprawled across the seat and couldn't move. I didn't have my own gun, anyway. Frost lurched to the front of the car and fell, hiding behind the fender.

Gordo stood up and put the gun against my head. "Señor, you are dead!" he shouted.

Tello rushed up, grabbing Gordo's arm. The gun fired and Tello fell, blood gushing from his belly.

Frost stood up with a .45 I didn't even know he had and began to fire wildly. I was still stunned. I heard a terrible scream and saw a man rush past me. It was Martinez shouting, "Don't shoot! Don't shoot!" Bo Taylor came rushing from his car and Gordo turned and started running, firing back at us. Everyone was firing in all directions.

Tello yelled up to me from the sidewalk. "Señor, get me to the American side, pronto! I am shot bad." I dragged him into the car and then yelled to Bo. "Take care of things. I'm getting the hell out of here with Raphael. He's hurt bad."

One of the laws in Mexico, I knew, is that if anyone is shot no one can move the injured party until the police arrive. I knew, too, that if I obeyed, Raphael would probably die. I took off like a dragster just as police cars started arriving. I gunned the motor, cutting down one dark side street after another, honking wildly. I had to find the main drag, which led to the bridge.

When I finally found it I wheeled right, forcing my way through the still crowded street. I didn't know it but the police had already called ahead and the Mexican border patrol had put up a roadblock although no one knew what had really happened in Boys Town.

I saw the blockade and hit it, breaking and ramming the boards aside and made for the far end. When I got to the American side I pulled up to the platform. By sheer luck Fred Patton, the Customs Agent-in-Charge and a friend of mine, was on duty.

"Fred, I have a man shot here!" I yelled. He didn't hesitate, didn't bother to ask me who was shot. "Move over," he ordered, taking the wheel.

Within ten minutes Raphael was on the operating table. It was to last five hours and when he came out of it half of his body was paralyzed. Happily, three months later he began to regain use of the paralyzed side.

The others arrived. The heroin and Gordo's worn sombrero were still in the back seat. Gordo had escaped completely. The case was a debacle.

I called Gentry who of course went into a rage, blaming me.

Fred Patton rubbed a little salt in the wound as we stood in the hospital corridor. "Hell, Jack, I wish you'd have let us know at Customs. We could have really helped out."

I nodded. "I know it, Fred, we'd never have had the shooting."

I had a call from Washington, D.C. the same week. They wanted to give Raphael the U.S. Treasury Medal for Valor. It was arranged that he was to fly to Washington and the Secretary of the Treasury was going to make the presentation. Then the Mexican government called it off, fearing, I suppose, the newspaper stories of Mexican and U.S. agents working together. I later had Jesse write him a letter in Spanish thanking him for saving my life. I never saw him again, although I did hear he later became Agent-in-Charge in Tijuana, then left the service. As for Mario Martinez, who ran that night, I now know I judged him too harshly. Two years later he was gunned down along with his brother during a narcotics bust on the streets of Monterrey.

The Mexican authorities went all out to get Gordo. They sent troops in, arrested Octavio and seized his car, closed the Aztec Bar and brought in everyone vaguely connected with Octavio. They asked me to come over and look at the prisoners to try to identify Gordo.

I wasn't about to return after running the blockade, knowing those police were just waiting for me. Then the U.S. Ambassador got involved and I ended up going across with an armed guard of Federales. I toured the filthy dungeons which they call jails looking at dozens of haggard, sick Mexican faces. Gordo wasn't there.

They held Octavio a few months and then released him. I am sure he is probably still operating from the end of the bar at the Aztec.

I returned to my Houston office after that dismal day wondering what was coming next. I guess I proved myself to be a softie because when I walked in all the agents and Darleen, the secretary, had mustered to shake hands and say how glad they were I'd come through it.

Of course, they knew what I had to face with Gentry. I'd given him the weapon to destroy me.

11

Showdown

I waited several weeks for the blast to come, convinced that Gentry was mustering his forces to accuse me of making a fiasco of the Mexican misadventure. Nothing happened. I couldn't understand. Then as the days passed I began to realize that Gentry was too canny to attack. After all, his own boys, Bo and Frost, had been deeply involved. Raphael was a hero in Washington, D.C. The case had involved the Ambassadors of both the United States and Mexico and there had been dozens of news stories. No. . .he was going to wait.

The climax was to come in 1962.

It was, in many ways, a routine case. Lorenzo Gutierrez was a squat, tragic little guy who was a heroin addict. His wife, Carmen, a flabby, orange-haired whore, was also an addict, her arms marked from years of shooting up. She spoke English, which he had never learned except for a few basic words. The few times I saw them he always had her nearby to translate and speak for him. We had a case against him and decided to try to use him as an informer. I wanted his source of supply.

He copped out, claiming he had a big source in San Antonio.

But the dealer demanded money in front which, of course, meant we couldn't deal with him.

We talked it over. I didn't want to make a case for Frost in San Antonio. I wanted to make a case for Kelly in Houston. Yet, if Gentry or Frost knew of it they'd steal my informant and take him to San Antonio.

I worked out a plan that seemed to make sense. I'd send Lorenzo to San Antonio to entice the source up to Houston with a big bundle. He agreed and, of course, took his wife.

I cautioned him before he left. "You're on your own down there. If you get busted there's nothing we can do." They agreed.

We arranged for them to call if they had the dealer from Richmond and we'd bag them in their car, seize the dealer and car, and let Lorenzo and his wife go.

Carmen called a few days later. She explained that they had a pound of heroin, were on their way back, and gave me a description and the license number of the car, arranging for us to make the arrest.

I happened to be at the moment with a friend of mine who—like my other friend—was also named Bill Jackson. He was the chief Assistant U.S. Attorney in charge of the criminal division. He helped me draw up the affidavit and obtain a search warrant. Unlike so many Assistant U.S. Attorneys, he was enforcement-minded, eager to help rather than try to invent sophomoric legalisms to show their knowledge—as well as their lack of experience.

We set up a team play. Buster Hightower, Jay Strickland, and others with the Houston narcotics squad were all set. Daily and Downing were ready to go to Richmond to spot the car and follow it in. I waited with Jesse and Cerda for the call, with Bill Jackson. About three that afternoon a collect call came from Carmen. "We got this far, Mr. Kelly, and we should be there in less than an hour. It's in the trunk."

"Go to the Lone Star Bar. Have your man open the trunk to give you the stuff and we'll hit him." She agreed.

I sent the men to Richmond to follow them in. We decided to pick up Lorenzo and his wife just to protect them and went to the bar to wait.

I left Cerda in front. He was dark-skinned and had passed successfully as Mexican, Italian, and Greek over the years although he was actually Puerto Rican. The calls started coming from Richmond from our men. Everything was working like a clock. They drove up to the Lone Star within seconds of when we anticipated them. The source got out, went to the trunk, and opened it. Lou and the others stepped forward and made the bust. We were all pleased at the ease of it and the size of the seizure. We booked the dealer, one Gilberto Parades, and I took Lorenzo and his wife back to the office with Bill Jackson. I took a statement from Lorenzo and Carmen and asked Bill to witness it. He started, then stopped. "Wait a minute. I'd better not. I may have to prosecute." One of the agents witnessed and we were done with a beautiful day's work. In the statement I saw that they simply said that they'd gone to San Antonio and called me from Richmond, not suggesting that I'd encouraged them to make the trip. Then we went out for a round of drinks and that happy moment of recalling all the details of our triumph.

The next day Gentry was on the phone in his anticipated rage. He accused me of undercutting the Bureau, a variety of devious tricks, and then began to bleat about what I'd done to poor Frost in San Antonio.

"Maybe if he did some work he'd make some cases," I replied crisply. "I can't help it if he doesn't come up with anything. There's more stuff down there than there is here. You keep telling me that yourself." Gentry hung up.

I forgot about it and a few days later when he sent me out of town on a case I thought little of it. I was gone two days. When I returned I found that he'd been to Houston. Further, he had grilled all my agents and browbeaten my secretary, Darleen, a sweet young girl just out of high school. She had finally broken into tears. He'd accused her of taking down the Lorenzo statement and told her he thought I'd made up the statements and that Lorenzo or his wife weren't there. She knew nothing of all this.

It was my turn to call up in a rage. "What the hell do you mean coming in here and making all those false charges and attacking this kid," I shouted. "If you have any quarrels they're with me."

"I think you've been lying in this case."

"In what ways?" I asked.

"I think you falsified that statement and the whole thing."

I felt vastly superior at having him so frustrated. "I'm sorry you feel that way. But I don't understand why you're looking for problems. It's a good case, the U.S. Attorney is satisfied with it, the police are satisfied with it, and—as a matter of fact—the defendant has already indicated that he wants to plead guilty. So, I don't see why you're trying to stir things up . . ."

There was a long Gentry silence. "You haven't heard the last of this," he then said softly. I knew he was right.

A few days later Lee Spear, the Assistant Commissioner, came walking into my office. "Mr. Gentry has preferred charges against you and wants to have you fired," he said for openers.

It was here at last. "Okay," I said. "What's the biggest problem?"

I knew already what was in the mill. The switchboard operator in our building had tipped me off, that Gentry had queried her and asked for the toll slip showing Carmen had called me.

Spear went on to explain the charges. Gentry had a pattern. When he talked to anyone on the phone he'd hang up, then teletype you immediately the same questions he'd just asked and demand that the answers be repeated for the record. After our angry talk the day after the arrest he'd sent a teletype immediately: "In reference to the case of Gilberto Parades in your memorandum report you state that you received the phone call from Gutierrez from Richmond, Texas. Please tell me who placed the call." I had teletyped back immediately that Carmen Gutierrez had placed the call. The reason, which I didn't mention in the teletype, was that Lorenzo had gone to the phone, but the operator couldn't understand him and his wife had to place the call.

Now, it seemed, Gentry was charging me with using a female as a special employee—meaning an informer—which was against regulations in the Bureau at the time unless one had special permission. So, I'd been ready with the right answer on the teletype report.

Spear sat down and began reading the other charges against me. Falsifying the statement, dictating the statement myself, giving the statement to my secretary when neither Lorenzo nor Carmen were present. As for the agent who witnessed the statement, that was dismissed as simply chicanery. I listened to it all, told Spear that I considered Gentry a sick man, and then dropped my own little rebuttal.

"I think I have an excellent witness to answer that," I said. "The chief Assistant U.S. Attorney was there and put the questions to the guy. He formulated the questions and I typed them personally sitting right in my chair here."

Spear leaned back. "You mean that Bill Jackson was there at the time?"

"All the time."

Spear paused. "What about the unauthorized use of Carmen Gutierrez?"

"What are you going to do?" I asked. "You have a man who speaks very little English and can't understand it. I wasn't using his wife and she wasn't working for me. He was working for me. If he wants to take his wife with him what can I do? He was using her, not me."

Spear nodded. "I guess you're right. I guess it's the way one looks at it."

"No!" I interrupted. "I don't think it's the way one looks at it. I can say positively that the women didn't work for me."

Spear went through the motions, interviewing Bill Jackson, Lorenzo and Carmen Gutierrez, all the agents in the office. Then he came in to see me. "Jack, this is ridiculous. I'm going to tell the

Commissioner that it's all wrong and Gentry is all wrong." He paused. "It's ridiculous, but he's throwing all kinds of trumped-up charges at you and everything he can find into the furnace to get a fire going. Why?"

I threw up my hands. "He was against me the first day I got here because he had no say in my coming here."

Spear left, but came back a short time later. "Do you know a man, an informer in Beaumont named Jack Carson?"

"Yes. He's made a couple of cases over there and Daily and Downing have been working with him along with some detectives."

"Do you know anything about Gentry buying a shotgun from him?"

I shook my head, wondering what he meant. Then Spear dropped a remark that showed he'd been digging in. "No, that's right. You were on vacation in the East at the time."

I was puzzled.

"I'll level with you," Spear went on. "I've been told he bought this shotgun off an informer who was also a defendant at the time, a known burglar. There's a damned good chance the shotgun was stolen."

Spear didn't leave it there. He investigated and Gentry nearly was fired. But he produced a receipt showing he'd paid $50 for the gun and knew nothing of the man's record. Then I received a curious call from the detective who'd been working with my men. He asked about a job with the Bureau.

"What job?" I asked.

"Mr. Gentry promised to have me appointed as an agent if I would give a statement for him on that shotgun."

So, I mused, that's the way Gentry smoothed it out.

What went on in Washington as a result of Gentry's attack I will never know. But I suspect they leaped all over him. After all, some 27 agents had either been fired, had quit, or had just faded away because of his endless harassment. All I know is that one day Gentry suddenly appeared in my office trying desperately to smile and seem pleasant. He had an affectation of a Southern accent when he was trying to be friendly and it was all drawl and a yard wide as he asked to shake hands with me.

"What for?" I asked bluntly.

"Well—let's let bygones be bygones."

"That's all right with me," I replied coldly. "But I'm not shaking hands with you. You try to get me fired, then you come over and want to shake hands! What the hell is this?"

"Look, Jack," he went on with his Alabama accent. "What do you say you and me go out and have dinner tonight and talk this over."

"No, sir. If you have any business with me, fine. We'll discuss it here in the office officially."

"Well, I want to talk to you unofficially."

I felt like an ass. "You can't talk to me unofficially," I said sternly.

"Well, socially then?"

"Look, through a misfortune, I had to work for you. But there's nothing in that manual that says I have to have dinner with you."

"What about dinner if we don't say a word about work?" he suggested. "I'm down here all alone. If you can have dinner with an informer you can certainly have dinner with me."

What the hell is this, I thought. Crazy! "Okay," I said suddenly. "Let's go."

We went to a seafood restaurant and ordered a cocktail. We both tried to make conversation about baseball, Texas, the weather, and it wasn't coming off at all. The waiter brought the sole and fried shrimp. Gentry sat staring at the plates moodily for several minutes. Then he seemed to explode.

"You lied! You lied! The only reason you beat those charges I had against you was because you lied!" He was apoplectic, his face was scarlet, and he looked as if he was ready to go to pieces.

What can I say to this man, I thought. What is there to do? Then all the hatred I had for him was more than I could stand. I leaned close to him and said in a whisper: "You know, Gentry, you're right. I lied all the way. But only you and me will ever know it."

He turned purple and waved his arms in rage. A waiter rushed over. I began to laugh. I got up and walked out, leaving him gasping with fury alone at the table, with the bill.

It was the last time I ever saw him. In less than a week I opened an official envelope from the Office of the Commissioner. "You are hereby transferred to Albuquerque, New Mexico. Please report within thirty days."

I was stunned. Gentry had got me after all!

12

In the Sticks

Albuquerque! I didn't even know how the hell to spell it. I thought it had something to do with Indian cliff-dwellers and cowboys and cacti but that's about all I knew. It just didn't figure as a place to find heroin peddlers. I got out the Bureau's roster and found one man stationed there, Weldon Parks, but he had been transferred to Los Angeles. I'd worked with Parks in New York.

My mood ranged between bitterness and anger during the next hour. Here I was leaving a ten-man office to take over a hick assignment in the sticks. I knew I'd done a good job despite the endless conflicts with Gentry. I also knew that he was the one who'd finished me off. It could be no one else. I went down to a bar alone, avoiding the other agents, and sat in the dark drinking martinis and wondering just how to tell the family. It was going to cause a lot of problems. My two daughters were in high school, one in her junior year. If she finished the junior year it meant she'd have to leave all of her friends and do her last year in a strange school. It wasn't so bad for the youngest, who was a sophomore.

I went home and broke the sad news. We talked it over and decided I'd go on to New Mexico and my wife would stay in Houston until the school year was over.

183

During the next four weeks I went around saying goodbye to the many friends I'd made in the four years in Houston. Then the day came to depart. I'd decided to take the train for the simple reason that I could haul all kinds of gear for the four or five months of bachelorhood in Albuquerque. The government paid my transportation and that was all. The more stuff I could carry myself the more I'd save. I went aboard the train looking like an animated second-hand store. I had suits, boxes, cartons, kitchenware, and even a television.

The ticket said Albuquerque but the train stopped at a little town called Belen. The conductor came along ordering everyone off. I was furious. "What the hell is this?" I demanded from behind my barricade of household gear.

"This is as far as the train goes," he explained. "Albuquerque is ten miles from here. You have to take a bus from here."

"Why didn't someone tell me?" I groaned.

I started unloading the boxes, foot lockers, TV set, suitcases.

I arrived in Albuquerque at two in the morning in the middle of a blizzard. Parks' family was still living there although he'd reported to Los Angeles and he'd told me he'd leave a government car in front of his house and had given me the address. I took a taxi to the house, found a white Cadillac, and went back to collect my gear in the ten degrees below zero darkness, cursing Gentry every few minutes. I checked into a motel and fell asleep in my clothes.

The next day I went to the Federal Building and was given the keys to my office. It was really a closet. There was one file cabinet and the desk took up most of the remaining space. A door led into the next office and I'd just sat down when there was a knock. A crewcut lad stuck his head in smiling, "Hi, I'm Johnny Jones, Secret Service."

I looked up and sighed. "So this is the wide open spaces, huh!"

During the next few days I called on the local police and found an apartment to settle in. I was deeply depressed thinking of how I'd been banished from a ten-man office to this dismal dump without even a secretary. When I groused to Johnny he cheerfully told me he'd lend me his secretary once in awhile.

My first meeting with the town's narcotics men was a wary encounter. Lieutenant Fred Gallegos was in charge with two men, Manny Aragon and Bill Proffer. We studied one another appraisingly. I guess I looked rather silly. In Houston I'd turned into one of the ubiquitous ersatz cowboys and affected a cowboy hat and boots, mainly because anyone in Texas who didn't looked like a dude. I was sure it was the perfect wardrobe for the desert wilderness of New Mexico. Yet, they looked on me as if I were an eccentric of some sort. Here everyone wore dark business suits and when they took me to lunch that first day I was politely given a tie to put on before the maitre d' would let me in the restaurant!

As I had the entire state I decided a first order of business was a tour. It was one of the better moves in my mood of deep depression. I didn't find any heroin on the junket but I did fall in love with New Mexico. I felt closer to history than I ever had in North Carolina, New York, or any other place in the East. People in Taos would talk about Buffalo Bill, who is buried there, as if he had just been in the bar last week and you'd hear arguments about Billy the Kid as if he'd had a shootout that afternoon. The Indians were all there, living and part of your daily life. It delighted me every moment.

Bill Proffer and Manny Aragon broke me in to the local narcotics scene. It had a curious local touch. In the cities the peddlers preferred the cover of night to work and agents generally adjusted to those hours. But in New Mexico the tradition was to peddle drugs in the morning with the crowd—just like farm produce and baskets! Manny explained to me that the peddlers liked the daylight so they could see if anyone was watching them. Well, I mused, everyone to his own bag of tricks!

My new life presented some tiring problems. We'd make a buy in the morning and another in the afternoon. I'd have to go to the office, write up purchase memos, process the evidence, weigh it, seal it, fill out the evidence form and, if we had an informer, do his statement and have him sign it. I'd spend hours typing and fall into bed at one or two A.M. only to be roused at eight the next morning by Bill and Manny, anxious to go out and find some more cases.

We'd make coffee, I'd shave, and we'd be out on the streets again.

We found cases everywhere, making some 65 arrests in the first few months. I got to know and admire the Mexican-Americans who made up the majority of the people in New Mexico, it seemed, and also I slowly lost my bitterness and anger. Then one day Tom Andrews, the District Supervisor, stopped by. "Congratulations, Jack," he said simply.

"On what?"

"On your promotion. You've been made a GS-13 and I guarantee there isn't another Agent-in-Charge of a one-man office in the Bureau history who ever did that!"

I was so delighted. I couldn't believe it. It not only meant more money but also that the Bureau was apologizing to me in its own way for the Gentry fiasco. That was exactly it. Not long after, Charlie Siragusa arrived to make a speech in Roswell and we had a long talk. "You got your 13 because we all felt terrible about the raw deal you got in Houston. You did a hell of a job there and you've done a hell of a job here."

I took it at face value although you never knew with Charlie. He told me that there was an ugly rumor going around that he was going to retire as Assistant Commissioner. Dirty Bureau politics in Washington, he said loftily. "There's no way I'm going to retire." A few days later he returned to Washington, D.C., immediately retired, and went to the Illinois Crime Commission as Executive Director.

As the case load increased I realized that New Mexico had been entirely overlooked as a narcotics center. Albuquerque ranked 35th as a city in recorded addicts. This statistic was based on a tabulation of a Bureau of Narcotics form which we and the local police filled out when we encountered an addict. When I left Albuquerque it ranked ninth in the U.S.—in a state with only a million population! Why? Simply because I went to the Police Department and kept reminding them to fill out the form as well as meticulously doing so myself. And so one can conclude from drug statistics what one wishes!

These contact reports made for delightful browsing when one had free time. I was always particularly taken with the answers to a bureaucratic, banal question on the form: "Reason for addiction?" The explanations would bemuse any psychiatrist. Sad, comic, tragic, and always superficial, they were, nevertheless, now and again revealing. The standard replies were unhappy love affairs or domestic and business problems. But others were unique.

I recall the unhappy youth who noted "Penis cut off." A medical check showed his penis was intact, but tiny. He preferred to believe he'd lost part of it. Tragic, too, was one Korean vet where the same reason was given, but true.

Others were quaint. "Nothing else to do," was one reply. "Wanted to quit drinking to lose weight," was another. "Something to spend my profits from burglaries on," was a nice reverse ploy. My alltime favorite involved a Las Vegas jazz musician. He'd married a showgirl who, as soon as she had the gold band, starting nagging him about his broken and chipped front teeth, demanding that he have them capped. He finally did and came proudly home to go to work only to find he couldn't blow a note on his trumpet! The upshot was he lost his job, she divorced him for non-support, and he took to the needle in despair.

We developed a routine with one Irish informer, Danny. He lived with his woman in a groundfloor apartment with an alley running along one side. He'd ask the dealer to deliver the stuff and also bring a wife or girlfriend. While the two women talked, our informer would ask the dealer to step back to the bathroom to complete the deal. We would sit beneath the bathroom window, listening to the arrangements, and Danny would excuse himself and step to the back porch. We'd search him, give him the money for the buy, and he'd return to the bathroom, explaining he had to go outside because he had the money hidden there to make the buy. The case would be made. We added a fillip by having Danny leave the drug on the window sill and we'd open the screen and take it. Danny could honestly testify in court that he hadn't even touched the drug and the case would be wrapped up.

While we made many busts, few were for large amounts. The reason was simple. The border was a short run away and peddlers didn't have to keep a big supply. They'd take orders, run down in the morning, and be back that evening. It all made for many smalltime peddlers but few big dealers. If a man scored with a burglary he'd take the loot to Mexico, buy heroin, and return to be a big man for a day or so—only to be replaced by another.

If the bigtime didn't exist I did run into one remarkable situation which ended with my being sued for $160,000. It all started when we got word that one Pete Luera was pushing a lot of marijuana. We found an informer and set up one buy, but couldn't get back to him. We didn't know why. We suspected it had something to do with our conflict with the Sheriff's Office. Neither the state, local, or federal agents could get along with Lester Hay, the sheriff. There were bad feelings. One reason was that the sheriff was publicity-mad and would go on television with anything he might have. He'd blown several cases in his desperate need for new stories or a television interview and we were all wary of bringing him into a case.

The time came when we were ready to nail Pete Luera. We hit him at his house and found a variety of items. He had a .25 caliber pistol in one pocket, a tear gas gun in another. As we had a search warrant we were able to shake down his house. We found some stalks of marijuana, 897 marijuana cigarettes, some heroin, a .45 pistol, three stolen radios, a set of expensive foreign-made silver. But, most important, we found some of our testers issued by the Bureau of Narcotics! These were made for us by the U.S. Chemist, small glass capsules which contain sulphuric acid and for- maldehyde. An agent simply breaks one and drops a few grains of heroin in it. If it turns purple it's heroin. As a courtesy we gave them to local police and sheriffs. I found a half dozen boxes of these in Luera's apartment. I was deeply concerned. A few hours later he was out on bail for $12,500 and I began pressuring him to work for us as an informer. He was reluctant and finally explained why. "I work for the Sheriff's Office and set up cases for them."

He grew expansive. "You know those big stalks of marijuana you found at my place? Do you remember the Sheriff being on television and showing them a few weeks ago? It was the same stuff."

"Do you mean you got them from the Sheriff's Office?" I asked incredulously.

"Sure, he said happily. "That's where I got those testers, too."

"Who gave them to you?"

"Deputy Sheriff Joe Chavez. In fact, all the narcotics you got today was stuff he gave me."

I couldn't believe it. "Why?" I asked.

"To sell."

"You mean he gives you that stuff to sell for him."

Joe shook his head. "No. He gives that stuff to me. I get people for him."

I was puzzled. "What do you mean?"

"Well, he gives me this stuff to sell," Joe went on. "You know, I'll tell you the truth. They don't have money to pay informers so they give me the stuff to sell and I make a buck and at the same time come in touch with people I can turn over to them."

"Will you make a statement to that effect?" I asked.

"Why not?" he replied.

I got an affidavit and took it to the U.S. Attorney. "I think you should take this to the District Attorney. I just don't want to handle it. I think it should be handled in a State Court."

They sent me to the District Attorney. "I want to talk to you about a possible crooked Deputy Sheriff," I explained.

The District Attorney shook his head. "I don't want to talk about it."

"What do you mean?"

"I just don't want to get involved in any of that stuff."

It was an Alice in Wonderland answer. "Look, buddy, you're the District Attorney. It's supposed to be your job to prosecute people like this." I went on to outline the case. "Okay," I ended. "If you want to drop it I'll go to the newspapers and tell them we are going to let this peddler go because the District Attorney refuses to discuss it."

He glared at me. "Okay, you win. I'll come over to your office." He went with me, read the statement, and was amazed. "I've got to talk to the Sheriff and Joe Chavez," he said. I'll bet you do, I thought, because I was now convinced he was somehow involved and trying to cool it.

He got a statement from the Deputy which said that he'd given Joe marijuana and heroin only to prove he was a dealer. It was a ridiculous argument. But the District Attorney refused to prosecute as did the U.S. Attorney. I discussed it with the Bureau and was told to drop the matter. I was furious, but helpless.

The case against Pete Luera was dismissed. He gave a statement that he'd given us all the information and made an effort to tell us his source of supply.

I decided I was going to follow through on the Deputy Sheriff on my own. I had a friend, Dave Gilmore—a private detective—who was a close friend of Floyd Bachman, a reserve deputy sheriff. Both Bachman and Deputy Sheriff Chavez owned saloons and were close friends. One day three things fell into place. Gilmore told me that Chavez and Bachman were going to El Paso for a brief vacation. Word also came in from the street that Joe Chavez was going down to score a load of stuff. The coincidence was remarkable.

I called Jack Salter, a Customs Agent in El Paso, and he agreed to put two men on them to see what was happening. He reported back later. Chavez and Bachman had crossed over to the Boys Town section of Juarez on foot, returned to get their wives, and then disappeared again into one of the back alleys of the whorehouse area. They concluded some narcotics deal was in the offing. Two days later when the two couples departed El Paso the Customs agents let them get to the edge of town, then stopped them. They shook them down completely, including a body cavity search, and found nothing.

Shortly afterward, they filed suit against me in State Court for false arrest for $160,000, charging illegal search, assault, battery, forced to disrobe, submit to indecent search, humiliation, suffering physical pain, mental pain, loss of time, and loss of reputation. The case was moved to Federal Court, and I was more or less arrested and released on a $5000 Surety Bond. They also charged poor Dave Gilmore, who'd had no part in it. As for Customs, they could not sue as the agents were acting under the law. U.S. Senator Clinton P. Anderson posted my bond and eventually it went before U.S. District Judge Howard Bratton, who dismissed it, stating that anything I did in the color of my office and employment was under my authority under the law. I was safe at homeplate!

Subsequently, Sheriff Hay was indicted on charges of embezzlement by the Grand Jury but beat the case and later was reelected. As for the District Attorney, he died and it was discovered he'd been drawing two salaries for all those years.

About this time I was drawn into an elaborate case which started with a most unique problem. On December 1, 1963, Tommy Thompson, Chief of Police in Roswell, New Mexico, called. "I've got a very confidential situation. Can you come and see me?"

The next day I was there and we met over coffee. He explained that he had a sergeant, Wilson Wheeler, who'd been on the force for years. He'd hurt his neck in an accident and while he was in the hospital a local bigwig Gary Hammill, who owned a laundry, drive-in, airplane, and several large cars and was considered a town tycoon, came to visit him. When the sergeant had complained of the pain Hammill had blithely said, "I'll get you some stuff." He'd started furnishing the sergeant with barbiturates.

I interrupted. "Isn't all this strange? Unusual for a small town, I mean?"

Tommy nodded. "There's talk all over town that the sergeant is addicted. He came to me and told me the whole story. He wouldn't have if he were really an addict. But I want you to talk with him. Hammill told him he could get any kind of narcotics he wanted. That's why I called you."

He brought in the sergeant and we chatted. I didn't feel as sanguine as the chief about the sergeant's condition. He had a dry mouth and the difficulty in talking that goes with a heavy barbiturate user. He repeated the story and said the chief had suggested he continue to buy from Hammill.

"Wait a minute," I interrupted. "No one told me you were buying from him. I thought he was giving them to you."

The sergeant shook his head. "No, no! I always bought them."

"For how much?"

"A quarter a pill." I sat back wondering at this weird situation: One of the town's wealthiest men sells barbiturates to the town cop for a Shylock shakedown price! I couldn't make sense out of it all.

I grilled the sergeant for an hour. He explained that Hammill had told him he planned to branch out in narcotics and was already flying stuff in from Mexico. But why would he brag to a police officer about it?

I asked the sergeant if he could introduce us. He was reluctant but agreed that if I could come up with a plausible story to explain myself, he would.

I drove back to Albuquerque pondering the new idea of having a cop for an informer and wondering what cover I could invent to get into the case.

Then I remembered I'd done some undercover work a few months before at the State Fair in Albuquerque during the race track meet and in order to do this I'd gone to the New Mexico Racing Commission and obtained identification as a horse owner. My name had been B. F. Owens of Denver, Colorado, and I'd discovered a couple of jockeys were involved in the narcotics traffic at the track.

Also, I had my grand cowboy gear from Texas, which I'd stored away. I decided I'd be the horse owner again. I put on my cowboy clothes, a set of Colorado plates on the Cadillac, and drove back to Roswell a few days later. I called Tommy. "Can you and the sergeant come over to the Holiday Inn to see me?" I gave him the room number. "Come in the back way." He agreed.

I sat out in the car until I saw them arrive and then went up to them. They were startled to see me in my "disguise". I used a

Western accent. "Now, Bill, you reckon you can set me up with this man or not?" He laughed as I explained my plan. "Sun Land is open," I said, a track near the Texas-New Mexico-Mexico border. "This is what you do. Tell Hammill I'm a horse owner just passing through town and you know me and arrange for the three of us to have dinner."

The sergeant balked, but finally we went over to Gary Hammill's restaurant. He was an odd sort. He affected what must have been his idea of the style of a bush pilot, with a scarf, flying jacket, and the style of Robert Taylor in a World War II movie. He apparently fancied himself as a most romantic figure—even if he ran a drive-in for a living. In no time I was sitting in the booth with Hammill acting the part of a bigtime horse owner on the way to Sun Land. I also dropped enough hints to let him know I wasn't too straight, cursing the way they were testing the horses. "I used to have a good connection for doping my horses," I complained. "But I've lost it."

Hammill took the bait immediately. "How would you like some half-grain morphine sulphate tablets?" he asked.

I paused and meditated. "I don't know about half-grain but I could sure use some quarter-grain."

Hammill nodded eagerly. "I may be able to get some."

"You can?" I said with enthusiasm. "How many?"

"I don't know offhand."

"Could you get me a hundred?" I asked.

"Sure," he replied. "I can get you all you want for a buck apiece."

I pulled out my flash roll and peeled off a hundred. "I'll pay for a hundred right now."

"Okay," he said, getting up. "You go back to the Holiday Inn and I'll be back with them soon."

I shook his hand. "Gary, you're some kind of a sport! You're really something the way you come through."

He blushed. "Sure. There's no sense in fooling around," he said awkwardly.

I couldn't quite understand this little guy, dressed as he always was like a bush pilot with his leather jacket and handkerchief tied around his neck. He swaggered and had studied gestures even when ringing up milkshakes on the cash register. I always felt when I talked with Gary that he was waiting for the cameras to start rolling at any moment.

I took the sergeant back to the room and explained that I didn't want him there when the deal went through. The chief came in. "Let's bug the room," he suggested. We did, renting the room next to mine and quickly running the bug through. It worked beautifully. I put the mike under the bedcover and stretched out. In less than an hour there was a knock. Gary swaggered in and dramatically tossed a bottle of pills on the bed. "Well, boss, I told you!" he said.

"My God, that's wonderful!" I gasped. "I didn't know you were really that big a man."

He leered contentedly. "Hell, I handle a lot of stuff."

"If I could get a lot of stuff I'd unload it myself," I said.

Gary took a quarter out and began flipping it nonchalantly. "What would you say to a pound of top heroin?"

I suppose people in every occupation have their first loves: musicians who love Bach; stockbrokers who love AT&T; jewelers who love rubies. Mine is heroin, as you've no doubt gathered. To me it's always been the No. 1 curse and I'd rather make one good heroin bust than a dozen cases of other kinds of drugs.

"Gary, where in hell would you get a pound of heroin? Have you any idea how much that's worth?"

He quit flipping the coin and caught it with a flourish. "I've got it. I've got it in my safe right now!"

"You're kidding!"

"No shit. I deal with a lot of people—in Chicago, L.A., San Antonio."

'Where did you get it?" I asked with flattering fascination.

"I own a plane and I've got a partner. We've been doing a little gold smuggling. I've been running gold back. Then we started with a little heroin and found we could make more money."

"How much do you want for that pound?"

He made a magnanimous gesture. "You can have it for $50,000."

I knew then I was dealing with someone who thought I was an amateur or a boob. No heroin could bring that price. "You're putting me on," I said grinning.

"That's my price. I already got a buyer."

"Look, you can get a pound in Mexico for $10,000—so why five times as much? And you're supposed to be a dealer."

"This is pure."

"I'm talking pure, Gary."

I backed off, suddenly fearful I'd make him look too much a fool.

"Well, I got a buyer," he went on stubbornly. "A buyer from Chicago. I'm going to fly it up there."

I just couldn't tell if I was dealing with a nut or what. So I decided to stall. I gave him an undercover phone number in Denver and told him on the way back from Sun Land I'd give him a call. There was no further mention of the heroin. We parted with a casual handshake.

Something reeked, something was off. The chief and sergeant came in from the other room and we played the tape, which was perfect. But right there I cut the sergeant out of any further involvement. "Just go on as if nothing has happened," I cautioned him. I was afraid of him. He left and the chief asked me if I thought he was using. "Look, you're the chief," I said a bit impatiently. "Why don't you send him to a doctor and find out." I left for Albuquerque.

I processed the morphine sulphate and started checking back on the wholesaler. It turned out the triplicate forms showed it came from a drug house in Cincinnati that in turn dealt with only one drugstore in Roswell, the Five Point, owned by a man named Ben Cathey. I called the chief and asked if he could establish a tie. Gary had mentioned a partner.

A day later I put on my cowboy gear and returned to Roswell and called on Gary at his restaurant. I was, of course, on my way back from Sun Land.

After smalltalk I remarked, "Don't try to tell me you unloaded that heroin for fifty grand!" I laughed.

He chuckled, "Naw, I was just putting you on. I already had the stuff sold. I was just, you know, kidding around..."

He scratched his chin and ordered a piece of chocolate cake from one of the waitresses. "But I'll tell you what. I'm flying down to Mexico on a gold deal. If you tell he how much you want I'll bring back some more heroin."

"How much do you think you could bring back?"

"Oh, a couple pounds, easy."

"I'll take it at $10,000 a pound," I said.

"You know, there's just one thing that's got me worried about you," he added slyly. "You ever hear of a jockey named Rodriguez?"

I shook my head. "Well, I talked to him and he says there's no way you can dope a horse with morphine. Nobody dopes horses with morphine."

"What makes him an authority?" I asked blandly.

"He's a big jockey. He's been around horses all his life."

I decided to bluff it through. My voice became hard and angry. "Look, jockeys work for me. I own horses. What do they know?" I went on to explain how I used the morphine to make a special speedball by mixing it with other drugs. Gary listened, nodding and fascinated. "That's why jockeys work for me," I concluded. "I know what I'm doing." I left, telling him to let me know when he got back with the heroin.

I called Gary twice after that and he stalled. Then a funny thing happened. Jess Sosa made a small case in Roswell. The smalltime peddler said that Hammill had approached him to make a trip to Mexico to get some heroin. What was it all about? His story about flying the plane down to Mexico seemed untrue. Yet he was obviously trying to get the heroin for me!

I spent a month waiting, then obtained arrest warrants for Gary and Ben Cathey at the Five Point drugstore. Then I called

Gary and said I was coming through Roswell and would like to get some more morphine.

"Sure, I'll get my partner and have it for you. By the way, I haven't had much luck yet on that heroin."

I met him in his restaurant. He said he'd go get the morphine and to wait at the hotel, then departed. It was simple for the chief to tail Gary to Cathey's house. They then went to the drugstore, opened up, and departed. Gary called me soon after and I met him at his restaurant.

"My partner is all out of morphine," he explained. "But he said he had some stuff that would do just as well."

"What is it?" I asked.

"Dilaudid tablets."

"Oh, yeah," I nodded. He arranged for me to wait until he closed the restaurant. "You got the money?" he asked.

"What the hell!" I said hotly. "I always got the money."

He went to his safe and returned with the bottle of pills. I saw the seal wasn't broken.

"Well, Gary," I said. "I've got something to tell you and I don't think you're going to like it. But it's just one of those things. I have no choice but to tell you."

He looked puzzled. I had quietly pulled my gun from my leg holster, took it out from under the counter, and opened my wallet. "This is my gun and this is my badge. I'm a federal narcotics officer."

Gary began to sob. I opened the door and let Dick Robinson and the police in. We handcuffed Gary and then went to pick up Cathey.

At the jail I read them the warrants. Cathey started cursing Gary. "You son of a bitch! I should have my head examined. I'm not a criminal. I'm insane, that's what I am, to have anything to do with you. How I ever let you talk me into this thing. . . ."

Cathey turned to me. "This bastard! He came to me with a scheme and was going to smuggle gold out of Mexico. He got me in on that and I put up five thousand dollars. All that happened is that they swindled both of us out of our ten thousand dollars! We never even saw any gold. Then this son of a bitch is going to smuggle heroin and he gets me into that and nothing ever happens. Now I find all he's going to get me into is jail."

They processed Gary and Cathey and just as I was leaving I heard a plaintive little call, "Jack Jack . . ." I turned. Gary was standing there in a heroic pose. I walked over to the door. He gave a brave little tug to the scarf around his neck and smiled bravely like Cary Grant facing a firing squad. "Jack, I guess we just can't win them all. You lose some and you win some." He gave a little gesture of finality.

I couldn't even answer. This idiot who wanted so desperately to be a romantic smuggler and bigtime heroin dealer who'd led me down the primrose path! I'd wasted weeks, assumed disguises, worked out fancy plans—all to get a few pills from the local drugstore!

13

Running from Death

I was getting restless. Much as I liked New Mexico I missed the action in a big city. My little hole in the wall had grown. I had moved into bigger quarters, had a secretary and a young agent, Dick Robinson, was assigned to the office. About the time that the itch was getting unbearable I had a conversation with my old partner, Ray Enright, who was now Assistant Commissioner of the Bureau.

"It's about time you quit playing around in the streets and start thinking about becoming an administrator. You can only claim that gray hair of yours is premature for fifteen or twenty years, you know."

"I'm not very damned interested in becoming an administrator," I said.

"If you want to get bigger jobs with the Bureau and get in bigger offices you're going to have to start changing your image," he replied.

"Gawd, you sound like a press agent."

But I was in a rut, no question. I needed to move. Then an opening came up in St. Louis. I jumped at it. "You won't be there too long, but it is a stepping stone," I was told. This was true. The

199

last two Agents-in-Charge had been promoted to bigger offices.

In August, 1966, I moved in. There were four other agents and a secretary. For eighteen months I was back to the fast pace of a city again. There were high moments of excitement. During a period of three days, for example, we arrested 20 heroin peddlers. Our case load grew so rapidly that St. Louis, which was rated sixth in the nation in heroin activity when I arrived, was down to twelfth when I left. The climax came with busting John McWilliams, who we estimated was selling $15,000 of heroin a week. Our break came when we made a case on a man named Andrew Lyles. Because of his record we were refused use of him as an informer but his girlfriend, Kimberly Robinson, volunteered to help us nail McWilliams, the city's top dealer. The manager of the Diplomat Motel, Bob Wesley, was a personal friend and when I approached him with the scheme to take two rooms and use one for surveillance he was so delighted that he had a hole cut in the door between the adjoining rooms.

We planted Kim in one and bugged it and then had her call McWilliams, who agreed to visit her. She explained that she was having so many problems with Lyles that she wanted a fix. He left and returned soon after with some heroin. We'd arranged the plan for the buy. She told him to put the heroin on the bureau and take the money from the top of the bureau. This way she didn't touch either the money or the drug and we witnessed the entire transaction through the hole in the door.

We arranged for a second buy but something had made McWilliams suspicious. He came to the room and returned the money he had taken the day before, explaining that he was just being friendly and wasn't a peddler. It seemed he knew the room was bugged. We simply stepped in and arrested him.

But more was to come. Kim returned to the apartment with her boyfriend. The next night three men arrived and beat the couple badly. One tried to shoot her but the gun misfired. "This is for Mac, you little bitch," one yelled. "We got orders to take you out and kill you." When Lyles tried to fight back as they were dragging her from the apartment they shot him. During the melee she escaped, rushed to a neighbor's phone, and called us. We arrived in time to catch two of the three gunmen. In court the judge cancelled Mc-Williams' bond. When he went to trial he was fined $8000 and given 25 years in prison.

It was luck and comedian Buddy Hackett's ingenuity which aided me when I ran into another dilemma. We had spotted a peddler in a section of St. Louis called Gas Light Square. But we knew he was only a petty street man and had a supplier, a mysterious figure we were able to identify only as "Joe." We knew we could bust the peddler with a John Doe warrant but it would be rather futile. We wanted the supplier, to know where *he* lived and to find out his source. We knew only that he loitered around the Square and let his mule peddle.

Buddy Hackett and Eddie Fisher had opened in a downtown theater. I'd known Buddy in New York and gave him a call. It's not well known, but Hackett is a staunch law and order man who abhors narcotics. He'd worked with other agents before and when we chatted on the phone he asked if I was working any interesting cases. I mentioned that we were going to make a buy that night. Buddy asked if he could come along. I went over to get him, meeting Eddie Fisher for the first time, who was to become a longtime friend.

That night we made a buy in a bar when Buddy was with us. We also saw the mysterious "Joe" standing a half block away. I'd told Buddy of our problem. "He's so elusive we can't trace him to an auto to get a license number," I'd explained. "He's like a phantom and even the people who work for him don't know his name."

"I'll bet I can get it," Buddy announced.

"How, for God's sake," I asked, amused.

"Lemme show you," and with that Buddy took off at a rolling gait and I followed. I couldn't imagine what he had in mind. He simply walked up to our man and stuck out his hand "Hi! I'm Buddy Hackett. What's your name?"

Our quarry, a dark, thin man, started and gawked in awe at the thrill of meeting a celebrity. "Joe Brigliano," he replied, ardently shaking Buddy's hand.

We strolled away. Within a week we had a make on Joe Brigliano and made a good seizure of heroin. He never knew how we found out who he was.

A short time later I received the call I'd been expecting from Ray Enright. "Well, here's your chance," he announced. "You've been selected to go to either Chicago or San Francisco as Enforcement Assistant." He then asked in a mock, officious tone, "Which will it be?"

I chuckled. "Are you kidding?"

"San Francisco it is then. I'll be in touch."

I reported to my new post on March 4, 1968. The District at that time was made up of Arizona, California, and Nevada, with Dan Casey in charge. It was a fortuitous break for me as Casey was the finest administrator I was ever to work under. He was to teach me the subtleties of handling people and I, in turn, tried hard to break my habit of being too abrupt and direct, which I know had made enemies in the Bureau.

Better still, he started to harass the Bureau for a promotion and I was boosted soon to Grade Fourteen, a high position in the old Bureau and the same as Dan held.

Little did I realize that events were at work which would mean that I was never really to live in San Francisco. It started in an unimportant way. On my birthday, April 9, 1968, I felt something under my tongue bothering me, the feeling of pain one gets when a chicken bone pierces the inside of the mouth. I promptly forgot about it.

We had other things more important to consider at the Bureau. The day before, President Johnson had signed an executive order putting the Bureau of Narcotics and the Bureau of Drug Abuse Control into one agency, the Bureau of Narcotics and Dangerous Drugs. At the same time he took the Bureau of Narcotics out of the Treasury Department and the Drug Abuse organization out of the Department of Health, Education and Welfare and merged them under the Department of Justice.

The move had actually been brewing for several years. The Bureau of Drug Abuse Control had been formed a year or so before. The simple reason, in retrospect, was that Henry Giordano, who had replaced Harry Anslinger, made a fatal error. In the early 1960s we all had watched the drug scene slowly change. The abuse of barbiturates, LSD, the amphetamines, was everywhere. We seldom made an arrest without finding these drugs along with heroin and the like. Congress asked the Bureau to take over on the whole problem of hallucinogenic drugs. Giordano refused, explaining that the Bureau had enough to keep it busy already. Congress then formed the new Bureau of Drug Abuse Control.

It set up an automatic new rivalry in the field. The people in the new Bureau were not professional narcotics agents—most came from other government agencies outside law enforcement. John Finlater, who came from the government supply organization, The General Services Administration, was made Director. He knew nothing about enforcement, the law, or drugs—and never learned. His agents began appearing, transferred from the Department of Agriculture, from the Food and Drug Administration, and just about any other agency you could name that was not connected with law enforcement. They added to this a sprinkling of narcotics agents and some police and this was the nucleus. Too, they had a vast number of people known in bureaucracies as "jumpers." They had already worked for three or four bureaus and then leapt to the new government opening to stay ahead of the tide, before being fired. They are usually, by the nature of the game, incompetents.

We viewed all this at first with scorn and a wry humor. When we made seizures of amphetamines, barbiturates and LSD we'd call the new Bureau and turn our take over. It was a standing joke that we were making most of the arrests and they were, now and again, seizing heroin or marijuana and turning it over to us. It is perhaps even unfair to call our conflict a rivalry, which implies a certain healthy competition. It was a bitter dislike for one another and a most unhealthy situation. Now, with the signing of the Presidential order, the personnel were to merge! The big question was who would seize the power, Giordano or Finlater? Giordano was a competent professional, Finlater a skillful politician who'd spent his career in Washington, D.C. and knew everyone. The infighting never really surfaced but must have been lively. For the result was that both lost out and a newcomer, John Ingersoll, Chief of Police of Charlotte, North Carolina, was named Director.

I was stunned at the choice because I had once been offered the same job, as had others, when I was in North Carolina and turned it down. In law enforcement it was considered a small, low-paying post. What he had done to be elevated to such an important new assignment had everyone bewildered.

We agents in the field sat back wondering what would happen next. There had been no effort as yet to merge the two bureaus physically and we operated as before. But we assumed changes would come soon.

A month to the day, May 9, when I'd first felt the pain under my tongue I became aware of it again. "It's been a month," I thought. "It should have healed by now." I went to the mirror and raised the tip of my tongue. I saw a large white growth with tentacles growing out of it. My God, I thought, I've got something serious. I was temporarily living in a room at the Hotel Embassy, waiting for the kids to finish the school year in St. Louis before moving to San Francisco. That night I lay awake all night getting up every few hours to stare at the growth again.

The next morning I went to the office and asked my secretary if she knew a doctor in the city. She arranged an appointment that day. The doctor took one casual look. "My God, son," he said. "I can't help you. There's nothing I can do. You've got cancer."

"What do you mean there's nothing you can do?" It was as if I'd been knocked over by a .45.

"I can't, that's what I mean."

"You mean all I can do is just sit around and die? There's no treatment?"

The old general practitioner shook his head. "Well, I know a young doctor here who they say has had some success. But I don't hold much with these young doctors."

"You worthless old bastard," I thought, getting the name of the young doctor.

A day later I called upon Dr. Alfred Marquez and told him of the diagnosis. He was amazed. "There's no one who can just look at you and say you have cancer. I want to do a biopsy and put you in the hospital."

I felt a bit better, convinced that—hopefully—the old doctor was an alarmist. "When?" I asked.

"Now, today," Dr. Marquez replied. I felt my panic return.

"I can't today, but I will tomorrow," I replied.

The next day they put me to bed and the following morning took me to the operating room and took a piece of the lump. The doctor told me to go to the hotel and wait until he called with the report. I went back to the room, pacing, turning the television on, then off, starting to light my pipe. "You must be crazy," I thought and collected all my pipes and tobacco and threw them in the wastebasket. I haven't smoked since.

The phone rang. It was Dr. Marquez. "I don't know how to say this except by being direct and straight. It's malignant."

I had been secretly expecting it. "What do I do now?" I asked.

"You have to go back to the hospital and I'll operate and see if I can remove it."

"When?"

"I thought tomorrow."

I gasped. "You don't understand. I have my family back in St. Louis and they're getting ready to move. I just can't leave them like that."

"I understand. But you have to understand that this is your life."

"I have to go back there and make sure they're moved before you operate."

Dr. Marquez hesitated. "All right. But you've got to make it fast."

I called my wife and told her the bad news. A day later I flew to

St. Louis and had just arrived when Dr. Marquez called. "I've made all the arrangements for you to go to the hospital in St. Louis. I have a friend there who'll operate."

"What are you talking about?" I asked in confusion.

"This is one of the fastest growing cancers I've ever seen. It's the squalis strain. I just refuse to be responsible for you unless you go into the hospital immediately."

I regained a bit of composure. "Look, you're my doctor. You did the biopsy and you are going to operate. No one else."

"You have to go to the hospital," he repeated. "You have to come right back now."

I was frightened. "We've got the house sold and the movers are due tomorrow. Then we're leaving for Albuquerque."

"All right. But call me each day. I'm very, very concerned." His voice was somber.

We shipped the furniture to San Francisco and left for New Mexico. We still had a house there and had decided it would be best for the family to move back until after the operation. By now the kids knew.

I'd suddenly become fatalistic about it all. As soon as the family was a bit settled I started for San Francisco. But I did a dilly thing on the way. I stopped in Las Vegas for a day and night of crap shooting, a favorite pastime, I felt I might die and wanted to enjoy once more the things I liked. Thirteen days after I found that I had cancer I checked back into the hospital.

Dr. Marquez explained that he was going to do a skin graft taking skin from my left armpit. He added that he anticipated doing a tracheotomy and prepared me. I was on the operating table five and a half hours. During that time Dr. Marquez came out and told my wife, who'd come with me, that he'd determined I was a nose breather and had decided against the tracheotomy as it would weaken my throat. She agreed to this and he went back in, only to return later.

"I'm not going to do a skin graft either," he told her. "I'd like to take a chance on doing it another way." She agreed. Later he explained what he'd done. He had removed the floor of my mouth and three salivary glands, then sewn my tongue, after removing the lower half of it, to my bottom gum.

I spent nearly two weeks recuperating, then, when he released me, went to Reno to once again shoot crap. I couldn't talk and had to write everything down. I went on to Albuquerque to recuperate.

The doctor had told me that I'd learn to talk again but I'd never give any after-dinner speeches. "You may have difficulty making people understand you," he went on. "So you might as well be prepared for that."

During the next three months I tried to forget, repairing the roof of the house. My tongue was still swollen three times its normal size and it was to be a year before it felt comfortable again. I tried to talk again, feeling the small tug on my tongue as it moved. I had difficulty eating. Slowly, I progressed until I was talking a bit with a slight lisp. Today, I still get annoyed at myself when I slur some words and a listener cannot understand me. But I had my happy revenge on Dr. Marquez and his warning. A year after he released me I was in Honolulu and appeared on a panel television show on drugs. When it was over I went to the telegraph office on the way back to my hotel and sent him a nightletter: "YOU'RE ALL WET. I JUST DID MY FIRST AFTER-DINNER SPEECH!"

14

The New Breed

San Francisco was a city already deeply immersed in a frightening drug tradition. The 1960s had brought the crisis of a new type of narcotics and new type of user. LSD, STP, hash, were added to the lexicon of drugs and the users were not unfortunate ghetto addicts but college kids, runaways, teenage dropouts. We can take the blame for this whole new culture, introducing LSD from San Francisco to the rest of the world, first to London, then as a plague to other countries. Kids who had taken a chemistry course in college started producing LSD in their bathtubs much as their grandfathers had made bathtub gin. It was all to be called the "Flower Child Conspiracy," which started as a wild, gay romp with the kids feeling like dangerous criminals of a special sort. All was merry at Haight-Ashbury for a time. Then came chaos. Bemused youngsters with their funny clothes and heads were found murdered. Poisons were mixed in the concoctions. Criminals after profit moved in exploiting the Love Children. Bodies were found daily in tenements, parks, alleys. Our office burgeoned from six agents to fifty. The city and state added still more agents. Bigtime crime took over. Nothing slowed the tide. This was the background when I returned to San Francisco, eager to be part of the battle and the excitement. The first week John Ingersoll, as the young, new director, visited us. I was struck by his easy, soft-spoken charm. When we shook hands he immediately suggested I call him Jack. "No, I can't call you Jack. You're the Director and you'll have to be Mr. Ingersoll," I replied. Perhaps it was the feeling that I was older that had prompted the gesture. He simply shrugged and laughed.

He immediately had his intramural woes. One was that his combined budget of about $8 million came from the old Bureau. We had been allocated $3 million and the Drug Abuse Control had $5 million. It made for automatic enmity. The people we considered amateurs got more money and faster promotions. Some of our agents had quit and gone to them and were promoted immediately from, say, Grade Nine to Grade Eleven and a year later went to Grade Twelve. The former colleagues of this turncoat would still remain at Grade Nine.

Despite such concerns, Ingersoll had everything going his way. His budget was to be increased in time to $72 million, he personally was making far more than Commissioner Anslinger had ever dreamed of getting, and he was well liked by the politicians who controlled our destiny. He could have been the top law enforcement officer in the United States. Unfortunately, it didn't work that way. He took bad advice. He surrounded himself with people with no background in narcotics enforcement and soon everyone lost sight of the simple fact that this was an enforcement agency. Yet at the time I was filled with enthusiasm as he explained how he planned to expand and operate. I was ready to put undercover work and roaming the streets behind me and try to be an administrator who would advise his agents, keep up on the cases, approve the purchases of evidence and payments to informers and all the other chores of "doing paper" as it was dismally referred to in the Bureau.

About then Dan Casey went to Washington, D.C. for a series of reorganization meetings. The power struggle was intricate and brutal as offices throughout the country were merged, selections made of who was to be in charge. The old Regions were wiped out and new titles were given to personnel. We, for example, were told that Arizona would be dropped, but we'd add Hawaii to Region Fourteen. Dan survived as Regional Director during the infighting and selected me as his Deputy Regional Director. They also moved our headquarters to Los Angeles. So the Kelly household's furniture wasn't even unpacked but sent on to Los Angeles where I moved to set up the local office while Dan decided to linger on, cleaning up in San Francisco for a month or two.

It was a tremendous task, putting the two bureaus together. We found space and moved the personnel into one big office. We set the chore of merging these embittered agents into groups with Group Supervisors. Tension ran high as people who had come into the work only six months before with high grades but no real experience were mingled with oldtimers who, under our lower budget, had not been promoted. This enmity was never really to pass. Even today, years later, the conflict and jealousies still emerge.

About this time Ingersoll made a fateful decision. He decided he didn't want Henry Giordano as Associate Director. He forced him to retire and Finlater became his deputy. It was ludicrous. One man was pushed out who'd spent a lifetime in narcotics enforcement. The other, who had never worked a day in law enforcement, let alone narcotics, took over. Finlater, of course, was to repay Ingersoll for his faith in him by releasing a statement as soon as he retired that he advocated the legalization of marijuana, adding that when he'd been with the Bureau he'd been forced to keep his mouth shut. This just wasn't so. In the field veteran agents were frustrated and bitter, remembering their companions who had been stabbed, shot, and beaten while this Johnny Come Lately with an important title made such carefree statements.

Now, a new policy began to seep out of Washington, D.C. and a new type of agent began to appear. He had at least one college degree, often several. Not that a college education was the problem. But the theory of what should be done was. Few had any law enforcement experience and priorities drifted more and more away from making arrests. Scientists, sociologists, physicians emerged. Their concerns, important and significant as they were, were with facets other than law enforcement—the root cause of crime, genetic factors in addiction, new drugs to use on addicts. Success and advancement hinged more and more around administration. The field agent making the bust, bringing in the heroin, was relegated to an unimportant role. Think tanks, discussions, long-range planning became primary functions. The street trade became unimportant as grandiose theorizing took over.

A variety of other changes came. When we had less than 300 men we had agents overseas controlling investigations. The State Department became involved in this process as has the CIA. The control was lost, not to mention the dangers of mixing drugs with international politics and intrigues.

In 1972, I went to Mexico City for a conference and was amazed to discover how deeply the State Department and CIA were involved. The CIA, for one thing, has to know the background and names of every informer we use in a foreign country. Yet, our narcotics agents can know nothing of CIA informers. This obviously presumes that the State Department and CIA officials are experts on drugs.

Trends on the domestic scene had become equally dismal. Ingersoll's new people started making innovations at a frantic rate, none of which had to do with enforcement. One such change was the "systems concept," as Ingersoll proudly dubbed it before a meeting of the Congressional Appropriations Committee. It called for our offices to outline the top "situation" or area, such as Tijuana, where problems existed. We were to give details on the top people in smuggling and peddling. All this sounded grand on paper and smacked of the romantic ideas about the drug trade found in movies and television, going after the big fish in the big pond. The Mafia leader in his big mansion, the warlords of the drug trade. As a practical result, however, it ended up with the Bureau losing its informers, its contacts on the street, what the gossip and the rumors were. Rather, we puzzled over position papers which were duly written, discussed, and filed. The old idea of working our way up by making a small case which would lead to the top layer of selling was forgotten. It reached the sorry point where we no longer even knew the going price of heroin on the street and had to call the local Police Department to find out what was going on. This led, quite understandably, to fewer cases, fewer arrests. I watched with frowning apprehension as these young so-called agents spent their days at the desk working on the growing piles of administrative detail papers and then going home at five o'clock, hours before the drug action on the street started. I had grown up in the world of the night, every night, prowling the bars, street corners, alleys, and junkie hangouts. Most of these newcomers had never seen a peddler. Was I wrong—a dinosaur of the past?

The vacuum had to be filled as the Bureau went more and more astray. It was Congress who finally forced a change through the President. It found form in a new organization, Drug Abuse Law Enforcement, known as DALE. Miles Ambrose, with a long and distinguished career as coordinator of all the Treasury law enforcement agencies and a former Commissioner of Customs, became head of DALE. It was to burgeon into what the old Bureau had been, finding the informers and making the cases, doing that which had been vacated.

The systems concept was to go through endless modifications and evolve into little. Today, some $730 million is the total budget of the anti-drug battle, yet the Bureau of Narcotics and Dangerous Drugs revived its estimates upward recently, numbering heroin addicts at 600,000 from 30,000, ten times what it was ten years ago and added the estimate that ten tons of heroin is being sold each year in the U.S. Hardly success!

Our projection seemed equally dismal. We blamed Turkey for many years for the flow of drugs into the U.S. We initiated a program to pay cash to stop the growing of opium poppies and aid the small farmers of that country in converting to other crops. Production dropped dramatically. But this, too, failed. Turkey announced in the spring of 1974 that it was returning to the old ways and cultivating the poppies again. Meanwhile, the United States had invested $35 million in the ill-fated effort.

The so-called Golden Triangle—Burma, Thailand, Laos—took over as the production centers during those years of Turkish calm. The CIA seemed to only wink at what was going on there as it seems the U.S. had allied itself with the remnants of Chiang Kai-shek's Army leaders, the Laotian generals who are leaders in exporting the opium crops from the backhill growers such as the Shawn and Meo Hill tribes. Its result can be found on the streets of Los Angeles today when one arrests an addict who has the fine, fluffy heroin known in the trade as China White. Since President Nixon's visit to China there has been a remarkable about-face in our official attitude toward Chinese drugs. For years every agent in the field was told repeatedly that a tremendous amount of opium came from Red China. Today the official line is that none comes from China, only Burma, Thailand, and Laos. I find this hard to believe. Recently in Hong Kong, police raided a heroin factory on the Chinese border and seized heroin valued at four to six million dollars based upon New York street prices. A half dozen similar raids have followed in the same area. Did all the opium for these labs come only from the Golden Triangle? If you'll forgive the pun, poppycock!

An added bit of chicanery involving domestic economics and lobbying is involved in the production of amphetamines and barbiturates. Quotas should be cut at least in half—which could easily be done under the 1970 Controlled Substances Act.

A final irony came in the 1970 legislation which both eliminated the mandatory sentence and reduced the crime of possession of such drugs as heroin and cocaine from a felony to a misdemeanor, punishable by not more than one year in prison. I find it particularly frustrating that "mere possession" of heroin is now a misdemeanor. Anyone who has dealt with the narcotics traffic knows that every addict is a potential peddler. In the midst of this cacaphony of politics, public relations, and cronyism the claim is that more drugs are seized than ever before. Why not? Today, there are five times the number of agents—1,500 as compared with 300 a few years ago— and a budget which went from $3 million to $70 million. But one can easily forget that the old Bureau placed the nation's top hoods in prison, Louie Lepke, Lucky Luciano, Vito Genovese. What has happened to the anonymous hoods who inherited their empires?

It has been nearly five years since I have gone out on a case. I have lost touch with the street. My elevation to Enforcement Assistant dimmed my perceptions of the daily drug fight. I became an administrator.

I mention this only to clarify that what I've said is not sour grapes. There's an expression used by regulars in the marines: "The Marine Corps ain't what it used to be and never was." I know that a patina of glamour comes with time as veterans look back to the old days. This is not the case in what I've said. The unhappy records show all too clearly that drug enforcement has gone down, down, down in the past few years.

15

The Brotherhood
of Eternal Love

In April, 1967, a team from the Bureau's office in Denver arrested a man who was manufacturing LSD in a laboratory in the back of a mobile van. The tablets were the ubiquitous Orange Sunshine. The Bureau had already analyzed these tablets by what one can call—for want of a better name—the ballistics system. By microscopic comparison it was possible to determine whether individual tablets were punched out of the same machine and, in some cases, we could even determine in what area the tablets had been made. If we were fortunate enough to seize a machine we could even determine the extent of distribution of these tablets through comparison with tablets throughout the U.S. By then we knew that Orange Sunshine tablets made up about 50 percent of all the LSD in the country. It was the beginning of a case which was to last six long years.

The suspect in Denver was running an elaborate plant, which he could move at a whim even if the weather was unpleasant. He had started in Oakland and moved slowly East. An agent in San Francisco had told our people in Colorado to be on the alert, and when they caught him, they found a quantity of LSD as well as a tableting machine and other equipment.

A Federal Court was to overturn the seizure on the basis of insufficient probable cause and go on to say that the search of the mobile lab was unconstitutional. There was nothing to do but release the man and give him back his mobile lab. He blithely drove off and went back to work making his regular rounds to supply local dealers. But one bit of lore did emerge from the seizure. The man belonged to an organization known by the poetic name of The Brotherhood of Eternal Love. In Region Fourteen a file had been growing on this mysterious group for months. In Los Angeles a young agent, Don Strange, had started collecting material on the Brotherhood more or less as a hobby. He was in our intelligence group and came to me one day in April, 1972 to outline his work. I was fascinated. Strange thought he'd pinpointed the base of operation, Laguna Beach, a quiet, seaside resort town in Orange County, south of Los Angeles. I told Strange to drop all his other duties and confine himself to the Brotherhood.

A few weeks later I asked the Orange County assistant District Attorney, Ed Freeman, to meet with us. Out of the talk grew a team we dubbed the Orange County Task Force. It included Internal Revenue Service Agents, U.S. Customs agents, California State Bureau of Narcotics agents, the Laguna Beach Police Department, the Orange County Sheriff's Office, the Newport Beach Police Department and the San Clemente Police Department and even the Maui, Hawaii Police Department. Ed Freeman took over as coordinator and I assigned two additional agents to work with Strange.

A few weeks later John Ingersoll, director of the Bureau, visited our office and told all the agents that he was anxious to change the enforcement thrust of the Bureau to task force operations concentrating on specific problems. When I told him we had one in progress already he was delighted and asked for a full report. In June, a week or so later, I had my report ready and forwarded it to Philip R. Smith, the Bureau's Chief of Special Projects. It outlined our team's organization and objectives and gave in detail what data we'd collected. I recommended a total complement of ten agents be assigned to the Brotherhood, two from San Francisco, one from Honolulu, three from Los Angeles and four from other regions and asked that the task force be funded with $100,000. With all this I included a report by Don Strange, the unofficial historian of The Brotherhood.

It was heady, even romantic, stuff. In 1963, Dr. Timothy Leary had departed Harvard University with a flourish. An iconoclast traveling under the banner of intellectual, he created such a furor that he'd been bounced by Harvard in the midst of wild publicity of a semi-religious sort. Leary not only advocated the use of LSD and marijuana but told students to drop out, turn on, and tune in on the great mysteries of the universe through the use of these drugs. If it was gobbledygook to the general public it enthralled thousands of kids who wanted nothing more than such academic and quasi-intellectual endorsement for their antics.

Leary moved on to Milbrook, New York, and started experimenting with other hallucinogenic drugs and founded the League of Spiritual Discovery which of course was derived from the initials LSD. It drew its religion-oriented ideas from the New American Church, the Southwest Indian cult which based its metaphysical concepts on the use of peyote as a way to gain mystical insights into life. Leary, now hailed as the High Priest of Mystical Thought, moved on to Berkeley, became the guru of the drug set and was lionized by faddists. In addition to such theatrics he was also to find his chief chemist in the years that followed and the manufacture of Orange Sunshine became a massive commercial project centered in San Francisco. To add an ironic touch, on October 26, 1966, the Brotherhood of Eternal Love became a legal corporation and was granted a tax exempt status by the California State Franchise Tax Board due to the religious nature of the organization as set forth in the articles of incorporation.

A year later the Orange Sunshine tablets began appearing all over the world. As they spread the LSD street price plummeted. In San Francisco, for example, a gram, which had cost $5000, dropped to $300. In cities across the country, depending upon their distance from the Bay Area, prices ranged between $850 and $1000. Too, the

Brotherhood started manufacturing LSD in another form and merchandising it as mescaline and STP. The unsuspecting never knew they were buying the same drug.

The market established, the Brotherhood began to look for new products. Marijuana, which had been the cornerstone of Leary's drug structure, was rather passe and available everywhere. So the Brotherhood came up with hashish and began importing it in massive quantities. Between 1966 and 1972 the Brotherhood brought 24 tons of hashish into the U.S.!

Moreover, from 1968 to 1971 they didn't lose a single pound through seizure until, late in 1971, U.S. Customs did manage to grab 800 pounds.

In December, 1968, Timothy Leary was arrested by the California narcotics unit in Laguna Beach where he was living with some members of the Brotherhood. The organization was by now a massive operation with an estimated 3000 members, although only about 400, it appears, were actively at work handling LSD and hashish.

Leary's arrest started a new surge of LSD production to finance his legal defense. He lost an array of appeals and was sentenced to California State Prison. In 1970 he was to escape the Men's Correctional Colony in San Luis Obispo and flee the country. (Supposedly the escape was arranged by the Weathermen faction of the Students for a Democratic Society for $5000 paid by the Brotherhood.) Leary, as was widely publicized, moved on to Algeria where he was welcomed by Eldridge Cleaver and elements of the Black Panther Party. When Cleaver and Leary fell out he fled to Switzerland. Somewhere along the line Leary's pretty wife, Rosemary, disappeared and he picked up with Mrs. Joanna Harcourt-Smith, a British subject who proclaimed their meeting as "instant love."

Leary was reported everywhere, Algiers, North Africa, Palestine, Lebanon, Austria. Then he emerged in Switzerland. U.S. officials tried to have him deported. The Swiss simply said he would have to leave but left the date of departure open. Rumor had it that

Leary was running the worldwide network of drug operations from overseas and that his attorneys visited him regularly.

This was the background when our task force was formed. I was pleased that I'd been a jump ahead of the new policy the Bureau was promoting and, when I went East for a few weeks, I awaited some grand results. I returned, was busy with other matters for a day or so, then thought I'd check progress with Don Strange. I called him for a report. He came into my office looking puzzled. "What do you mean, a progress report? Don't you know it's all been cancelled?"

It wasn't possible. "Hell, there's some mixup. I received approval for the $100,000 fund," I said. "I told the Orange County district attorney to go ahead before I left."

"Well, while you were away, Mr. Kelly, the head of the Intelligence Unit cancelled the task force." For administrative purposes the Task Force was under the Intelligence Unit's control.

I was in a rage. "Who the hell is he to cancel something approved by the Director!"

Don Strange shrugged. "All I know is that Mr. Freeman is mighty upset and waiting to talk with you. We've got leads in Maui and San Francisco and things happening in Costa Rica and the Honduras. But we are bogged down without money."

I ordered the intelligence head to my office. "What the hell is going on?" I demanded.

He explained that he just didn't think it was a good idea and had cancelled it.

"I want you to call Director Ingersoll on the phone and tell him he's been mistaken about this and that he's been misled. Tell him there's nothing to this Brotherhood of Eternal Love and that you decided to cancel it. You are going to countermand *his* orders as well as mine and tell him so!"

It was obvious his real motivation was simple jealousy. I went to see the Regional Director, Frank Pappas, and asked that Strange and other agents in the task force be removed from the Intelligence Unit and placed as a separate task force. He agreed. I then arranged

for a group supervisor, Lloyd Sinclair, to be placed in charge, then
called Ed Freeman to assure him that our plans were going on as
before and that we'd have funds available for making buys and
travel expenses.

We already had an outline of the Brotherhood's operations. It
was split into two elements: San Francisco handled LSD; Laguna
Beach arranged for the hashish smuggling. We knew the man in
charge of the hashish logistics. He was the focal point when a
syndicate of both Brotherhood members or outsiders put together a
fund to buy some hashish. He would take the money, arrange the
smuggling operation, and take a profit from the advance that had
been given him. The usual method was to have campers built in the
U.S. with various secret compartments. These were turned out by
one firm. They'd then be shipped overseas and the man in charge
would arrange for a hashish buy in Kabul, Afghanistan. A mule
would be given a passport with false identification. This was vital in
the operation as the Brotherhood could avoid prosecution by this
means. When Brotherhood members were arrested by local narcotics agents they'd simply use the false identification to obtain
release on a low bond. They'd then skip and it wouldn't be found out
until later that the identification was false. This happened again and
again.

The liaison man for the buy was known as the "load man" and
his mission was both to deliver the money and to oversee the
shipment back to the U.S. The campers would go to various locales,
perhaps Spain or maybe India. The load man would pick up the
vehicle, drive it to Afghanistan, load it with the hashish, and then
return it through various points of entry, usually ports which were
known to have minimum U.S. Customs security. Mexico and
Canada were also used at times. When the vehicle arrived, Customs
would notify the load man and a cleancut college youth with a
business suit and short hair would arrive to pick it up. Once cleared,
he'd notify the load man, who'd arrange with the investors to meet
him with the balance of the money at a prearranged spot and the
deal would be completed. It was estimated one load a month was

being shipped. Too, they'd sometimes go through Hawaii and bring the smaller loads in on domestic flights.

Some arrests were made. Customs seized 1330 pounds of hashish in Seattle and arrested four members of the Brotherhood. The Royal Canadian Mounted Police seized 720 pounds in Vancouver in a camper which was bound for Santa Barbara, California, and traced it directly to the leader in Laguna Beach. Mexican police picked up 1000 pounds in another camper. We could only guess how much more was getting through.

The Brotherhood dealt exclusively with two brothers in Kabul, Amanullah Salem Tokhi and his brother, Hyatullah. Both had visited the Los Angeles area and we'd obtained clandestine photos on them in December, 1971. The special Agent-in-Charge in Kabul, Terry Burke, had copies of the photographs.

He'd been working on the Brotherhood since its inception and had charted the pattern of operation.

The Brotherhood began to spread about this time, apparently deciding that hashish was also getting to be old hat. Hash is actually the resin of marijuana and, theoretically, about ten times as potent. Now the Brotherhood began experimenting with a more romantic version, hashish oil, a derivative that isn't too toxic and that has a not unpleasant odor. It's made by extracting the hashish with one of several volatile solvents including denatured alcohol. The liquid at one stage appears dark brown with a large amount of gray sediment which is made up mainly of cystoline hairs, small leaf fragments. As the solvent is evaporated the material becomes more viscous until it eventually looks like dark brown grease after the liquid solvents have been burned off in three processes of decanting. The finished product is poured into small containers and sold for $100 for ten cubic centimeters or about $300 an ounce. Afghanistan hashish has a concentration of oil to about 20 percent of the original weight of the hashish and is about three times as powerful as hashish or some 20 to 30 times as strong as marijuana. Obviously, it was in immediate demand when the Brotherhood began to market it.

Our task force was accumulating data, gathering names of members involved in the manufacture and sale of Orange Sunshine, LSD, hashish, hashish oil, and some cocaine. The LSD had been encountered in almost every state in the U.S. and 12 foreign countries. The task force, too, had obtained 24 federal indictments for passport violations. Our entire thrust was in three principal categories, violations of Federal narcotics laws, California laws, and passport regulations.

It was all to come to a head on July 29, 1972. After weeks of testimony before the Orange County Grand Jury, federal, state, and local narcotics agents began a roundup of indicted individuals at six in the morning. Assault teams included federal agents, IRS and customs agents, and the state and local narcotics agents. Arrests were made in Maui, Hawaii, Santa Barbara, Oregon, San Jose, San Diego, and other California cities. Agents such as Terry Burke had to be brought from all over the world to testify. The amount of drugs seized or purchased up to that time was 4,500 pounds of hashish, 1,500,000 Orange Sunshine tablets, three LSD labs and four hashish pill labs with 30 gallons of hashish oil. On August 3, 1972, we arrested 45 people and seized two more hashish oil labs, three autos, $40,000 in cash, and an unlimited quantity of controlled substances. Timothy Leary in the original indictment had bond set at $5 million. Agents were being dispatched to such places as Vermont and Costa Rica and Australia and another special agent, Gary Elliott, seized still another LSD lab in Honduras.

As for Leary, he was recognized by our agent, Terry Burke, in Kabul with Mrs. Joanna Harcourt-Smith. He persuaded Afghanistan officials to put Leary under house arrest. Mrs. Harcourt-Smith was to explain what had gone on. They had driven from Switzerland to Vienna in Leary's yellow Porsche to make an anti-addiction film, she said, explaining that she and Leary were opposed to heroin, cocaine, television, and autos and "anything else that is addictive."

They had been asked to leave Austria, gone on to Beirut, then flown to Kabul. Burke brought them back through Frankfort and

London to Los Angeles and fittingly, Don Strange, who had first collected the lore on the Brotherhood, took them into custody. When Leary was brought off the plane 50 police officers were needed to hold back the fans. He was put in a Volkswagen bus surrounded by twelve patrol cars and taken to jail. He was charged with escape for fleeing prison and still faced the original one-to-ten-year sentence for possession of narcotics in Laguna Beach. He was charged with nineteen counts for smuggling and conspiracy to smuggle narcotics, faced tax evasion charges filed by both California and the Federal Government which were estimated at $76 million! The Brotherhood itself had been involved in 130 passport violations.

In 1974 an array of defendants went on trial in San Francisco and the convictions came pouring out.

It is safe to say the Brotherhood is no more. In fact in 1974 the State of California announced that the Brotherhood was no longer a valid corporation. It wasn't non-profit after all, a spokesman explained.

16

Coke

The crisis of the Flower Children and LSD as an epidemic has slowly faded away. But it's been replaced in 1974 with a new virulent social infection of perhaps worse proportions.

What now seems centuries ago in New York, I knew a gangly black con man with the unlikely name of Spider. He was a comparative oddity in the world of drugs at the time, a cocaine sniffer. He was a fine informer, holding heroin addicts in scorn and he was also an outspoken advocate of his own habit. "I been using it for 20 years and never had a cold," he would brag to me. It may have been true. But the septum of Spider's nose had been eaten away, presumably from cocaine sniffing.

Today, bankers, businessmen, people in the film business—all use coke in fashionable Los Angeles. It's the "in" thing to do. They have all heard the street stories: heroin is addictive, cocaine isn't. (That there is such a thing as habitual addiction as well as physical addiction is something they'd prefer not to understand.) In Beverly Hills and along the Sunset Strip expensive silversmiths sell tiny spoons to be worn on keychains. One may look like a Rolls Royce radiator, another an erect penis, another a heavy silver container ("so if you have to throw it away in a hurry") attached to a ball and chain.

227

Even if there was a law to cover such implements used for sniffing cocaine, no one would care.

The price of coke changes almost daily, varying from $900 to $1500 an ounce.

A heavy coke user can want fifty good hits a day and even a moderate user will take eight or ten a day. Sniffing is the accepted etiquette but it can be smoked, shot up with water, rubbed in the mouth or even on the genitals or put under the eyelids where it burns for a euphoric high. At parties a group may use a mirror. The cocaine is poured out on the mirror on a table, sectioned off into "rails" and snorted through the end of an eyedropper. This ease is one of its fascinations. One user told me "I've even watched people use it on network talk shows and no one realizes the guy is taking a hit."

With the wild and fluctuating market today street coke is often only 30 percent pure and cut with speed, but 50 percent is considered good. There are ways to test it. If rubbed on the gum you can tell by the numbness if it's been cut with procaine. If it's been cut with speed it can be mixed with Clorox and the degree of redness will tell its purity. Other cuts are B12 and a baby laxative, Mineta.

This new drug of preference offers what users call a "soft speed." Unlike heroin, which creates a state of being "on the nod," coke leads to a wild activity, a sense of euphoria, and increase in the sex drive. Medically, since it is not an opiate, it's classified as a stimulant. Spider once explained to me this sense of wild perception and awareness. "I was going ape with a scratching noise and couldn't figure where it was coming from. Then I saw it. A cockroach was crawling along the floor . . . "

Some users claim it helps their work. One told me, "It makes you very sharp. You feel you are on top of everything, you think you have it all licked." His wife didn't feel the same. "He pretends to work but nothing really happens," she explained.

In 1971 our Los Angeles office received word of Operation Eagle. It was a concerted drive throughout the U.S. to round up Cubans, the major smugglers, involved in the cocaine traffic. It was also official recognition that we had a new major peril at hand.

Our agents did their best in Los Angeles but we were only able to produce six Cuban peddlers. The Bureau complained, pointing out that other Regions had found scores of peddlers. The reason was simple. There were few Cubans in Southern California. But that was soon to change. Not only was there a rapid influx of Cuban peddlers but a shift in other crimes indicated that the use of cocaine was burgeoning. While heroin addicts tend to be passive and steal for their habit through burglary and shoplifting, cocaine addicts prefer crimes of violence while on a high. Muggings, purse-snatching, attacks of various sorts become their choice. Indeed, when the killers of Murder Inc. were finally rounded up it was found that the gang always sniffed cocaine before they went on one of their missions.

In New York cocaine has made massive inroads. With the temporary closing down of Turkish imports and the conclusion of the case of the French Connection the prices for heroin more than doubled on the Eastern seaboard. But cocaine was another matter, even though the price today fluctuates wildly. It was to be had everywhere and hundreds of entrepreneurs were in the act. While newspapers reported heroin doings almost daily, cocaine came quietly in the backdoor and was soon the silent market leader in many major cities.

It also became the preferred drug among addicts who use more than one drug. For the users of speed it offered a fast and exciting high without a needle. Affluent black users soon made it the fashionable "in" drug in colored areas and it is even considered proper for dealers to sniff cocaine while they look down on heroin users as only necessary scum. Latin Americans adopted this same attitude and among white users such as writers, artists, and rock singers it became a chic luxury item.

Users emerged everywhere. They had only one thing in common—money. Even while supplies of cocaine leapt so did the users and the prices went higher and higher. Today, a pound of cocaine will bring upwards of $16,000 in the Eastern cities; on the street it bounced between $7 and $10 for a grain and the inflation continues.

It costs more, too, for a user to maintain a high. A cocaine user must snort a dozen times a night to stay up. A heroin addict can go on the nod for the same length of time with one shot. Such a night of fun for a sniffer costs between $75 to $100.

To add to the dilemma, the coca leaf (not related to the cocoa bean) grows wild over much of South America and when cultivated in such areas as the Andes the bush starts generating the coca alkaloid within two years and the crop of leaves can be picked six times a year and will produce for up to 30 years. More than that, it is intricately woven into the customs and economics of many South American countries. Peasants have used the leaf to chew for centuries as a pacifier. To try to stop its growth would be to try to police an entire continent.

The survivors of Batista's days who escaped to Miami when Castro took control grabbed the cocaine market first. But they soon found themselves in competition with scores of top dealers in Chili, Peru, and other countries. Hundreds of small landing strips across South America became the focal points for cocaine smuggling. The planes, flying at low altitudes and with extra gas tanks to give them up to 2400-mile ranges, beneath radar monitoring move the cocaine into Mexico, Louisiana, Texas, and on to New York, Chicago, and Los Angeles. Like big heroin dealers, cocaine operators often never even see the cocaine, moving it north through mules and simply handling the financial transactions as the prices soar as it comes into the U.S.

One problem has emerged for the big dealers. These mules or couriers in their employ tend to become ambitious and form their own operations. They'll make a few runs to New York, for example, then start branching out on their own. Perhaps they'll arrange with relatives to make some charter flights to visit South America where a kilo of cocaine will cost $2000. Back in the U.S. it's worth $30,000.

This splintering has presented a new problem. Hundreds of small-time operators are in the act on their own. The old approach of working up to a big supplier often falls apart. The peddler you arrest may be the total "organization" as this new army of freelancers swarms about.

In terms of sociology of the underworld it has even wider implications. If the trend continues it means that the Mafia, which has had control of at least half of the drug traffic in the U.S., will continue to lose ground to these amateur operators. In organized crime snuffing out a rival gang is one thing. Trying to contain hundreds of smalltime dealers is another. Since the source of supply is the whole massive continent to the South there is no way to keep control there. Since refining cocaine requires no expensive secret lab, there is no way to channel the product. All it takes to go into the cocaine business is a few thousand dollars and some nerve. The spectacle of what is to come is awesome.

17

Hollywood Stars

In Los Angeles I soon had to face head-on the confusions of Hollywood as a social and economic force. While much of our task involved enforcement in greater Los Angeles we heard almost daily wild rumors and tales of goings-on among film people. In New York, years before I'd face some of this with endless gossip about Broadway stars or other celebrities who were supposedly buying or peddling. I learned then to take such stories with a large grain of salt. In dealing with Hollywood this same situation applied, but to ludicrous extent. It seemed half the informers and addicts had some story of some star who was shooting heroin or sniffing coke. The efforts to identify their own forlorn drug habit as fashionable by such claims of celebrities doing the same were endless.

Yet, even as we tended to ignore such gossip, there was the problem of leaning so far backwards that we could fall on our butts. We had to listen when we'd hear the same story repeated again and again. Certain things were true. The daughter of a famous movie sex symbol is a peddler in Beverly Hills right now. There's a former child star who has the reputation of being a large cocaine peddler although no arrest has been made. We hear again and again of several stars who were regular buyers. Generally, we discovered, the children of stars seemed particularly likely to be involved with drugs, perhaps because of the difficult family life so many had faced.

Past this negative aspect, however, there were scores of film leaders and top actors who were the first to step forward to aid in the fight against drugs. Almost by osmosis I soon found myself involved as a liaison man between the Bureau and some of these people eager to help us.

One was Paul Frees. Dan Casey and I first knew him in San Francisco where he was a lieutenant in the Sheriff's office working fulltime and donating his salary to charity. We had recommended him as a consultant for the Bureau to help us in tying us into the entertainment industry in television, training films, and movies.

Paul, who was a "voice", had done hundreds of television commercials, many of the voices at Disneyland (such as all the pirates when they are shouting at one another in the Pirates of the Caribbean show), and the voice of Dr. Phibes in the movie. Most important, he understood police work as well as most facets of the entertainment industry and had volunteered his services. He could have handled the daily requests the Bureau received from companies wanting to use our name or seal in some production.

Paul took this all very seriously. The Bureau, for example, was looking for a likely movie or television series to promote the new image. Paul started discussing the idea with Jackie Cooper at Screen Gems and Vaughn Paul, the former husband of Deanna Durbin, who headed still another production company. They offered to do free training films for the Bureau. A variety of proposals were made but nothing happened. Frees finally gave up in despair. "I'm defeated and completely beaten down," he explained to me. "They just won't move on anything."

About this time the Bureau started a recruiting drive to get more agents from minority groups. We badly needed good undercover agents to work with minorities where most of the action took place. But Mexican-Americans and blacks are generally disillusioned with law enforcement and, if they had the education, still weren't interested. The Bureau, frustrated in the drive, sent a letter to all field offices taking us to task for not fulfilling the recruiting needs.

I decided an appeal through radio might help. We had all kinds of taping equipment and trained personnel and I started asking minority celebrities if they'd lend a hand. Almost to a man, they volunteered. Sammy Davis, Jr., Greg Morris, Ricardo Montalban, Juan Marichal, Jose Cardenal all offered their services free. I outlined my plan to the Bureau. We'd record the spots on our own tape casettes and send copies to all of our major offices. They, in turn, could duplicate them and ask local radio stations to play them as a public service in the drive for recruiting minorities. It would cost the Bureau practically nothing.

I waited for a reply to my proposal. Silence. Finally, I called Joe Flanders, the Public Information Officer.

"What's happened?" I asked.

"I'm afraid they turned it down," he replied.

"Why?" I asked, flabbergasted. "It's all free, using people who could cost a fortune."

"Well," Joe said weakly. "They turned it down."

"Who are 'they'?" I demanded.

"Mr. Ingersoll's staff voted against it."

I hung up in disgust, thinking of the time I'd spent trying to develop the project and the confusion of having it rejected without the simple courtesy of even being notified. Later, I was to find, there was a separate section which handled such matters made up of the non-professionals. Their singular policy was to reject anything that didn't originate with them. I sat back musing over my annoyance and frustration. Had I turned into one of those "oldtimers" who grumble about everything? Was my growing apprehension plain old sourgrapes over changing times? Were things really going to pieces or was I too simple-minded to recognize the "big picture" out here in the field?

I thought of another suggestion we'd made in the field of public relations. The Customs Agency Service had a program on the border which paid informants who reported shipments of narcotics. They had a set chart of figures they'd pay, $500 for information that led to the seizure of a kilo of heroin and the like. We suggested a similar program offering a reward for the apprehension of narcotics with posters in airports, railroad and bus stations and piers. Only silence.

Again, Andy Williams approached me. Ardently interested in the drug fight, he'd worked out a spot idea for television with Jonathan Winters, who would donate his time. I wrote the Bureau explaining Williams' idea. Again, there was only silence. Williams, after several efforts to find out what had happened, dropped it.

Meanwhile, both Ingersoll and Finlater asked me about a television series or, perhaps, a movie based upon the Bureau. I brought up the disenchantment of Paul Frees. Ingersoll agreed that this had been unfortunate, but to keep trying.

Some weeks later I happened to be with Buddy Ruskin, a onetime Los Angeles Deputy Sheriff, who had created the television series, "Mod Squad," written the screenplay for the movie, *The Clay Pigeon* and a book, *The Decline and Fall of Beverly Hills.*

I told him of Ingersoll's request. Buddy mused over it and concluded, "That sounds interesting. Let me see what I can do."

Not long after, he submitted to me a presentation titled "B.N.D.D.", a television series idea which would have called for the use of the Bureau seal and the like. I forwarded the material to Finlater, as Ingersoll was away, in July, 1971.

Shortly afterward, Ingersoll wrote Buddy and said the idea seemed sound. Buddy went to Filmways to talk with Richard Brown, then in charge of television. I was called into several meetings, Brown and Buddy worked out their separate financial deal, and things seemed ready to move ahead. I notified Ingersoll. As he was due in Los Angeles a luncheon was arranged at the Polo Lounge at the Beverly Hills Hotel. We met and Brown brought his then wife, Eva Gabor. All went well and Ingersoll agreed to everything Richard Brown explained.

At last, I thought, something has come off. A series of phone calls followed and Brown called me, explaining that he, the President of his firm, Martin Ransohoff, and their attorney were flying to Washington to sign the contracts between the Department of Justice and Filmways Studios. He asked me about coming back with them. "Hell, you set the whole thing up," he said.

I called to ask permission but was told that Ingersoll felt it was all too premature and didn't want me to come back. They departed. The contracts were signed and all looked right with the world.

Brown called me soon after he returned. "You know," he said, "I'm kind of astounded at your Bureau. I really don't understand them."

"Why?"

"This fellow Finlater just called me. He told me that I am not to talk to you anymore and that if I want anything I'm to call him personally. I asked if you could be assigned as technical advisor and he turned me down."

I felt deflated but decided they didn't want me involved in projects outside the office. Then, to rub a bit of salt in the wound, an agent in the office, Mike Antonelli, came in. "Finlater just called to tell me I'm going to be the technical advisor on that television series—but not to tell you." I didn't know whether to laugh or cry.

That same month came a sort of coup de grace. Finlater was to arrive at Disneyland for a convention of the International Association of Chiefs of Police. Many of the Bureau's personnel were going to be there and have a Regional Director's Conference with Ingersoll.

Finlater called. "My wife and I have never seen a film studio," he explained blithely. "Do you think you could set up a tour?"

I marveled at his callous gall. "Sure," I agreed.

"Call me back and let me know," he requested.

I thought a touch of irony was in order. I called Richard Brown at Filmways and asked if he could arrange a tour since the series was to be produced there.

"Sure, that's no problem at all," he agreed immediately. "In fact, I'll tell you what! I'll arrange for Eva to call some friends and we'll have a dinner party for the Finlaters. You and your wife are invited now and we'll have some stars too."

"That's wonderful, Dick," I said. "That's far better than this guy deserves."

I called Finlater in Washington and told him of the plans. "That's very nice," he said happily. "Do you have Richard Brown's phone number?" I gave it to him.

The next day I received a call from Brown. "You know, I've said all along there's something odd with that Bureau of yours. Now I know damn well there is. It isn't just the Bureau, it's the personnel in it. This guy Finlater just called me to thank me for the dinner party but he only had one request. That you and your wife not be invited!"

"You're kidding me, I hope," I said.

"Nope. He said that he was the Deputy Director and you were only a Deputy Regional Director and he didn't think it was right that the two of you go to the same dinner party."

All I could do was chuckle a bit hysterically. "Okay. I don't want to put you on the spot. Thanks for telling me. Forget it."

Brown's voice was abrasive. "Forget it is right! There isn't going to be any dinner party. This is the end of it as far as I'm concerned."

There was no dinner party. The series never came off.

18

Scapegoat

The Los Angeles Police Department is the finest police department I've ever encountered in the United States. Professional and honest, the officers are well educated and well trained. The department has a program to adjust shifts in order that any officer can go on to college, get graduate degrees or law degrees. This is encouraged and promoted.

Naturally, there are a few bad officers. The Internal Affairs Bureau moves in quickly when trouble emerges. There is no effort to cover, to pussyfoot. The Department is the first to prosecute a bad cop.

One of my agents came into my office to outline a case that involved a screenwriter and film editor named John McCarthy and his partner, the peddler, Adolph Shaffee. The agent had set up a buy from Shaffee in a rather brazen gesture right across from our office in a Colonel Sanders Kentucky Fried Chicken stand for two the next afternoon. The idea: to photograph the purchase with a movie camera from the second floor.

I was with the cameraman to watch it the next day. Our undercover agent, Bob Sternaman, was loitering in the parking lot when Shaffee drove in. He parked, got out, and chatted a moment with Bob, who handed him the money. The peddler then returned to his car, got a package, and handed it to Bob and drove away.

It was all so simple and we were delighted. The case grew as agents made added buys from McCarthy. Then one day the agent handling the case explained to me, "We have information a cop is involved."

"How come?" I asked, rather amazed that an LAPD officer would be on the take.

"Shaffee just keeps hinting that a cop is in on it. We've tried to tail him but had no luck."

"Stick with it and put intensive surveillance on both McCarthy and Shaffee from now on," I ordered.

A week later the agent was back. "We've found the cop they're meeting with. He's Hardy Lee Furnaman, a sergeant in the Intelligence Division."

This puzzled me more. The Intelligence Division is where superior officers are assigned and it's considered an elite unit. It was sticky. Was he working the case, too? If so, why? I didn't want to jump into the middle of some delicate situation. "Just keep building the file," I said. "And don't talk about it."

It soon became clear Furnaman was the source for the other two. His toll calls indicated he was in the drug trade and whispers began coming in from informers and street people that a cop was moving drugs.

I decided it was time to move. I called Charley Reese, commanding officer of the LAPD detective bureau and an old friend. I told him what we had. "I want to cooperate with the department on this," I explained.

A few minutes later two officers from Internal Affairs arrived. We worked out a plan, arranging a buy from Shaffee on a corner in Van Nuys, a suburb. LAPD narcotics officers joined in, we got search and arrest warrants, and tailed Shaffee to McCarthy's apartment in Hollywood, then to Furnaman's house in Van Nuys. When Bob Sternaman made the pre-arranged buy of 35 ounces of cocaine we moved in, grabbing McCarthy, who had three more ounces, and then raided Furnaman's house, taking him and his wife into custody after finding ten ounces of heroin in the refrigerator and another six in a paper bag on a nightstand. The rest was handled with efficient alacrity by the Internal Affairs Bureau. We released a joint statement on the arrest, Furnaman resigned and later was given a long sentence in federal prison.

I admit to being rather pleased with the way I'd handled it all. There were no ruffled feelings and bureaucratic diplomacy had been preserved. I was indeed becoming an administrator, I decided. Little did I suspect that I had a long way to go.

Some strange twists emerged in Los Angeles. We received data through the duplicates of wholesale drug firm order forms of a massive amount of amphetamines being ordered by one doctor. A bit of investigation showed he was a hopeless alcoholic who was working for a promoter of four weight reducing parlors in satellite towns around Los Angeles—Long Beach, San Gabriel, El Monte, and Montebello. Unsuspecting housewives were being charged huge fees by the "consultants" whose only treatment were amphetamines and methamphetamines. Soon the good ladies were hooked and, naturally, lost weight because they quit eating.

An undercover man was assigned who managed to make buys at all four establishments, then managed to meet with the owner, who had a previous conviction for abortion in Pomona Superior Court. Our agent asked him bluntly, "I've got a lot of friends who'd like to get in on this. How many pills can you sell me?"

The quack saw a fast buck. "I'll tell you right now, I wouldn't sell you less than a hundred thousand."

Our agent agreed and soon after bought 100,000 amphetamine tablets and 60 vials of 30 cc liquid methamphetamine, known as "speed" in the drug traffic. He paid $4600 for the lot although the legal value was about $45.

That transaction completed, we arrested him and his day of glory was over.

In December, 1971, Dan Casey was transferred to New York to a bigger assignment, Regional Director of Region Two. It was a sad parting. The two of us had been jokingly called the Irish Mafia in the Bureau as we were so close. He asked me to go with him as his Deputy. I discussed it with my family and we decided against returning to the living conditions of the East. A month later Frank Pappas was named the new Regional Director, a man I'd known for years and one with a reputation for being a top administrator. I had nothing against him but had always felt he had two major flaws. He knew little about enforcement work and was inept at handling men. But, if he left me alone to handle enforcement work I saw no reason for conflict.

Then a series of incidents began to accumlate. I was proud that we were obviously going into the best year in Region Fourteen's history in terms of enforcement. Yet, I sensed the deterioration setting in as the emphasis shifted more and more toward administrative procedures.

Morale among field agents is always a delicate problem. Some can act like prima donnas, others revel in a chance to feel hurt. But most are firm realists. One day we were gathered around the radio in our communications center in high excitement as we listened to a drama. Some of our agents had chased a man in a camper who they knew had five hundred pounds of marijuana. Now, he had turned the caper on them and was trying to ram them off the edge of a cliff. They were firing back. All this was coming to us over the car radio.

Pappas strolled in. "What's going on?" he inquired.

"A couple of agents are involved in a shootout," an agent replied hurriedly.

Pappas nodded. "Is that right?" he said absently. "Have you seen the administrative officer?"

Word of his nonchalance about his own agents swept through the office in minutes.

Pappas brought in a new Assistant Regional Director and Intelligence Director. A concerted policy began to undermine enforcement as the agents' morale declined. Trying to play the administrative game, I submitted an enforcement study I'd started under Casey. It was ignored. A Friday ritual had always been the meeting on enforcement. Dan Casey, who'd been swamped with administrative chores, always enjoyed these sessions when cases and busts were discussed. He felt it was somehow the ultimate purpose of all the paperwork. Not Pappas. At the first meeting he attended he announced to the group supervisors, "I don't want to know anything about enforcement. I'm only interested in administrative problems." The men were shocked. It was much like a colonel telling a frontline soldier that what they were doing wasn't important, that keeping the records straight was what really mattered.

One factor was apparent soon after Pappas arrived: the sticky problem of minority discrimination among agents. The Regional Director usually reflects the mood of the office on such matters. Minorities are used freely in undercover work but a subtle change develops in promoting them to executive jobs. There is, for example, only one black Regional Director, Art Lewis in Philadelphia, who started as a clerk in New York City. There is some feeling that tokenism was the major reason he was given the Philadelphia post. As for Mexican-Americans, there is no Regional or Deputy Director in the U.S. and only one Assistant Regional Director, Joe Baca in Los Angeles.

Pappas told me soon after he arrived, "I'm transferring a fellow out from Washington, Ike Wurns. He's a protege of mine and will be your backup man as an Assistant Regional Director."

"Come on," I complained. "You can't do that. Wurns hasn't been in the field for four years. He's a paper-shuffling inspector in Washington. It would mean he'd be running enforcement when I'm out of the office for the entire Region. He's just not qualified."

"I can put whoever I please in," Pappas replied.

"Joe Baca is the senior man. He's spent his entire career in this Region and knows the personnel and the area inside out."

Pappas simply shook his head. A short time later Wurns was transferred. Soon after Pappas told me that Wurns was to handle all the branch offices except San Francisco, which came under my jurisdiction.

I complained again. "You're making a mistake. Joe Baca speaks fluent Spanish and we have two offices at the border—Calexico and San Diego. We have to deal with the Mexican Federal Judicial Police. Joe knows them all. And remember, all the defendants are Spanish down there."

Pappas simply repeated himself. "I can put whoever I please in." This continuing policy was, of course, a terrible blow to Joe's pride.

Still another top agent was Sergio Borquez. He's an electronics expert, a wiretapper, a lockpick expert and one of the finest undercover agents. He, too, had blood like ice water. Several years ago he killed a man in an undercover situation. Soon after a framed picture of the victim appeared in his office.

"He must be wacky," some agents said. I asked him one day why he kept the picture on his wall.

Serge grinned. "I know they think I'm off my rocker. But I keep it there to remind me never to relax or let down my guard. Every time I look at his picture I remember again never to turn my back."

Serge was promoted because of his excellence to a Grade Thirteen, which Dan Casey got for him. There was no opening as a Group Supervisor so he was known as a Street Thirteen, filling in when Group Supervisors were on vacation until the day an opening came. Then when Pappas took over he brought in a new man from Baltimore to head our intelligence unit, a man who'd never worked in a large Region. Serge was simply outflanked in the unit where he'd been Acting Group Supervisor and, to add more injury, Pappas refused to even allow Serge to be the backup man, taking a Grade Eleven for the post.

In March, 1974, Vincent T. Oliver, deputy personnel director for DEA testified before the subcommittee on Civil Rights and Constitutional Rights of the House Judiciary Committee. He stated: "I submit to you in good conscience and in my best professional judgment, the Drug Enforcement Administration is currently engaged in a conspiracy to limit the number of blacks and other minority Special Agent candidates hired to no more than token proportions. . . ." He went on to accuse DEA of being guilty of conspiracy in violation of the Civil Rights Act of 1964, outlining a variety of specific cases and general policies.

Such discrimination seemed commonplace. One young agent nicknamed Chili was a fine undercover man but enjoyed his fun. He failed to show for radio duty one day. He was suspended for a few days and received a letter of reprimand. He'd theoretically paid his price for his minor wrongdoing. From that time on, however, he has never received a promotion. He was scheduled for an in-grade raise that he didn't get. The Mexican-Americans ask, "Why does it always·happen to us?"

Such tensions grew and rumors spread. I heard through the grapevine that Washington knew and was concerned about the discontent. The day came when Ingersoll visited. I was called into Pappas' office for a conference.

"Would you like a transfer?" the Director asked.

"No," I replied. "I like Los Angeles."

"How do you get along with Pappas?"

"Pretty good," I said hesitantly.

"What do you mean by that? I don't want you to get along pretty good. I want you to get along real good."

I glanced at Pappas, who sat stony-faced. "We get along all right," I modified.

"I detect you don't get along as well as with Dan Casey," Ingersoll added.

"That's true," I agreed. "Dan was a personal friend. Frank and I never will be. We are two entirely different types and just never will get on socially. But that's no reason I can't work with him." I resented the whole tone of this inquiry.

"Has Frank a complaint against me?" I asked bluntly.

"Oh, no—no."

"Well, I don't understand this. Are you dissatisfied with my work?"

Ingersoll shook his head. "Definitely not. You've done a fine job and can stay here as long as you wish." It was a bewildering encounter.

A few months later a nuclear blast was to come. Ingersoll received an anonymous letter from our office. It was bitter and angry, saying that enforcement was being completely ignored. Worse still, copies of it had been mailed to a number of police and sheriff's offices in the area. The implications were jarring. Although I had no idea who had sent it, I felt somehow responsible.

A few days later Ed Kelly, the Director's Executive Assistant, arrived. I'd already seen the letter and told him so. In addition to complaints it called for a moratorium on drug seizures, grievance with Civil Service, and the suggestion that the "facts" be sent to Los Angeles political leaders and the news media.

Before the questioning began I made a statement to him. "I don't think I should be questioned. I don't know who wrote the letter. If you want to talk to any agent, fine. But unless this is official questioning, I think you should talk to them."

Kelly shrugged, indicating that he felt the whole matter involved only a disgruntled agent or so. He started his interrogations. Fifteen agents later, he came to me, deeply upset. "I didn't realize things were that bad," he murmured.

I suggested he also confer with the former Executive Assistant, Dick Callahan, who was in San Francisco. Kelly departed. We heard nothing more of the letter.

An uneasy peace settled in until September, 1972. Then a second letter arrived at the Director's desk filled with bitter details and complaints.

It was bad enough as it was, but the timing made it worse. About this time the Agent-in-Charge of the FBI in Los Angeles had received a barrage of bad publicity. He'd been reduced in rank and transferred. He didn't report for duty and was going to be fired. Then he resigned. The press flurry had been nationwide.

Ingersoll was fearful of the same sort of scandal. An Inspection Service team came to Los Angeles. Long interrogations of all agents began. Their report showed that Pappas and the team of aides he'd brought in were harassing my enforcement agents and even following them.

About that time I went to a meeting of Deputy Regional Directors in Washington, D.C. I met with the Deputy Chief Inspector, Walter Panich, an old friend, in my room to find out what was happening. He explained: "Something has to be done. I think Pappas should be transferred but there are two things against it. First, what can happen if an agent's anonymous letter can get a Regional Director transferred?"

"I don't see it that way," I replied. "It's the inspection that would cause the transfer. Not the letter."

"Well, there's a more important reason. Ingersoll selected him for that office and Ingersoll doesn't like to be wrong. Ingersoll won't transfer him."

Dim as I was in operating in such intrigues I suddenly had the feeling that a scapegoat was a serious likelihood. And I thought I knew who it could well be.

"That leaves a couple of alternatives," Panich continued. "I could recommend that the Deputy Regional Director and all three Assistant Regional Directors be transferred as well as the two Group Supervisors."

I was furious at such a suggestion. "I'm really going to be pissed off if that happens. It's completely unjustified and I'm not involved in this thing."

Panich shook his head. "Sure you are. The thing is all the men are following you, not Pappas. That makes it very bad for him."

"Are you suggesting I'm trying to undermine him?" I asked heatedly.

"Absolutely not. There's no indication of that. But it doesn't change the fact that the men are in back of you."

"I thought one of the prerequisites for a job like this was leadership qualities. So I have it and he doesn't. That's not my fault but his. And it sounds like I'm likely to be the victim."

Panich sighed. "Yeah, but I don't know what to do."

Someone did. A few months later I received orders to transfer to Washington, D.C. along with one Assistant Regional Director and a Group Supervisor.

From my viewpoint it could only be interpreted as a demotion and that I had become the sacrificial lamb. Further, I was still under constant medical care recuperating from my bout with cancer. I wrote Ingersoll, explaining that I was under the care of three physicians and was having extensive dental work that required changes involving the entire structure of my mouth. "I have never been notified of any deficiency in my work and this reduction in rank is embarrassing and humiliating to me," I noted.

His reply some two weeks later gave no quarter. He pointed out that there were adequate medical facilities in Washington, D.C. and disclaimed any idea that the chaos in morale in the Los Angeles office was a factor. "With respect to any implied reduction in rank, I can emphatically assure you that a responsible staff position in Headquarters can in no way be viewed by me as a reduction in responsibility or performance requirements." He ordered me to report January 7, 1973.

I saw no alternative but to claim sick leave and enclosed letters from three doctors outlining my condition, adding that I would notify the Bureau when I was able to return to work.

In June, 1973, I received a service pin in recognition of my 20 years' service from Ingersoll. It was really a fitting and appropriate finale. For I'd received a 20-year pin in 1968 and was only three months short of being eligible for a 25-year pin when I retired.

It was my last word from Ingersoll, this silly but so significant bit of foulup. A short time later he departed the Bureau and went with IBM overseas.

19

Drug Enforcement Today

I retired June 30, 1973. So, by amazing coincidence, did the Bureau of Narcotics and Dangerous Drugs! Effective July 1, 1973, pursuant to a Presidential Directive Order, BNDD, the U.S. Customs Agency Service, the Drug Abuse Law Enforcement Service, and a section of the Justice Department—allegedly a Drug Intelligence function—all merged into an office called the Drug Enforcement Administration.

The very name should have been an obvious tipoff to the agents. For the road to heaven is being an administrator and the emphasis shifted away from enforcement completely.

Ingersoll departed with bitterness. He called a press conference and tried to involve himself in the backlash of the Watergate debacle by condemning Nixon's aides, Haldeman and Ehrlichman, for the crisis which had descended upon him. To the end he refused to face up to his own deficiencies and recognize his lack of leadership. Miles Ambrose—a notorious job-jumper from the New York Waterfront Commission to U.S. Treasury Enforcement Coordinator to Commission of U.S. Customs to Director of the Office of Drug Abuse Law Enforcement—decided, in the face of certain difficulties that had been aired in the press, to enter private law practice. He had been in open conflict with the Bureau of Narcotics and Dangerous Drugs again and again and his running feud with Ingersoll had flared up again and again.

When President Nixon ordered the merger Ambrose was the leader in structuring the new organization. As a result he took his revenge for his years of frustration with his enemy, the Bureau of Narcotics. He started by appointing his assistant, John R. Bartels, to head up the new Drug Enforcement Administration. His next step was to place U.S. Customs agents in charge of the key offices such as New York, Miami, Dallas, Seattle, Los Angeles, Mexico and South America. I am sure he departed chuckling. He'd left those agents in federal law enforcement who had annoyed him for so many years in ruin.

Today, the Drug Enforcement Administration faces horrendous problems which stem from the endless concern with administration and bureaucratic politics.

John R. Bartels is a former Strike Force attorney in his late thirties, the son of a federal judge in New York. He is strongly oriented politically but it would appear won't remain for long as Administrator of the DEA.

One of the purposes of the merger of these various agencies was to give one Bureau the total responsibility and authority for control of internal, border, and international drug traffic. It would seem, in theory, that this has been accomplished. Unfortunately, nothing of the sort has happened. Up until this time there has been no delineation of duties. U.S. Customs is in a quandary as to its powers, and the DEA has no clear idea of what it can, and cannot, do utilizing the powers of U.S. Customs. Meanwhile, Customs and the U.S. Treasury Department are still fighting over the loss of border powers which, in turn, defeats the very prime purpose of the merger.

A conflict of basic philosophies has added to the crisis. Over the years the Bureau of Narcotics and Dangerous Drugs has believed in infiltrating the narcotics traffic by the use of undercover techniques and attempting to work up to the major traffickers. This is the tradition and the expertise which has worked for them and is the prime concept they respect.

The Customs Agency Service, on the other hand, does not believe in the undercover concept. Their expertise rests in working paper conspiracy cases. I call these "paper conspiracy cases" in no snide way. Rather, I mean their method of tracing all seizures to different customers. The seizure of narcotics has already been made, the case follows. When one of these involved cases is put together it is ordinarily very effective. However, such cases are made infrequently and have no real effect in removing narcotics from the street. As one can see, the former agents of these different agencies simply don't believe in the fundamental methods of the other. There is a constant lack of cohesion within the DEA itself with endless conflict and jealousies. Too, the former narcotics agents believe that while they cooperate with local law enforcement agencies they do not depend upon them. Rather, they concentrate on sources of supply and the interstate and international traffickers. Former Customs agents openly rely on local enforcement agencies and dislike making any move without them. This concept can be traced back to the days when Customs agents had little or no authority except at the border and had to use local law enforcement as their authority to work cases of internal traffic. Such traditions die hard.

An important thing happened at the time of the merger. Customs agents' names were put in a computer. Those who had spent most of their time working narcotics cases were transferred to the new DEA. If they didn't like it the arrangement was that they could return to Customs but only to work on cases other than narcotics. Many tried the new job for a time and returned. Some stayed on with DEA but generally are discontented. The BNDD agents resented this as they had no choice. Today there is dissention in all the offices of DEA, particularly along the border. The differences are emphasized by a complete lack of focal leadership. Today, the Regional office with a former narcotics agent in charge operates in a way that is completely different from the office with a former Customs agent in charge. In headquarters there is even more confusion, which is blamed on Bartels' lack of understanding and leadership. His penchant for indecision is notorious within the DEA. Typically, now, nearly a year after the merger he has yet to designate a Deputy who should by now be deeply involved in solving the complicated enforcement problems. At the moment no one knows who is in charge with the result that no one accepts responsibility.

Rumors and gossip of impending change, of demotions, forced retirements, shifts of power go on endlessly. There are no teletypes originating from Headquarters, no explanation of major cases being investigated, no official word explaining shootings even when an agent is involved. This, of course, feeds the rumor mill and wild stories become standard. Similarly, communication between the Regional offices is absent—which adds to the confusion.

When Bartels took over he changed the nomenclature and the various Regional Directors became Regional Administrators and their assistants the same. There was such a cry of anguish that he was forced to relent and return to the title of Directors. But the turmoil continues. Two Regional Directors, for example, have requested demotions to smaller and relatively unimportant jobs simply to escape the chaotic working conditions. At least one of Bartels' high-ranking assistants requested and received a reduction in rank to remove himself from headquarters and return to the field.

Agents in the field are openly hostile to Bartels. He has the unfortunate habit of disciplining agents by means of the press conference. Agents feel that, if they are to be punished or suspended, it should be within the Bureau, not by public chastisement. In effect, they see this consistent policy as clear proof that Bartels is not ready to support them or back them up in times of crisis.

The handling of the unfortunate case of the ten federal and local narcotics agents who made the mistaken raids in Southern Illinois and were brought to trial last spring is typical.

No one questions that Bartels has a most difficult job. It would be a Herculean task for one who was qualified and fully understood the problems of enforcement. It remains sure that he can, at best, only be adequate with his background and lack of expertise.

Ideally, for the work of the Bureau, a man who understands narcotics enforcement such as Dan Casey, George Belk or Jack Cusack—all eminently qualified and in the DEA at the present time—should be appointed as the Director. Yet, this isn't likely to happen. The position has become a political one with the concerns centered around dealing with Congress and the patterns of shifting administrative tasks.

Meanwhile, I cannot help but see a parallel with those battles of Dad's those many years ago in Atlantic City. He faced the enemy of corruption and crooked politics in his career as a police officer. Today, a more insidious and subtle disease has set in. It finds expression in the harassed and frustrated agent who spends his hours in meetings discussing organizational changes and filling out charts and forms.

The prime target still remains the peddler. It seems this has somehow been lost in the hall of mirrors of the Federal narcotics enforcement program. Maybe what's needed is a little less organization in the organization.

1 2 3 4 5 6 7 ← P Y → 9 8 7 6 5 4